D1486382

# LUCKY JACK

# LUCKY JACK

## SCOTLAND'S FIRST MINISTER

## LORRAINE DAVIDSON

BLACK & WHITE PUBLISHING

First published 2005
by Black & White Publishing Ltd
99 Giles Street, Edinburgh, Scotland

ISBN 1 84502 050 2

Copyright © Lorraine Davidson 2005

British Library Cataloguing in Publication Data:
A catalogue record for this book is available
from the British Library.

Printed and bound by Creative Print & Design

# CONTENTS

# ACKNOWLEDGEMENTS

I am most grateful to the dozens of people who gave up their time to speak to me about Scotland's First Minister, Jack McConnell. Many of them are quoted in the book while others chose to remain anonymous but were equally helpful. I could not single out any particular source for special thanks as everyone I interviewed was remarkably generous with their time. Their insights were all invaluable and their patience in helping me check facts was much appreciated. I only hope that I have done justice to the views of all those I spoke to.

However, I would like to thank Shaun Milne of the Scottish *Mirror* for giving me the idea to write the book. Campbell Brown, Alison McBride and Patricia Marshall at Black & White Publishing were a joy to work with and helped to make the experience such an enjoyable one.

Thanks also to my mum and dad without whose support I could never have managed to write the book and to David for putting up with me while I wrote it.

*This book is for Jonathan and Jenny*

# INTRODUCTION

In November 2001, Jack McConnell became Scotland's third First Minister and, at the time of writing in spring 2005, he is already the longest-serving one. Jack was elevated to the most powerful job in Scottish politics just eighteen months after he was elected as an MSP and this was despite being him being embroiled in 'Lobbygate', one of the early scandals to affect the new Scottish Parliament. Although it is now more than twenty years since Jack McConnell first became an elected politician at local government level, most of his political work had been carried out while he was in the unelected post of Labour Party General Secretary.

The first First Minister, Donald Dewar, had been an elected MP for thirty-three years before he came to lead his nation and he was a well-known figure in Scottish public life through much of that time. He was appointed Secretary of State for Scotland in Tony Blair's first cabinet and was responsible for taking the legislation that set up the Scottish Parliament through the Commons. Jack's immediate predecessor, Henry McLeish, had also served as an MP – in his case for thirteen years, the last three as a government minister – before he became First Minister. But Jack McConnell's apparently meteoric rise to the top meant that Scottish voters knew little about the man who was given the keys to Bute House when he became First Minister.

I decided to write this book at a time when Jack McConnell was being criticised for cronyism and for a lack of vision. He was being painted as a machine politician who was expert at fixing votes but, when it came to directing his country, he was at a loss. At best, I viewed that as an over-simplistic assessment and, at worst, it was just plain wrong. I hope this book will shed some light on what Scotland's First Minister stands for and what we can expect from his leadership. I started this project as a sympathetic observer who has known Jack McConnell for the best part of a decade and that is what I have remained. I have tried to make this a factual account of his political career. However, I know there are several people who have clashed with him over the years and, regrettably, they have declined to give their side of the story. The account, therefore, of some incidents may appear one sided. In researching this book, I asked for an interview with Jack McConnell. He decided not to be interviewed. However, I was able to gain unprecedented access to his closest allies and for that I am most grateful. I was also able to check facts with a family member as well as his close political contacts.

# 1

# TOO CLOSE FOR COMFORT?

It is often said that there are no true friendships in politics but, if there are exceptions to this, it appears Jack McConnell's case is one of them. He forged strong bonds with fellow student activists at Stirling University and many have remained firm friends as well as acting as his most constructive critics. Professor Mike Donnelly, his former lecturer, is one of his strongest supporters, as are Neil Stewart, whom he met through student politics, and Douglas Campbell, another fellow student who is now his official spokesman. However, one or two relationships have fallen by the wayside. The Labour MSP and former Scottish Health Minister Susan Deacon was an ally of Jack during the Scottish Labour Action period but ended up out of favour by the time he became First Minister. Tommy Sheppard, who was close to him from the late '70s until the late '90s, is someone else who is still waiting to be invited round to Bute House.

But the friendship which has aroused the most interest is the one with the BBC *Newsnight* presenter Kirsty Wark. The man with the most powerful job in Scottish politics often enjoys the company of one of the most influential broadcasters in Britain. Until Christmas of 2004, not many people realised the extent of the friendship but all that changed when the *Sunday Mail*'s political editor Lindsay McGarvie discovered that Jack and his family had been invited to spend that New Year with Kirsty and her family at their villa in Majorca. The paper dealt out some mild criticism of his decision not to spend the festive season in Scotland.

At the last First Minister's questions of 2004, the SNP's Parliamentary Leader Nicola Sturgeon could not resist having a dig. In what was a jovial exchange before the end of the parliamentary season, she wished the First Minister a good holiday 'wherever he might be spending it'. The Nationalists thought it was worth having a go at the First Minister for appearing to turn his back on his nation's Hogmanay celebrations. They did not appear to think that what they were on to was to become one of the biggest political rows of the year but that is exactly what ignited in the weeks that followed.

During what is traditionally a light time of the year for news, picture desks were excited by the prospect of snatching a shot of Scotland's First Minister on holiday with a celebrity. Three newspapers dispatched snappers to photograph the two families on their Spanish break but *Scotland on Sunday* was the only one to be successful. It duly ran a photo of the First Minister and his family, along with Kirsty Wark's family, out for a holiday stroll. The image of the two families sparked an incredible backlash. Despite the fact that the Asian Tsunami had claimed the lives of over a hundred thousand people including many Brits, the First Minister's holiday dominated the headlines in Scotland for the next two weeks. The story ran on two fronts. There were attacks on the professionalism of Kirsty Wark. Unnamed BBC insiders criticised her decision to holiday with the First Minister when she might be expected to interview him in the future. In doing so, they appeared to overlook the fact that, as the presenter of *Newsnight*, the UK current affairs TV programme, Wark is likely to interview McConnell as often as she would be expected to probe the President of Catalonia. But the attacks focused on the fact that she also hosts the Scottish general election coverage every four years. Although McConnell would not be a candidate in that election, he could be expected to be interviewed in his capacity as the Leader of Labour in the Scottish Parliament.

That was enough to spark calls for Wark to be removed from the election coverage.

Kirsty Wark and her husband Alan Clements are shareholders in a successful media company, IWC Media, which has been the recipient of public money to develop educational websites. The media turned on McConnell for accepting hospitality from a couple whose company bids for public contracts. Accepting that the First Minister played no part in making such decisions, the media argued that it was not necessarily about a conflict of interest but about the public perception that there might be one. Day after day, new lines emerged which kept the story going. It had become such big news it was predictably dubbed 'Villagate'.

When the attacks on Kirsty Wark and her husband began to subside, there was the question of the hospitality that McConnell enjoyed. Under the Scottish Parliament's rules, MSPs must declare receiving all gifts worth more than £250 each. In theory, this means that any birthday or Christmas presents they get over that value must be declared to the public. The man responsible for drawing up the rules, the former chairman of the Parliament's Standards Committee, Liberal Democrat Mike Rumbles, said that, in his view, McConnell was in breach of the rules. Instead of being beaten into submission, the First Minister put up a robust defence of his actions. He insisted that staying overnight at the home of a friend did not constitute a gift and, therefore, the question of declaring it did not arise. His bullish response paid off. In May 2005, the parliament's Standards Committee ruled he had done nothing wrong.

Finally, there was the question of the programme that IWC were making about the building of the new Scottish Parliament. The programme had attracted Scottish Arts Council funding and contained interviews with the late First Minister Donald Dewar and the architect of the Holyrood building, Enric Miralles. The inquiry into the Holyrood building project, headed by Lord Peter Fraser, had requested the tapes of this programme but he was refused access to them. The copyright was owned by the BBC, not IWC, so it was for the corporation, not Alan Clements, to decide if they should be made available to the inquiry and it ruled they should not.

However, even those who are friendly towards Jack said that, because his friends had made the programme with public money and they had backed the BBC's decision not to make the tapes available to a public enquiry, his relationship with Kirsty Wark was now difficult to defend.

Instead of giving in to the pressure heaped upon them, the two families fought back and defended their right to maintain a friendship of almost twenty years' standing. Although Jack and Kirsty were the two people who attracted the headlines, in reality the friendship was not born of a bond between McConnell and Wark but began when McConnell got to know her husband Alan Clements, at a time before Clements had even begun a relationship with his future wife. Alan had just returned from a spell living in the States and had landed a job as a researcher with BBC Scotland when he met Jack. The two men are similar in age and, in the mid '80s, shared similar political views on devolution. Clements was a Labour Party member at the time and he met McConnell through Scottish Labour Action (SLA), attending a meeting of the fledgling group in McConnell's Stirling flat. Clements was interested in some of the ideas being floated by the group but he was also aware that attending political meetings could present a conflict in his new job with the BBC. Shortly after SLA was formed, Alan decided to take a step back from political activity. From then on, he continued to take an interest in the group in a professional capacity only but his friendship with Jack McConnell remained. Over the years, Alan and Jack would regularly meet up for a drink. As avid football fans, they would often arrange to get together to watch a game on TV and their shared interest in golf is another thing that brings them together.

Bridget McConnell also became firm friends with Kirsty and, although the Clements' children are ten years younger than the McConnells', Jack's kids adore the younger ones and vice versa. Jack and Bridget were guests at Alan and Kirsty's wedding in 1989 and Alan and Kirsty were one of the few couples close to Jack who were invited to attend the wedding reception for his younger brother Iain in the late '80s. The Clements family know Jack's wider family and the McConnells know Alan's parents who also holidayed with the families in Majorca.

Given their mutual interest in politics, the Clements and the McConnells invariably end up discussing the subject but both claim there are certain lines they never cross. For example, Jack has said he has no idea how Kirsty votes and would not dream of asking her. And Alan says that, despite the fact he and Jack were on opposite ends of the argument over the Dewar–Miralles tapes, McConnell never raised the issue with him directly. 'We never talked about it – Jack didn't raise it with me and I value that,' he said. But there are plenty of MSPs who feel that McConnell should have used every means at his disposal to secure the tapes – presumably even if that meant abusing a friendship. The First Minister did publicly call on the BBC to release them, which put him at odds with the argument being made by his friend Alan who defended the corporation's decision not to. But the holiday with Alan Clements and Kirsty Wark only served to heighten suspicions that he could have tried harder.

After learning of the holiday, Lord Fraser added to that suspicion by speaking out about his doubts as to whether Jack McConnell had done everything in his power to get the tapes. Both families were well aware of the dangers of highlighting their closeness by going on holiday together. They knew before they booked the flights that the decision could provoke media interest but it was not a difficult decision to make. They cared more about their friendship than they did about the perception of it. The two families had been on holiday together before and were not prepared to sacrifice their relationship for the sake of appearances.

Speaking just days before they left for Majorca, Alan Clements said, 'It would probably have been easier for both families if we had said that the friendship could not continue and that we couldn't go on holiday together but we feel strongly that we cannot allow our friendships to be dictated for us.' Alan and Kirsty were also close to the first First Minister Donald Dewar, prompting critics to claim the friendship is a power-based one. But the friendship with Dewar developed because he was a neighbour of the couple.

It is not uncommon for friendships to develop between politicians and journalists. Most weekdays, Edinburgh restaurants near the Parliament will have tables reserved for journalists taking their favourite contacts to lunch. On Thursday nights, it is traditional for the two sets to get together for a few drinks at the end of the week. Politicians need journalists and journalists need their political contacts. The Scottish Parliament is not alone in this and similar relationships develop at Westminster and in Washington. There are those who argue the relationship between the journalist and the politician should be akin to that between the dog and the lamp post. However, in a country the size of Scotland with its considerably smaller pool of people, MSPs and journalists do get to know each other better than the average Westminster backbencher would know the political editors in the lobby.

Many links between Scottish journalists and politicians can be traced back to university days when they came across each other through an involvement in student politics. Jack

McConnell first met Peter MacMahon, *The Scotsman*'s government editor, while they were at university. He was also close to the BBC's senior political producer John Boothman while he was studying. That said, people who work on opposite sides of the political divide tend to respect the boundaries they must operate within.

When Alan and Kirsty get together with Jack and Bridget both couples say some issues are off limits. Although they do 'talk shop' sometimes, their relationship is essentially one in which the two families enjoy each other's company. 'Of course we sometimes end up talking about politics but it by no means dominates our time together. I am friendly with Jack because he is a good guy who has never let me down,' says Alan.

Alan Clements was one of many people McConnell sounded out before deciding to challenge Henry McLeish for the leadership of the Scottish Labour Party following Donald Dewar's death. Like most of his friends, Clements told him he had to stand for the leadership. He didn't believe McConnell would win and told him so but he advised him to run the race as a way of putting down a marker for the future.

Despite their long-standing friendship, Clements would not claim to be a big influence in the life of the First Minister. He appreciates that McConnell has many friendships, both political and non-political, and will take a wide range of soundings before he arrives at a decision. Clements says:

> I don't think there is any one person who he listens to above all others. He is an extremely good listener and people's opinions matter to him. I have known Jack for sixteen years and I think I know him reasonably well but does anyone really know all of Jack McConnell? He keeps his own counsel – there is a bit which he holds back from everyone.

The address book in the First Minister's mobile phone is jam-packed with names of friends and contacts he will regularly send text messages to as a way of staying in touch as he travels the country on official business but there are few friends who are trusted as much as the Clements family or who have the same level of access to him. The Clements family were the first friends to be invited to stay at the First Minister's official residence Bute House after Jack was elected First Minister. McConnell wanted to share that first weekend with his family who had been through a difficult leadership campaign and with friends in whom he felt he could confide so he picked the Clements. During that weekend, Jack told Alan of his much-derided plan to 'do less better'. The new First Minister was convinced the biggest challenge facing him was to put some stability into the running of the new institution. Since the Parliament was set up in 1999, it seemed to Jack as if there had been a crisis every week and he feared for the institution's credibility with the voters. He felt the single most important thing he could do was to draw a line under the chaos that had dogged the Parliament's first two years. And, during their discussions that weekend, his confidante only served to reinforce that view.

According to Clements, a strong supporter of home rule, Jack stopped the whole devolution project from 'going wrong'. Alan readily admits that that is not the epitaph his friend would want etched on his grave and he believes that McConnell is now keen to speed up the pace of change. It is, therefore, not surprising that Clements comes to Jack's defence amid criticism suggesting that the First Minister lacks vision. Alan believes McConnell cares passionately about Scotland and its problems and will make a difference in the areas that matter. He said:

Jack feels strongly about antisocial behaviour. He has no time for the chattering-class liberals who have never had to

10

experience what it is like to be terrified of walking home with a bag of shopping. That kind of situation makes him incredibly angry.

Given Scotland's advances in research and development and science, Clements claims one of Jack's biggest gripes is with people who 'talk Scotland down'. It is the criticism he is most likely to level at the SNP. Apart from claims that he lacks vision, Jack McConnell has also suffered from a perception that he is a ruthless operator who will let no one stand in his way of achieving his goals. It is also largely accepted that he has a large circle of enemies as well as a large circle of friends. However, in writing this book, I have found that well-known figures in the Labour Party, who I have always understood to feel a degree of animosity towards him, have become unusually silent in their criticism. In some cases, it is clear people do not want to speak out against him because they still want to be promoted by him. In other instances, there appears to be a genuine thawing of frosty relations.

It is also obvious that the First Minister has spent a lot of time cultivating people over the years sometimes because he thought they would be able to help his career in the future. That is not to say he does not hold them in some affection. Unlike many politicians who bad-mouth those they see as intellectually inferior, this is not a trait associated with McConnell. It would not be true to say that McConnell has never briefed against a colleague but his criticisms tend to be based on what he sees as bad political decision-making rather than personality-based issues.

During his years as General Secretary of the Scottish Labour Party, Jack McConnell built up a reputation as a bit of a slippery character who couldn't be trusted. At the time, it suited him to be regarded as a wheeler and dealer but it is an image he has struggled to cast off since becoming a government minister.

Alan Clements doesn't recognise the descriptions frequently attached to his friend. He says:

> People say he has no moral compass. I just say look at his family. He has brought up two of the nicest young people you could meet. They respect him and seek his advice and he gives them unstinting support. They are such a loving, warm family and he is a very loving and loved dad.

For some politicians, the long hours involved in climbing the greasy pole mean that family life gets neglected but anyone who knows Jack says his family matters to him above all else. He travels back to Arran whenever possible to see his parents and never misses an opportunity to speak proudly about his children or to spend time with them. Despite the fact that his daughter Hannah is now twenty-six and son Mark is twenty-two, he seems if anything to have become even more protective of them since taking on the role of First Minister.

Alan Clements is one of the few people who has witnessed Jack's family life closely in recent times. He has seen them as a family together on holiday and has also witnessed the McConnell family during some times of stress. One Saturday night, the Clements family arrived for dinner at Bute House to be greeted by a bemused McConnell who posed the question, 'What would you least like your daughter to be doing this weekend?'

This was at the time when the accusations surrounding the TV personality John Leslie were at their height. Leslie was at the centre of rape allegations (something he was subsequently cleared of) so Clements joked, 'Dating John Leslie?' But, as it later transpired, the TV host had, in fact, asked the McConnells' daughter Hannah out on a date. Jack had spent most of that day fielding questions from the press about the liaison and several newspapers carried the story the next day. By coincidence, two newspaper executives, Colin McLatchie of *News International* and Andrew Jaspan of the *Sunday Herald*, were also at the Bute House dinner. Hannah McConnell was furious that they were going to be running the story and she told them so. According to Clements, it wasn't an out-of-control outburst but an articulately argued case as to why she believed this was not newsworthy. Hannah was involved in student politics and worked in the House of Commons for Michael Connarty MP. She understands the game and can hold her own. Her younger brother Mark is, by all accounts, a more private person and finds the media scrutiny of his family more difficult to deal with.

Ironically, the family holiday the McConnells enjoyed with the Clements family was to have been a way of spending quality family time away from the pressures that the role of First Minister brings. It was the McConnells' first family holiday abroad for two years and Hannah and Mark had been looking forward to the escape and spending time with their dad somewhere that he could relax. To find photographers had followed them there left both young people bitterly disappointed that their private time together had been invaded.

While the Clements' children were not subjected to taunts at school, they were worried about the effects of the row on their parents. And Hannah and Mark both found the aftermath of the holiday stressful to deal with. It was perhaps their reaction which made McConnell all the more determined to take on his critics rather than give in to them. The row over 'Villagate' enraged him and he was determined not only to stand up for his own rights to a private life but also to ensure that devolution does not mean precedents are set which prevent future generations of politicians from leading normal lives.

One of his fears is that talented young people will be deterred from going into public life in Scotland if they feel they would be forced to live their lives in a 'goldfish bowl'. 'Villagate' also prompted concern from two of Jack's closest political allies. Lord Robertson, former Defence Secretary and ex-Secretary General of NATO, often despaired of the Scottish media during his stint as Shadow Scottish Secretary. Speaking of the 'Villagate' saga, he said, 'We are afflicted by terminal self-criticism. In situations like this, people feel they have to pile in.'

When asked about the holiday issue at one of his weekly press conferences in Downing Street, the Prime Minister's advice to Jack was to 'ignore it'. And Leader of the House of Commons, Peter Hain, claimed 'Villagate' made the Scottish media look parochial. He said:

> When you look at the obsessive focus on issues like Jack's Christmas break when you are sitting in London, you can't help feeling that the Scottish media is worse than the London media. They seem to live in a self-obsessed little world and they are completely out of touch.

Despite his years of manipulating the media, Jack McConnell has never managed to develop the kind of thick skin that enables some politicians to get through the difficult times. While the late Donald Dewar could shrug off the criticisms of what he called the 'popular prints', McConnell takes their words to heart and often they wound him. It is clear that, on becoming First Minister, he made a deliberate decision to stand back from dealing directly with the media. For years, he had always been on the end of a mobile, ready with a quote or a put down. Familiarity between the politician and the press had rebounded on Henry McLeish and Jack McConnell learned from his predecessor's mistake.

When the going gets too tough, McConnell takes to the golf course. According to Clements, 'You can visibly see the tension lifting when he picks up a club.'

# 2

# ARRAN

Jack McConnell pushed his plate away, satisfied his appetite had been met. Neatly stacked at one side lay a small pile of carrots that hadn't taken his fancy. Like most six-year-olds vegetables held limited appeal for him. But Jack's teacher spotted his rejection of the carrots and told him he must eat them or he would end up being unable to see in the dark. However, the young McConnell refused to obey the order and, instead, chose to argue back insisting that he slept at night and, therefore, had no need for vision during the hours of darkness.

Even from his first days at school, McConnell had stood out as being argumentative. Some of his primary teachers encouraged his appetite for debate but, on this occasion in the dinner hall, it was not appreciated. McConnell was ordered to the headmaster's study and given the belt. It was an unusually harsh treatment for a six-year-old child and one seldom used at Lamlash Primary School on the island of Arran but, when it was, McConnell was on the receiving end more than most. His teachers remember him as a child 'who had an opinion on everything'.

The odd brush with authority aside McConnell enjoyed his time at school – even if his teachers didn't always enjoy having him there. He arrived at Lamlash in the summer of 1965. The 'school' consisted of three classrooms at the end of a corridor in the island's only secondary school, Arran High School. The unusual set-up meant the tiny five-year-old was dropped at the school gates to make his way through the building along with boys and girls in their teens. It was both intimidating and exciting for him.

The young Jack did well at school. He was good at most subjects but, from the start, it was obvious he had a talent for maths. Joyce Scott, who taught him in Primary 6 and 7, says that, in her thirty years as a teacher, McConnell's class was one that stood out:

> They were such a clever bunch. That happens sometimes in a small rural school – you just get a particular class which is full of bright kids. Apart from Jack, one of the class went on to become an actuary and one of the girls got a first-class honours degree in maths. For some reason they were all extremely good at maths in his year. Jack was a clever boy in a clever class.

It wasn't just academically that Jack McConnell made his mark. His non-stop chattering made him difficult to overlook. His teachers remember him as being enthusiastic and confident. If there was a debate to be had, Jack was at the centre of it. If a teacher wanted a contribution from the class, Jack would be first to put up his hand. His former headmaster David Oakes says, 'He was a very self-confident boy who was never afraid to speak up. He always made very positive contributions. Looking back, the evidence was there that his future might lie in politics.'

Jack's view of school was that it was there to be enjoyed. He tried to get the most out of what was on offer during the lessons and he also made the most of his time out of the classroom. To one side of the school lies the road to Whiting Bay and to the other side is a row of shops and these were the focal point of the village. Lamlash Primary, the bay and the shops soon became the centre of Jack McConnell's world. From early on, it was obvious that he did not have to work hard to master the academic side of life. His literacy and numeracy skills were among the best in the class and, because of this, he was able to devote a lot of his energy to having a good time.

Jack Wilson McConnell was born in Irvine on 30 June 1960, the oldest child of Willie and Elizabeth McConnell. He was given his mother's surname as his first Christian name. His parents were both brought up on farms and met through the young farmers' social scene in Ayrshire. It was a tight-knit community and both parents came from close families. Jack's maternal grandfather Willie Jack had married a local girl called Ballantyne McEwan and his two brothers married her two sisters. When Jack was born, the extended family were delighted but the joy of Jack's birth was to be tinged with sadness for them. His arrival had been eagerly awaited but, shortly after Jack was born, his mother's mother became seriously ill with cancer. The infant was a great source of comfort to Willie Jack during those long days and nights as he watched his wife fight for her life in the same hospital in Irvine where Jack had been born just a few months earlier. But Ballantyne Jack died at the age of fifty-three, leaving Jack's grandfather and his mother devastated.

Elizabeth McConnell had been extremely close to her mother and took her death very badly. The thing that kept her going during that period of grief was the birth of her first son. She felt Jack had been born to help her cope with the loss of her mother and she threw herself into looking after him.

Eighteen months later, Elizabeth McConnell gave birth to a second boy, Iain. The McConnells were living in a flat on Elizabeth's dad's farm, Biglies near West Kilbride, where Willie McConnell was employed. Elizabeth's twin brother, also called Willie, lived in the cottage next door. His wife Janey gave birth to a daughter, Alison, just nine months after Jack was born and, for the first two years of their lives, the two kids were brought up together more like a brother and sister than cousins.

But, as their family expanded, Elizabeth and Willie were keen to move somewhere larger and the couple decided to lease a farm on the island of Arran on which they could bring up their boys. Elizabeth's family were sorry to see them leave Ayrshire and were worried about how she would cope living in such a remote location without the support of the brothers and sisters she was so close to. However, she adapted well to life in Arran and her own family was growing. In August 1964, Jack's sister Anne was born and, two years after that, the youngest brother, Calum, completed the family.

The family home for the McConnells was Glenscorrodale Farm. It lay half way along Ross Road, a nine-mile-long, winding single-track road that linked Lamlash to Kilmory. The whitewashed farmhouse building where Jack grew up was demolished in 2004 by Buddhist monks who plan to replace it with a retreat. The fact that the First Minister then chose a painting of the farm building by the Scottish artist Hamish MacDonald for the front of his 2004 Christmas card reveals not just his anger at the building being torn down but also the great affection in which he held the family home.

The farm nestled high in the hills, surrounded by forestry land and gently rolling streams. A cleaner, purer environment and more breathtaking views would be hard to find anywhere. For miles on either side, there is not a house in sight. The young McConnells would spend their days fishing or swimming in the nearby streams or playing in the hills. On one level, it was an idyllic childhood, during which the children were free to roam around the vast hillside, but it was also marred, from time to time, by loneliness.

During the harsh winter months, Willie McConnell would put his offspring on the back of his tractor to get them through the snow to school. The rest of the year, at 8.45 a.m. each morning, the council would send a car up Ross Road to collect the four children and take them to school. On the way down the road, they would peer out of the windows to see if they could spot their father, who would be hard at work. They would see him, knee-deep in mud, planting trees by hand as he made an attempt to earn a little extra cash for the family. The children would wave excitedly out of the window, happy to have glimpsed their dad before going to school, but they were also deeply aware of how hard he was forced to work to make ends meet. The kids knew that the farm he had leased was failing to generate the income he needed to keep his family. Planting trees was just one of the ideas he came up with to keep the wolf from the door. From a young age, the children were keen to help their father in any small way they could.

Despite living on a farm, Jack had little affinity for the sheep, cows and horses that lived on the land. As a young boy, he was taught to milk the cows and round up the sheep but it was his brother Iain who would race out to help his father feed them when he got home from school – Jack would do almost anything else. He would clean out the fire, chop the wood or help make the dinner, happy to do those chores if it meant he could avoid having anything to do with the animals. It was the daily dropping-off at the school gate that gave Jack his greatest thrill. He knew that hours of chatting to his friends, playing sport and running along the beach lay ahead. School work was an easy distraction that he had to do to allow him to concentrate on the things that really mattered to him – sport and socialising.

Every weekend, Jack, along with his brothers and sister, attended Sunday School at Lamlash Parish Church. The religious aspect didn't interest him but the activities the Sunday School arranged did. The biggest attraction for him was the badminton classes they organised four times a week. He was also an enthusiastic attender of the youth club – anywhere he could meet people was a big lure. Jack made friends easily and he was one of the kids everyone wanted to invite to their parties, knowing he would be the life and soul of them. Even on school trips, Jack stood out as the character who made everyone else laugh. After one outing to Hadrian's Wall, his class stopped off at Gretna Green, the romantic setting for hundreds of weddings each year. The blacksmith asked for volunteers to take part in a mock marriage ceremony. True to form, Jack was the first to offer to marry one of his young classmates. Wearing a black top hat, he made his wedding vows and 'married' Rebecca Reid, one of his schoolmates. They were just thirteen years old. His former head teacher David Oakes said, 'When I heard about the mock wedding, it didn't surprise me that Jack was the groom. He would have been the one at the front speaking up and enthusiastically taking part in whatever was going on.'

Jack was excited by going to school and by everything it had to offer but the sound of the school bell at the finish of lessons signalled the end of his fun. The young Jack packed in the maximum amount of socialising to his day but the arrival of the council car meant he was forced to leave his friends and the buzz of the village to make the journey back to the isolated farmhouse. Although he did enjoy his own company, the drive out of the lively village into the wilderness could leave McConnell feeling that his fun was being stolen from him. To the dismay of his teachers, he dealt with the isolation that he felt at Glenscorrodale by being disruptive at school with his non-stop talking. Back at the farmhouse, he coped with his loneliness by spending hours reading or listening to music.

During school holidays, he would stay with his grandparents or on the farms of aunts or uncles on the mainland mainly in Ayrshire. One aunt and uncle, Margaret and Bill, lived in Wemyss Bay and he liked going there best because they had a milk round and he could rise early to deliver the milk and chat to people on their doorsteps as their day was beginning. Also, they did not have any children of their own so Jack enjoyed the extra attention he got there.

His Aunt Margaret, his father's sister, was a keen golfer and she first took him to Skelmorlie Golf Course when he was just eight years old. Jack loved the game. His mother's cousin was Sandy Sinclair, a former captain of the Royal and Ancient Golf Club and a captain of the Scottish team in the 1960s. His success inspired Jack but it was not emulated by him – Jack is noted more for his enthusiasm with a golf club than his skill with one. The First Minister now plays off a handicap of fourteen but suffers taunts from family and friends about his ability. Although he is not the best golfer in the family, Jack still loves to pick up a club and challenge relatives and friends to a round on the local course in Arran. But, even there, he is subjected to heckling. During one recent game, when he hit a ball off to the right, a cry of 'Typical – New Labour politician always going right!' was heard. There has been some harsh criticism of his dress sense on the course, too, where he has been spotted wearing black socks and brown shoes. But the criticism does not appear to affect him. His passion for the game has never diminished since Aunt Margaret introduced him to it as a small boy.

Jack also remained close to his aunt – or AM as he has called her throughout his adult life. She was diagnosed with cancer in 2002 and the First Minister would regularly travel to the hospice to visit her and would send her postcards or small presents on an almost weekly basis. When he spoke at her funeral in September 2003, it was clear what a major influence she had been on his life. Jack said:

> Margaret Howie shaped all our lives more than she ever realised. AM had a gift of kindness, an ability to see the sunshine every day and in everyone and a gentle but firm way of helping all of us to be all that we could be in every way.

But Jack's sojourn's from his island home also involved a taste of urban life. Jack's aunt lived in Edinburgh and the lure of the city meant he would often ask to stay with her so he could visit the attractions it offered.

Jack's father, Willie McConnell, is a skilled shepherd. He still regularly wins prizes at the annual agricultural show and the sheepdog trials on the island. It is clear that all his kids had the greatest of respect for him as they were growing up. He was also a fun-loving character who threw himself into community life and was generally regarded as the life and soul of any party. People liked to be around him, his enthusiasm was infectious and the kids were proud that he was their dad.

However, despite Willie's best efforts to make a go of the farm, he just couldn't make it viable and, in the summer of 1970, it was Jack's mother who came up with an idea that would change the family's fortunes. Elizabeth McConnell decided to open a tearoom at the farm. She erected half a dozen tables and put up a sign by the roadway to encourage passers-by to stop for coffee and home baking. Although travellers on the Ross Road were normally few and far between, news of the venture soon spread across the island and Elizabeth McConnell's tearoom became a roaring success.

That winter, Willie McConnell bought a wooden hut, erected it beside the farmhouse and created a car park alongside it. The following summer, the tearoom was an attraction come rain or shine and despite the fact it was in the middle of nowhere. Young Jack couldn't believe his luck – suddenly there were dozens of people arriving at his home. He threw himself into the fledgling family business, helping his mother in the kitchen and waiting on tables. As each car pulled up, Jack was eager to find out all about its occupants. It transformed his way of life during the summer months – what had once been the long lonely days of the school holiday that he dreaded were now replaced by frantic activity and noisy chatter. Jack also found that he could use his flair with figures to help with the accounts for the business.

By the mid '70s, the Ross Road tearoom had developed into a restaurant and it attracted tourists by the bus-load. The hut held fifteen tables and could seat forty-five people. It won a *Glasgow Herald* award and it was recommended in the *Egon Ronay Guide* as a great place for families on a budget to eat. It was also a family-run business. Elizabeth McConnell would start work, baking and cooking, at 6 a.m., often not finishing until 10 or 11 p.m.

Her own children along with her nieces made a willing workforce. Each summer, many of Jack's sixteen cousins would arrive from Ayrshire to help out in the tearoom. The girls were told they were being sent to the 'Arran finishing school'. They all looked up to Jack and, as the eldest, he was very protective towards them. To his young cousins, he seemed mature and sensible but also fun. However, there would be arguments over Jack's taste in music. He insisted on playing The Tremeloes' track 'Silence Is Golden' over and over to the annoyance of his young cousins. And they hated his Lynyrd Skynyrd records and his insistence on changing the TV channel from their favourite programmes so he could catch the latest news or current affairs programme.

And after a hard day serving in the tearoom, fights would break out among the cousins in the kitchen involving salt or ketchup. The kitchen would be a mess but Jack's parents rarely got angry over normal childhood fun. To the kids, the tearoom was a great laugh as well as a good source of pocket money. They all set up accounts at the bank bus that came round to the tearoom once a week and they watched their savings grow to proportions they would have thought unimaginable for teenagers.

With the restaurant well established, the McConnells' main source of income came from it rather than the farm. For the first time, the family had enough money not to worry how they would pay the bills and to start enjoying life a bit. People who know the family well talk of Elizabeth McConnell as a very capable woman who was talented but who also worked hard and was focused on achieving the best for her family. Jack is often compared to his mother in terms of his determination to succeed but he is undoubtedly much more of a party animal – a trait he takes from his father.

Although Jack enjoyed the buzz of the tearoom, he was always looking for his next challenge. In the summer of 1974, Willie McConnell received a call from a young cousin who had been on an exchange with a French family some years earlier. The French family had a fourteen-year-old boy called Bruno and they were looking for a fourteen-year-old Scottish boy to take part in a similar exchange. The idea was mentioned to Jack and he leapt on it without a moment's hesitation. The arrangement meant he would be going to live with a French family in Paris for three weeks. Not only did he agree to take up the offer, he also told his parents he would pay his own way from the money he had earned in the restaurant.

Jack sent the French family a photograph of himself so that they would be able to recognise him at the airport when he landed in Paris. The family had also agreed to send him a picture but, by the day of his departure, it had not yet arrived. Fourteen-year-old Jack sat on a train from Ayrshire to Glasgow, his stomach knotted with excitement and fear. It is unlikely this was the first time that the teenager had been on a train but it was the first train journey of his life that he could recall and it was only the first leg of a terrifying trek to Europe.

His plane touched down at Birmingham Airport en route to Orly Airport in Paris and even the bustle of this airport seemed like another world to the inexperienced country boy. As the miles to his destination evaporated, McConnell began to panic. In a couple of hours, he would land in France to meet a family he had never spoken to. He had no idea what they looked like or how he would find them. What if they didn't turn up? What if his own photograph hadn't arrived and they wouldn't know what he looked like? What if they didn't spot him? With sweating palms and a churning stomach, he got off the plane and started to make his way through the airport passing hundreds of faces. As he followed the exit signs, he travelled up an escalator. Midway up, he spotted a family with a boy around his age and they were clutching his photograph. The sense of relief he felt was overwhelming. They were there, they had found him and the best adventure of his life so far was about to begin in earnest.

He kept a diary of his experience in France. It is clear that he was very homesick in the first few days but soon got over it. The two youngsters hit it off. They spent the next two weeks visiting the Eiffel Tower, the Champs Élysées and Paris's art galleries. This was followed by a week in Berne in Switzerland.

By agreeing to the exchange, Jack knew he was taking a risk. Would he like the family? Would he enjoy France? Would he cope with the journey? Not for the last time, it was to be a risk that paid off. From early on, it was clear that the quiet island life of Arran would not always have enough to offer Jack. He was too adventurous and too academic to find a fulfilling life on the island. He was so desperate to find things to do that he would often hitch a lift to get him away from the farmhouse and down to the villages of Lamlash or Blackwaterfoot where the hotels and bars were a big attraction.

Like his son, Willie McConnell also craved company and was much sought-after company himself. He adored the island way of life and showed great commitment to local organisations and clubs. He would be the first to offer to take the youth club if they needed a volunteer and would put on discos during the Christmas holidays at the farm tearoom to entertain the local youngsters. Lamlash's ex-head David Oakes recalls a typical Christmastime:

> I remember several car-loads of children going round the village singing Christmas carols on Christmas Eve and, afterwards, we all ended up at Glenscorrodale. Jack's mother was busy making sausage, beans and chips for all the kids and we [the adults] all got something much better. Jack owes a lot to both his parents – they are lovely people.

The McConnells' farm was always a welcoming place and the children were often encouraged to invite friends to stay for the weekend.

The summer of Jack's seventeenth birthday was a very unhappy one because his girlfriend Mhairi emigrated to Canada with her family, leaving Jack broken-hearted. His cousin Alison offered Jack a shoulder to cry on as he tried to get over losing his childhood sweetheart. When he turned sixteen, Jack bought himself a moped to help him track down a bit of excitement on the island. The three pubs in Blackwaterfoot became regular haunts, offering McConnell the kind of opportunity to socialise he so badly craved.

If Jack was outgrowing the social scene on the island, he was also beginning to feel stifled in the classroom. Maths was his great love and he would often race through his own work so that he could devote the rest of the lesson to helping his colleagues who struggled with their algebra or trigonometry. But his disruptive influence continued to irk his teachers throughout his schooldays. By fifth year, all but McConnell and one other boy were made school prefects. In the autumn a boy left the class, creating a vacancy for another prefect and the teachers took a vote on which of the remaining two boys should be awarded the position. McConnell lost, leaving him as the only pupil in his class not to have won the endorsement of his teachers. Being blackballed in this way was a punishment too far for Jack the Lad who decided to get his own back on the school establishment. Traditionally, it had always been the role of the prefects to organise the Christmas dance at the school but McConnell embarked on a campaign to undermine their efforts and put forward an alternative programme of entertainment. The competing ideas were put to the fifth-year pupils to vote on. They backed Jack's ambitious plans and rejected the prefects as the dance organisers. Various performers took to the stage to ridicule the staff mercilessly. The youngsters loved it and Jack was elevated to the status he desired.

That summer, he was awarded four Highers in English, French, chemistry and, of course, maths in which he scored 98% and was awarded an A grade. He also got an A in accounts, which he sat at O-Grade, adding to the eight O-Grades he had passed the previous year. Jack's father had been encouraging him to go to university to study accountancy. Willie McConnell believed his son had a flair for business and a degree in accountancy would ensure he had a well-paid job free from the financial uncertainties that had dogged his own ventures. Jack was minded to take his father's advice and applied to Stirling University to study accountancy. It is obvious that both his mother and father were big influences on his life and he has respect and admiration for their achievements.

During this period, Jack was spending much of his time playing in a local football team in which his maths teacher, Jimmy Stewart, also played. That summer, Stewart convinced Jack that he should follow his passion and study mathematics instead of accountancy. Jimmy said:

He had a natural talent for maths and a nice challenging way about him. He had a twinkle in his eye, so you knew you had to watch him but I always thought he would have made an excellent teacher.

The young Jack had also being weighing up whether he should go back to school for a sixth year or leave for university that autumn. His teacher bluntly told him there was nothing more the school could offer him. Jack took his advice and left the security of island life to begin his career on the mainland. But his links with Arran were to endure.

When the local landowner announced he was throwing the McConnells off the farm they had leased for fifteen years, the future of the successful restaurant was also plunged into doubt. But Willie McConnell agreed to give up the farm, providing he could keep the restaurant they had built in the grounds. The deal saved the family from ruin and they would later be able to sell the business off to buy a hotel in Blackwaterfoot. The Rock Hotel overlooked the sea and was situated next to a golf course and a beach. It was a stunning location and, with the combination of his mother's cooking in the kitchen and his dad's personality in the bar, the place was soon one of the most popular places to go on the island. Even when he was at university, Jack would go back to work there in the summer.

But by the mid '80s, the work was becoming too much for Jack's mother. The McConnells decided to sell up once again and Willie began to run a bar in Whiting Bay. The Rock Hotel was sold on again a few years later and bought by the man who lived in the house next door. Nobody realised his motive was to destroy the business so he could live in peace and tranquillity without the comings and goings of a busy bar next door. So the new owner had the Rock Hotel pulled down and where it once stood, on one of the best sites on the entire island, there is now just an empty piece of land. This was a source of great sadness to the McConnell family. Jack's parents are now retired and both are well-liked members of the community in which they live. Islanders have now nicknamed Willie McConnell 'The First Shepherd'.

To this day Jack McConnell returns to Arran every summer and it is with great delight that he has brought his own children to the island for holidays. The locals take great pride in his achievement and are extremely protective towards him and his family, particularly if outsiders start to ask questions about them. And during periods of stress in his life or ahead of important decisions the First Minister will sometimes drive up Ross Road so he can walk in the hills around the farm where he grew up, now seeking the solitude that he once fought so hard to escape.

# 3

# STUDENT DAYS

It was a glorious autumn day in 1972. The Queen was due to inaugurate the new buildings on the Stirling University campus. The students had turned out in force to enjoy the sun if not the pomp and ceremony and most came prepared with a bottle of wine to mark the occasion. The Secretary of the University, Major General Lang, was looking forward to his own day in the sun. Proud of the new buildings and of the preparations he had made for the regal visit, the retired army major thought he could stand back and enjoy his brush with royalty. Perhaps he had not picked up on the discontent felt among the students who were angry about a rise in their accommodation costs on the campus as he splashed out on an upgrading of the facilities ahead of the visit or maybe he simply didn't care. Whichever it was, he did not foresee a need for extra security on the day. As the Queen made her way towards the university's library building, the crowd of students began to push their way forward. It's alleged that, amid the mayhem, one of the ladies-in-waiting was forced to start hitting students with her handbag to keep them back.

Major Lang could only look on in horror as the royal visit was marred by what appeared to be students staging a revolt. One mature student, Jackie McKee, came to symbolise the protest. As the Queen passed him, he raised the bottle of claret from which he was drinking and said, '*Slainte mhath*.' It is assumed that the Queen was far from impressed but it is probably fair to say that McKee, a gentle figure in his early thirties, did not intend to cause offence. However, the next day, the picture of the student, merry after a morning's drinking in the sun, thrusting his bottle towards the Queen made headline news across the world.

Stirling University was disgraced. The major lost his job and the university lost millions of pounds in endowments. Even the university's student radicals began to realise that a degree from Stirling would be looked down on by employers unless things changed. The scenes of chaos that day in reality amounted to little more than some jostling and pushing. It wasn't an organised protest. Linda Quinn, the Student President at the time, was a member of the Internationalist Socialist Students, an organisation with a similar ideology to that of the SSP of today, but she was not in control of the situation.

Although the disturbance wasn't exactly on the scale of the student uprising of Paris in 1968, the Queen's visit of 1972 marked Stirling University out as a hotbed of anti-establishment student radicalism. It was an exciting place to be in the 1970s, particularly if you were young and wanted to change the world. Students at Stirling, a relatively new university, were renowned for being radical and passionate about their politics. Most of those who attended the political meetings at Stirling were not aligned to any party. They were part of the broad left and built alliances in order to achieve their objectives. The level of student grants was a hot topic at political meetings, as were rents in the town. The Defence Secretary and former Health Secretary, Dr John Reid, was a mature student at Stirling and he became active in politics on the campus. He is remembered playing the guitar during a student occupation in protest over plans to raise student accommodation rents.

The Stirling students were quite unlike the students who came out of the more rarefied political clubs at Glasgow and Edinburgh Universities around the same time. For a start, the political activists at Stirling did not tend to allow the party political system to dominate their thinking. Unlike the Universities of Glasgow and Edinburgh who, in a right-wing backlash, had severed their ties with the National Union of Students (NUS), Stirling was still an NUS university. Because of this, its students were more likely to engage with activists at different universities throughout the UK. Around the same time as Jack McConnell arrived at Stirling, Bob McLean, a founder member of Scottish Labour Action, was studying in Aberdeen, as was Neil Stewart who went on to work in Neil Kinnock's office. Tommy Sheppard, who was to become Deputy General Secretary of the Labour Party, was also active in student politics in Aberdeen. John Boothman, a senior BBC political journalist and partner of Susan Deacon, was a student leader at Strathclyde – another NUS university. Because McLean, Stewart, Sheppard and Boothman were active in student politics, it wasn't long before McConnell met them and they soon became a potent force. They would hire a Transit Van and travel round the country, attending political meetings and sleeping on the floors of various student flats in order to do so.

It was into a rather sophisticated political environment that baby-faced McConnell came in 1977. A shepherd's son from the island of Arran, he could easily have been treated as a naive kid and confined to the sidelines of debates. Those who remember him at his first political meetings on the campus described him as 'unremarkable'. The fact that he looked younger than his mere seventeen years did not help him to be taken seriously but, instead of trying to compete with the more mature political heavyweights, McConnell quietly listened and learned from them. McConnell had chosen Stirling University rather than Glasgow or Edinburgh because of its out-of-town location and its campus-based ethos. It appealed to the country boy because it seemed a smaller, friendlier place than the bigger institutions. However, McConnell went from being the brightest in his class at Arran High School to feeling out of his depth at Stirling.

Most of the other students in his year had completed sixth year studies in maths and were more proficient at the subject. They also seemed more mature. For the first time in his life, academic study proved to be a tough challenge and he was forced to work hard to catch up. It was a valuable learning experience for him.

But, if Jack felt overwhelmed by his new environment, it wasn't obvious to those who studied with him. Fellow students say his smile marked him out as a pleasant, likeable guy. Some of the more mature students would try to take him under their wing and help him to make his mark. However, his political mentors struggled to get him elected to the political positions he craved. He looked so young that he tended to be overlooked by his fellow students. Former Stirling student Ian McKay says, 'It was obvious Jack wanted to be a politician. He was interested in politics beyond student politics.' Eventually McConnell was elected as the Student Association President 1980 and, instead of giving up at the end of the year as was customary, McConnell stood again and won the presidency for a second year – something which had never been done before.

Around this time, the university's political life changed. As student activists developed their politics along party lines, it moved away from meetings of the broad left. Jack had joined the SNP when he was a sixteen-year-old schoolboy. The Labour government of the day did not hold much appeal for McConnell who was attracted by the idea of a party claiming to put Scotland first. However, when he went to university, the SNP activists on the campus tended to hold strong anti-English views and Jack was turned off by their insular attitude. McConnell had worked out that, in order to achieve what he wanted, he must pledge his allegiance to the Labour Party and work within it to deliver the changes he strove for.

The district council elections in Stirling that year produced an administration of ten Labour councillors, nine Tories and one Independent. McConnell attended a May Day rally in the town's Albert Hall that year and, afterwards, John Reid took him aside and told him he must join Labour's ranks. Reid said that, in four years' time, the council could be a different place but it needed people like Jack to make that happen. Reid also warned him of the necessity to take on the hard left who had a strong grip on university politics. McConnell didn't need much convincing. The following day he called John Boothman, the president of the Student's Association at Strathclyde University, to ask him to send him an application form to join the Labour Party. He phoned Boothman because he was the most committed Labour Party student that Jack knew at the time. Within days of his conversation with Reid, Jack had signed up to the party that he would go on to lead in Scotland.

In those days, Constituency Labour Party (CLP) meetings were packed and the activists were enthusiastic. Mike Donnelly, one of Jack's university lecturers with whom he had formed a strong friendship, was the secretary of Jack's local branch of the Labour Party. The guest speaker at one of the first local party meetings Jack ever attended was John Reid. At that time, Reid was working as the Labour Party's research officer. He gave his analysis of how Labour had to change if it was to capture voters in the future and every word made perfect sense to McConnell. But activists who watched him then say that, while some budding politicos were eager to be seen to be putting the Labour Party first, McConnell's attitude was rather different. He gave the impression that he was less tribal and he showed a willingness to work with people who did not necessarily share his political opinions if it meant he could achieve some objective he was particularly concerned about.

It is clear that Mike Donnelly was a big influence in Jack's life around this time. Donnelly had lived through the party's internecine war following the '79 general election. He had taken part in the left–right battles that threatened to engulf the party. McConnell, on the other hand, was fresh out of school and eager to learn from this experienced hand. There is no doubt Donnelly was steeped in the Labour Party and wanted Jack to become so too but he also encouraged him to engage in debates with his student counterparts in the Communist Party. Donnelly's philosophy is that you have to be honest as you can only argue what you genuinely believe in if you are to be effective.

Getting results is what drove Jack back then. While watching the Moscow Olympics along with a friend in his room at the student halls of residence in 1980, he was cheering on Linsey MacDonald, the young Scottish athlete who went on to win a bronze medal in the 4 × 400-metres relay. At the time, there was a row over a lack of funding for young athletes and the speculation was that, following the games, MacDonald would have to move to the States to pursue her career. McConnell was appalled at the idea of Scotland losing such a talent just because the country could not give her the financial support she needed.

Instead of downing a few more pints, Jack hatched a plan to bounce the university into offering her a sports scholarship. He rang the news desk of *The Glasgow Herald* newspaper that night and told them that Stirling University was planning such a scholarship and that MacDonald could be the first recipient. The story wasn't true but Jack calculated that, when the paper phoned the university to get more details, the university would see the sense of going along with the plan. He wasn't far wrong. Although the plan came in to force too late for Linsey MacDonald, the university was the first in Scotland to introduce sports scholarships. Even at the age of twenty, Jack had mastered the art of spin.

As Student President, Jack was well known on the campus at Stirling and he was seen as an effective student leader. During Jack's time as president, the former Labour MP Jim

Sillars was the university's student rector. McConnell both admired him and liked him. By that time, Sillars had resigned from the Labour Party and lost his seat when he stood for his breakaway Scottish Labour Party. He had then joined the SNP. In the autumn of 1981, the two men attended a rally and spoke out against planned education cuts. Education was a passion the two politicians shared then and continue to do so now. After McConnell left the platform, he took his seat in the front row of the audience next to Sillars' wife, Margo McDonald, then a former SNP MP, to listen to Sillars make his speech. McConnell had never been introduced to Margo at this point. As he sat down, she turned to him and said, 'So when are you going to become a Labour MP?' The twenty-one-year-old student politician was stunned. Here was a respected political figure believing that a 'wee guy from Arran' could, one day, sit in the House of Commons. McConnell may have been shocked by the suggestion. But the very idea that someone like Margo McDonald thought it was possible gave him a huge confidence boost. At that moment McConnell realised what his ambition actually was – to become a full-time elected politician. More than twenty years on, he has remained good friends with Margo and Jim and often seeks their advice on big political issues.

Jack was also heavily influenced by University Principal Ken Alexander who was spearheading a campaign against planned government cuts in university funding. As he fought for the university's survival, he came up with a plan that funding should follow students rather than be divided up among the institutions. Stirling was a popular university and Alexander knew that he could attract enough students to make the university viable under such a scheme. Jack learned from Alexander, believing he was someone who could win arguments by adopting a realistic approach rather than by relying on emotional sway.

Away from the political scene, drug-taking was rife on the campus during McConnell's time there. There is certainly no suggestion that he ever dabbled and, given how seriously he took himself, it is unlikely he would even have been tempted. Even from his university days, Jack was always conscious of how he behaved and he went out of his way to ensure there were no embarrassing escapades that could be cast up later. If he fancied having a blowout, he would make sure the only people who saw him letting his hair down were people he could trust. In fact, although he is remembered for having lots of friends and being extremely popular and sociable, few can ever remember him even getting drunk. One former student stated, 'Women certainly liked him because of his charm but he seemed so naive I'm not sure he would have realised if someone was coming on to him.'

As a student, McConnell shared a house in the town with Douglas Campbell, a fellow student who is now his press spokesman. To this day, McConnell has remained close to many of the friends he made while in Stirling. He maintains a close relationship with John Reid. His friend Ian McKay went on to become a senior official with the EIS teaching union and, while McConnell was Minister for Education, he provided Ian with valuable advice. Mike Donnelly went on to become his chief of staff when he became First Minister and fellow students Eric and Eileen Turnbull, who went on to become teachers, have also remained close.

As well as spending time in political meetings, Jack would also regularly turn up at social events on the campus. He spent a lot of his time at the Gannochy sports club and he was a regular at Maisie's bar in the Student Union. Eric Turnbull says, 'Jack lived the life of a student to the full. He worked when he had to but that was all.' Jack also amazed his former student friends when he turned up to the surprise fiftieth birthday party for former student union president Tommy Geddes. The party was held on the same day that the McConnells were moving house from Stirling to Wishaw but this didn't prevent them from attending. One friend said, 'Jack gets loyalty from people because he values relationships and puts a lot of work into keeping his friendships going.'

# 4

# STIRLING

Jack graduated from Stirling University in February 1983 with a degree in maths and a diploma in education. His parents travelled from Arran for the ceremony and proudly watched as their son was awarded the degree that would enable him to embark on a career in academia – or so they thought.

With his carefree student days behind him, Jack went in search of a teaching job. For three months, he worked at Wallace High School in Stirling on a temporary contract before landing a permanent job teaching maths at Lornshill Academy, Alloa. The town of Stirling was where Jack lived his student life, began his working life and was first elected as a politician. It was also where he was to meet his future wife.

Jack was elected councillor for the Logie ward of Stirling District Council in May 1984. He continued to work part-time as a maths teacher at Lornshill and spent two days a week at the council offices where he soon made his mark. But, early in his local government career, he was accused of forming an improper relationship with a member of staff. The then leader of the council Michael Connarty (now the MP for Falkirk East) called McConnell to his office to make his displeasure known. Connarty told him that he deplored the idea of councillors, who were seen as powerful figures, forming liaisons with staff members. In McConnell's case, Connarty was particularly angry because the woman concerned was a senior official within the arts and leisure department and McConnell was Committee Chairman of this department. Connarty told McConnell that, if he was indulging in a casual fling with this member of staff, he was to end the relationship immediately. Connarty had steeled himself for what he thought would be an unpleasant meeting but he was left speechless by McConnell's response.

Connarty had McConnell marked down as a young guy about town, a bit of a Jack the Lad who would charm one woman before quickly moving on to the next challenge. People who remember him from this time say there were lots of girlfriends but none of them seem to have appeared serious enough for anyone to have taken much of an interest. However, in the case of the member of the council staff, McConnell told Connarty that, far from messing one of the staff around, he had fallen deeply in love with her and was extremely serious about the relationship. The name of the woman in question was Bridget Brown, the council's Arts Officer who had recently been poached from Fife Council. Connarty was stunned as, apart from anything else, Jack had opposed her appointment.

When the council was looking to appoint an Arts Officer, Jack had someone in mind. He wanted local arts expert Brian Beattie to land the job and was furious when the interview panel went against his choice and gave the job to Bridget. After a few uncomfortable weeks of Bridget holding the post, Bridget and Jack decided they needed to work together despite his reservations about her. One day in October 1984, he took her to the Barton, a bar and bistro in Stirling town centre, and found, to his surprise, that not only did she have many radical ideas about how to do the job but that he actually liked her too.

Bridget was in the process of leaving her husband and had two young children. Jack was only twenty-four years old and settling down had been the last thing on his mind. However, on their first proper date together, he left Bridget speechless when he raised the subject of marriage. Because of their positions on the council, Jack and Bridget tried to keep their relationship secret for a while but without much success. Their cover was blown early in 1985. After a council meeting, their colleagues decided to go out for a drink. Jack declined to go, saying that he had marking to do in connection with his job as a maths teacher. Bridget also turned down the invitation, claiming she had to go home to look after her kids. Jack and Bridget had already arranged to go out together for a quiet drink away from the town centre. As they sat enjoying a romantic drink in a pub out of town, the door opened and in walked the same group of colleagues they had just lied to. Jack tried to dig them out of the hole by pretending that they had just remembered they had some outstanding business to discuss but he fooled nobody.

Meeting Bridget was a big turning point in Jack's life. He had always been responsible beyond his years but, in forming a relationship which would also mean taking on Bridget's two children, Jack was aware of the need to provide them with stability and support. Almost overnight, he went from being Jack the Lad to Jack the Dad. But, shortly after getting together with Bridget, Jack fell ill. He had been working long hours trying to juggle his job as a maths teacher with his council work. He was diagnosed with having colitis and he lost a lot of weight. Bridget persuaded him to scale back his political work and to radically change his diet and adopt a healthier lifestyle.

Early on in their relationship, Jack and Bridget formed many friendships that have proved lasting. After McConnell confided in Michael Connarty about his relationship with Bridget, the couple became close friends with Michael and his wife Margaret. Bridget and Jack would often take Bridget's two kids, Hannah and Mark, to play with the Connarty children. It was a relationship that was to endure – after leaving university, Hannah went to work for Michael Connarty in his office in Westminster and the two families remain close to this day. The friendship between the two men has lasted despite the fact that, throughout Michael Connarty's leadership of Stirling Council, it was clear McConnell wanted his job. Connarty said, 'Jack was always smart enough not to challenge unless he thought he could win.' McConnell could probably have made a successful challenge in 1987 but did not go for the top job because he suspected Labour would lose control of the council – in the end, Labour retained control in 1988 on a cut of the cards.

It is difficult to say whether it was Bridget's influence that drove McConnell's interest in the arts or if it was a passion they shared. Whatever the case, the result was that the department thrived while they were there. Nelson Mandela's African National Congress (the ANC) had an artistic group that travelled the world putting on plays and musicals that highlighted the injustices of apartheid. One of the musicals was *Amandla*, which the group performed at the town's 'little theatre', and having been able to attract them there was seen as a major coup at the time. Instead of ploughing money into the traditional areas of arts funding, there was a move to invest in areas of the arts which would have particular appeal among people living in poorer areas of the region. Bridget was also responsible for attracting the children's theatre group The Singing Kettle to Stirling in an attempt to make the arts more relevant to a wider range of people. This is a strategy that is also very much evident in Bridget McConnell's leadership of the arts in her current job at Glasgow City Council.

McConnell was just twenty-four when he was elected to Stirling Council and, when he was still in his mid twenties, he was responsible for running the authority's budget and he was also working as a teacher at Lornshill Academy. Lornshill is a large secondary school with more than 1,000 pupils, many of whom come from backgrounds where they lack parental support, and Jack taught there from 1983 to 1992. As you would expect of someone interested in politics, Jack joined the teaching union, the EIS, but he quickly became disillusioned by the union's politics. He took part in the teachers' strikes but only reluctantly. His view at the time was that the children's interests were not being put first and he found that situation difficult to defend.

The industrial action aside, Jack enjoyed his time in the classroom. Teaching at Lornshill made for a challenging job and this was all the more so when the subject was one as unpopular as maths. But Jack was young and enthusiastic and his ability to relate to the kids by talking to them about their interests in music also helped. Most of McConnell's lessons took place in the school outbuildings where bad discipline was more likely to be a problem. In the main part of the school, the kids were aware of the presence of other teachers walking up and down the corridors but, in the hut situated in the playground, they felt free to push their teachers to the limit. That said, McConnell had a reputation for being firm but fair and rarely had problems with his pupils. After he was elected to the council, Jack was forced to cut back on his teaching to just three days a week. This caused some resentment among several colleagues who did not agree with McConnell being able to divide his time in such a way.

During his time as a teacher, Jack became friendly with the Assistant Head of the Maths Department, Andy Juroszek. Both men lived in Stirling and Juroszek was also a Labour Party member. The two teachers would travel into school together by car each day. Andy said, 'We had a lot in common at that time. We would end up talking about politics when we were at school and talking about school when we were at political meetings. Jack was a good friend and we have remained in touch despite the fact I moved to Aberdeen.' Although he shared Jack's interest in politics, Andy was amazed when his friend went on to take up a full-time political career. 'I obviously knew that he was very active,' he said, 'but he seemed so enthusiastic about his teaching it never occurred to me that he would give it up for politics. He always gave the impression that teaching would be his career.'

Jack also enjoyed a good working relationship with the Head Teacher Alastair McLachlan and this helped him to carry on doing his two jobs. McLachlan rated Jack highly as a teacher and believed he was committed to the school and cared about the pupils. McLachlan says:

> He had a strong commitment to young people and he never used the fact that he had other work commitments to try to get out of doing something. Even as First Minister, he has been back to the school and has come to leaving parties for former colleagues. To me, that is indicative of a genuine interest in the school.

However, Alastair McLachlan was never in any doubt that Jack's future would be in politics rather than teaching as he never hid the fact that he was serious about his politics and knew where he wanted to go with it.

Jack McConnell was marked out as a young up-and-coming political star from May 1984 when he became one of the youngest councillors in Scotland after he won the Tory–Labour marginal ward of Logie. The seat took in the wealthy Bridge of Allan area but it also covered the university campus with its 1,800 voters. Traditionally, the student vote in local government elections had been in the order of 5% of the campus turning out. After deciding he wanted to get elected, McConnell turned to the Stirling University lecturer Mike Donnelly, his political mentor and friend. Donnelly immediately set about securing the student vote for McConnell. The turnout among the town's undergraduates shot up from the usual 5% to an astonishing 50%. McConnell had made the transition from student activist to elected politician and he had Donnelly to thank for fixing it.

From the day he was elected, Jack McConnell was seen as the heir apparent to Connarty's position as council leader. Although the two men were friends, Connarty kept a tight grip on power and around half a dozen of Connarty's allies were suspicious of the young McConnell. In 1988, McConnell's close friend Mike Donnelly was persuaded to stand for election to the council. Donnelly was reluctant as he realised his academic career would suffer but, not for the last time, he was to give in to Jack's pleas. The arrival of Donnelly served to increase tension among the older hands in the Labour group who could see McConnell building his power base. Depending on whom you talk to, Mike Donnelly is either the greatest restraining influence in McConnell's political life or the man responsible for teaching McConnell every Machiavellian trick he knows. The self-effacing Donnelly claims it is neither and that his influence over McConnell is exaggerated. However, one former Stirling official said, 'Mike Donnelly plots everything twenty years in advance. He plays a long game and keeps his cards very close to his chest.'

Donnelly was a much more sophisticated political animal than McConnell when the pair met at Stirling University. He taught Jack about the discipline of the Labour Party but also warned him that it was not necessarily a case of his party always being right and he encouraged Jack to debate and challenge on big ideas. Unlike the more naive McConnell, Donnelly understood the factions within the Labour Party and was a highly skilled organiser. While it is certain that he fixed some deals and votes for Jack, he does not appear to collect enemies in the way McConnell does. Those who distrust Donnelly can rarely point to a reason why.

It is clear Donnelly remains a big influence on McConnell even today. Early in McConnell's local government career, Jack faced a tough dilemma. His close friend from student politics Neil Stewart decided to leave Scotland to pursue his political career in London and ended up working in Neil Kinnock's office while Kinnock was Labour leader. McConnell was apparently torn between staying in Stirling and heading south to learn the ropes at Westminster in a backroom job. He confided in Connarty who told him he should continue as a maths teacher and hone his political skills by serving people instead of becoming a policy wonk. Given McConnell's general dislike of London, it was probably not a difficult decision to make as Scottish local government was in its heyday and Margaret Thatcher was in power. It was only through local government that Labour could offer any improvement in the running of the lives of the millions of Scots who detested her.

Stirling prided itself on being a modernising council. Along with Edinburgh, it was the first to appoint a women's officer, it invited tenants to sit on its housing committee and it did not shirk from battles with central government. These two councils were seen as among the most left-wing and radical in the country. After the Labour group defied a government ruling by increasing the rates bills of homeowners in order to keep council rents down, all eleven councillors were surcharged to the tune of £10,000 when they were taken to the High Court. The late Donald Dewar was one of the first to come to their aid with a personal cheque for £500. The remainder was quickly raised by trade unions and those who agreed with their approach.

In 1987, Jack was chosen as the Labour candidate for the Perth and Kinross constituency at the general election. At the time, the Scottish Tories were in deep trouble and many people were casting their votes tactically to get rid of the sitting Tory MP, the controversial Sir Nicholas Fairbairn. The SNP's Jim Fairlie stood a good chance of taking the seat from the beleaguered Tories. The local Labour Party approached McConnell and asked him to stand to prevent their vote from collapsing. He was just twenty-six at the time but he ran an enthusiastic campaign which resulted in Labour's vote doubling. As a result, the SNP failed to take the seat and Sir Nicky was safely re-elected. Perhaps not surprisingly, the high-living Conservative MP and his wife took a shine to Jack while the Perth and Kinross Nationalists, understandably, took a strong dislike to him.

Then, in 1989, McConnell saw a chance to make it on to the Westminster stage. He threw his hat into the ring in a bid to win the Labour nomination for the Falkirk East parliamentary seat. He was up against his friend Michael Connarty, the prominent activist Ester Quinn and the influential moderniser Bill Gilby who was seen as the favourite for the seat. However, Gilby pulled out of the race, opting instead to work with Rodney Bickerstaffe at NUPE's HQ in London. Connarty won a crucial branch nomination and, believing Connarty would win overall nomination, Jack decided to withdraw from the contest. Another significant factor in his decision not to chase a Westminster seat was that Bridget had left Stirling to take up a job as Director of Arts with Fife Council and was working long days. By now, Jack and Bridget were living together. Jack was able to take the children to school in the morning and was first home in the evening and he did not want to upset a domestic arrangement that was working well.

In the Scottish Labour Party, rivals for parliamentary seats tend to become enemies from the day the process is triggered until the day they die. However, Connarty and McConnell have remained firm friends. When Connarty was selected for the seat he gave up the leadership of the council and he instructed all his supporters to back McConnell. With Connarty gone, at the age of just twenty-nine, Jack McConnell became the youngest council leader in Scotland. It was his first taste of power and with it came plenty of problems. Unsurprisingly, he appointed Mike Donnelly to the post of Deputy Leader. Between them, they set about thoroughly modernising the council. Chief Executive Bob Black, the auditor general, left and McConnell and Donnelly saw this as an opportunity to appoint one of their own. They picked Geoff Bonnar, a young manager who wasn't afraid of implementing change. Highly paid council directors were thrown on to the scrap heap as McConnell decided he could streamline the authority. Money was ploughed into setting up play areas to help families with young children, particularly those living on the schemes. McConnell poured cash into private sports clubs on the condition they gave access to the local community. As well as being the first council leader to order the wheelie bins that are now used by every council in Scotland, McConnell introduced Scotland's first council customers' charter. And one of his first acts was to freeze the council tax for two years. He wanted to send a signal that he was not a Labour Party tax-and-spend leader but one who could deliver better services without landing taxpayers with a greater bill.

It was a smart move. Michael Forsyth was the local Conservative MP and he had the ability to exploit his opponents' weaknesses ruthlessly. As McConnell declared war on the Tory government at Westminster, he was careful to ensure his shake-up of the council did not hand them any ammunition. One of Scotland's best-known trade union officials, Bob Thomson of UNISON, described him as the 'Ken Livingstone of Scotland' at the time. He explained why, saying:

> He was taking on the Thatcher government – the council was radical and visionary under his leadership. It had women's officers and crèches – he was a real trailblazer in the '80s. Unfortunately, he is not giving local authorities the same chance to make the sort of improvements that he made.

However, McConnell's reforms at Stirling did not please everyone. The unions resisted many of his ideas and feared for their members. During one council meeting, a banner was unfurled in the public gallery, declaring 'Come back, Michael, all is forgiven', a reference to Michael Connarty who had a more friendly relationship with the unions. Jack was also to clash bitterly with the unions after a scandal erupted involving Stirling Windows, a company set up by the council. In many ways, the idea behind Stirling Windows was ahead of its time. It was set up by Michael Connarty as a firm that took on unemployed local people to make and fit plastic windows in the area. It was run by a board that was made up of councillors and the manager became a close friend of Jack. Stirling Windows looked to be a great success story.

But, while he was out on a local visit one day, during 1991, Jack received a call warning him that a Tory councillor was raising serious concerns about corruption within the firm. It transpired that the councillor was right to be worried. Staff at the firm had uncovered a secret set of books showing that payments had been taken from contractors but had not been declared. Jack felt sick. He had wanted the firm to succeed and he knew that, if there was corruption within the company, his close friend could be implicated. However, he did not hesitate for a second to consider how the matter might be hushed up. In his view, public money was involved and he was responsible for making sure it was spent appropriately. Jack called in the police and his friend was later prosecuted.

At the same time as the scandal was uncovered, the council realised that the firm was in financial difficulty and half the workforce was laid off. The Transport and General Workers' union called a strike. The union was furious that a Labour council was laying off staff. McConnell went to the Stirling Windows factory to hold a meeting with the workforce. To this day, it was one of the most difficult confrontations he has been involved in. Feelings were running high but Jack stuck to his guns. As furious workers turned on him for making their colleagues redundant, he made the argument that, even though he was in charge of a Labour council, he was prepared to see some people lose their jobs if it meant the company would survive and continue to provide employment for others. It was a bruising meeting and one of the first times that McConnell had been forced to make a tough decision and stick to it despite the unpleasantness of the situation. His friends refer to that factory meeting as one that shaped Jack's character and his approach to his politics.

Jack's tough edge won him both admirers and enemies in Stirling. His ability to take on the unions was all the more surprising given his youthful looks. McConnell was dubbed 'young Jack' on the council. He was even persuaded to grow a moustache in an attempt to look older. It was an ill-judged move and his moustache had few admirers. Some observers believe McConnell always felt he had to prove himself as he struggled to win credibility because of his age. It may be because of this that the young McConnell seemed to act like someone far older. He was always attracted by the idea of responsibility from helping to do the accounts for his mother's tearoom to the leadership of Stirling Council and the office of First Minister.

As McConnell was making his name on the local government stage, he never lost his boyish sense of fun and, in the main, he was liked by the staff. As a young councillor, he would often burst into the council's press office and throw his arms round the staff. One said:

> There was nothing sexual about it. I don't think he would give it a second thought – he is a very touchy-feely sort of person. It's his way of making people feel good. I don't often hug people when I meet them but, if I bumped into Jack, it would seem a natural thing to do.

Even middle-aged male friends remark on his tactile behaviour.

Another of McConnell's trademarks which can be traced back many years is his addiction to risk-taking. The closer he sails to the wind, the more of a political buzz he seems to get. In 1990, he used council money to stage a celebration for Scotland. Officially, 'A Day for Scotland' was billed as a great family day out. Held in a park beneath Stirling Castle, it was a glorious summer day and literally tens of thousands of people turned out. However, it didn't take a seasoned political observer to work out that the day of celebration was a thinly disguised attempt to hold an anti-Michael-Forsyth rally in the heart of the MP's constituency. Despite the fact that all the guest speakers were warned against making obvious political capital out of the taxpayer-funded event, the STUC's General Secretary, Campbell Christie, appeared to get carried away by the atmosphere and laid into Forsyth. McConnell found himself at the centre of a blazing row. Not for the first or last time, one of his carefully hatched plans threatened to blow up in his face. As with all his political storms McConnell withstood the pressure and it blew over.

Unfortunately, Lord Forsyth has a personal policy of not speaking to biographers so his direct views of McConnell cannot be recorded. However, Tories, who were close to him during McConnell's reign at Stirling, claim that Forsyth rated his opponent highly and had him marked down as a politician who would make it on the bigger stage.

Friends and enemies alike agree that McConnell has always had the air of a young man in a hurry. He held the leadership of Stirling Council until the 1992 election when Labour tied with the Tories at ten seats each. As had happened in the previous election, the control of the council was decided by cutting cards but, unlike 1988, Labour was not lucky and the party was consigned to opposition. After the cards went against him, McConnell lost power. It was not a situation he could live with. The young Jack started to look around for his next challenge and it wasn't long before he found it, landing the job of General Secretary of the Labour Party in Scotland. The move meant he would gain a higher national profile politically but it would end his teaching career. His colleagues at Lornshill were sad to see him go although, by now, they realised where his real ambition lay.

In the month before leaving his teaching post, Jack had been off ill. The long absence sparked a frenzy of gossip in the staff room at Lornshill. Speculation ranged from the state of his health to the plots he may have been involved in to get his new job. The gossips were still not satisfied by the time of Jack's leaving do and he knew it. In an act of typical Jack bravado, he stood up in front of dozens of his former colleagues and decided to put them out of their misery. Jack said:

> I know many of you have been wondering why I have been off work for such a long time. Some of you think I have spent the time plotting. That would have been far less painful than the circumcision and vasectomy operation I have just undergone.

There were audible gasps from the crowd followed by much laughter that Jack had opted to reveal such personal and potentially embarrassing details. The decision to have the vasectomy was Jack's. He was convinced that it would be damaging to Hannah and Mark if he and Bridget had other children.

As Jack changed jobs, Bridget's career was taking off. She was highly rated in her new job with Fife Council and earning substantially more than Jack was. As a result, he spent as much time as he could looking after the children. From the time Jack and Bridget got together, it was inevitable that they would get married. Their close friends Kirsty Wark and Alan Clements were planning to marry in 1989 and Jack and Bridget were caught up in the excitement of the plans. Just months later, they decided to marry. Not unexpectedly, given that they both come from large families and that they are both extremely sociable, it was a huge wedding. The guest list was comprised of their friends from the council, the school and their universities. Jack's close ally from his student days Bob McLean was his best man and future MSPs Wendy Alexander and Sarah Boyack were both at the reception at Seamill Hydro in Ayrshire on 6 April 1990. They exchanged vows in the hotel with Jack's home island of Arran as the backdrop in the window behind them.

Both families were pleased about the marriage. Bridget's relatives were delighted that she was happy again after suffering a tough few years with the breakdown of her first marriage and Jack's family believed she was a good influence on him. No sooner was the ink dry on the wedding certificate than Jack and Bridget embarked on a difficult adoption process that was to end in the successful outcome of him becoming father to Hannah and Mark.

# 5

# JACK'S DEVOLUTION JOURNEY

Labour's election defeat of 1987 was, for some, the most devastating of all the losses party activists had to endure during the eighteen years of Tory rule. In 1983, they had expected it but, four years later, they believed Neil Kinnock's reforms would win over voters. They didn't – at least not in England and that was where it mattered. The story was different in Scotland – the Tories lost half their seats as the electorate sought to punish them over their poll tax plans. But Scottish Labour activists took little comfort from the improved showing north of the border, rightly realising that, if the party couldn't win in England, it couldn't be in a position to deliver a parliament for Scotland.

During the summer of '87, frustrated activists met to discuss what, if anything, could be done. It was a desperate time when many believed that their party would never be in power again. Then, that autumn, a young Labour activist, Ian Smart, came up with a brainwave – he believed an organisation, working within the Scottish Labour Party, could deliver home rule. Smart was a lawyer who became involved in student politics while studying at Glasgow University. He was close to Bob McLean, an Edinburgh-based activist with strong home-rule credentials. Between them, they had a formidable network of bright young things in the party and, when they set about canvassing support for the new organisation, they found huge enthusiasm for the idea.

The group was to be called Scottish Labour Action (SLA) and it was founded in the winter of 1987 at a meeting in Jack

McConnell's flat in Stirling. The organisation put together a manifesto that had the backing of eight signatories. They included Susan Deacon, Sarah Boyack and Frank McAveety, all of whom went on to become ministers in the Scottish Parliament, and leading activists of the time like Alan Bell as well as Smart and McLean. It is interesting to note that although McConnell hosted the inaugural meeting of SLA he was not one of the signatories. Opinion is divided over whether this was intentional or not. The group called for Labour politicians to stand for election on a 'dual mandate', which meant that, if they were elected to Westminster at the next election but found that another Tory government was returned, they would refuse to recognise it, remain in Scotland and work with other political parties to force the government to negotiate a devolved settlement. Although Jack was an important player in the group, as Alan Clements said, 'There was no feeling of there being a first among equals.' Soon after the SLA was set up, Clements decided to stop being politically active as he felt that, if he continued, it could potentially be seen as being in conflict with his job at the BBC.

Many of those who were attracted by the aims of Scottish Labour Action had been members of the Labour Coordinating Committee (LCC) but that group's leading figures tended to be older than those in SLA and not all of them were so passionately committed to a Scottish Parliament. As a result, the younger, more ambitious members were looking for a more radical vehicle that could deliver the changes they thought needed to be made.

The two organisations, however, worked side by side until the Scottish party conference of March 1988 when the party ruled out running a campaign of non-payment of the poll tax. The SLA was incensed at the decision which had been taken by the Scottish Executive of the party. They were even more irate that the LCC members of the Executive had not bothered to consult them.

As well as championing the dual mandate idea, SLA members were strongly in favour of non-payment of the poll tax. They saw the issue as being the strongest argument they could make to voters as to why a Scottish parliament was needed. Ian Smart said:

> We would travel up and down the country making speeches against the poll tax and we used that issue to make people see the case for home rule. Whenever anyone asked why we need a parliament, you only needed to say, 'To stop the poll tax' and the argument was won.

The LCC was nicknamed the Labour Careerists Committee because so many of its members went on to become MPs but latterly it was seen by some as too close to the leadership to force the pace of change. Smart said:

> We thought there was a danger that the world would pass us by unless we did something radical. The LCC seemed to be too interested in deciding who would be the Chair of the Scottish Labour Party in three years' time and we just didn't see that as important.

The poll tax row of 1988 prompted speculation that the Scottish Labour Party could split. In the event of that happening, several newspapers had pledged their support to the SLA wing of the party but Scottish Labour Action members were all too aware of the experience of the Scottish Labour Party and were determined not to make the same mistake.

Publicly both Donald Dewar while he was Shadow Scottish Secretary and George Robertson when he took over the post distanced themselves from SLA. However, neither politician dismissed the pressure group, realising that many of its members had the potential to become the next generation of Scottish Labour politicians. And there is a view that the internal pressure from SLA suited the party leadership in Scotland. Whenever Dewar or Robertson wanted to push the case for home rule with the party in London they would point to the threat of a damaging breakaway nationalist movement by the faction unless concessions were made.

Looking back, some of the ideas put forward by Scottish Labour Action appear extremist. However, the group realised that the devolution plan put forward in the 1979 referendum was unworkable. Labour MP John Maxton had put forward a private member's bill in the Commons in November 1987 in an attempt to tidy up the proposals.

Crucially, SLA decided that, unlike the 1979 proposal which set out the powers a Scottish parliament would have, a new plan should state that the parliament would be assumed to have all powers apart from those expressly stated. This change of emphasis was significant and it formed the basis of the Scotland Act which was passed in Parliament in 1997.

Although Donald Dewar quickly saw the merit of that argument, there were other areas in which he thought SLA was too extreme. Dewar was a cautious politician. The idea of Labour politicians standing on a dual mandate was for him a non-starter. He was a strict constitutionalist who could not counter anything other than winning the election in order to deliver his dream of a Scottish parliament. To him, there could be no use of shortcuts or threats to bring it about. And, in his view, the dual mandate could only serve to point up the impotence of his own party.

The setting up of SLA followed on from the work of the Campaign for a Scottish Assembly (CSA), which later became the Campaign for a Scottish Parliament. Many of the founding members of SLA had been part of the CSA which was a cross-party organisation. It devised the claim of right which stated that the Scottish people should have their own parliament. It wanted all the parties to form an electoral pact to defeat the ten remaining Tory MPs standing in the way of constitutional change and to support calls for a multi-option referendum on the issue.

While members of the LCC would have been more resistant to the idea of working with Liberal Democrats, the SLA people believed that, without cross-party effort, a parliament would never happen. Ian Smart again:

> We had this idea that we could get hundreds of thousands of people into the streets to demand their own parliament. But we thought that it would be impossible to gather that kind of support for a parliament set up by Labour to serve Labour's interests.

Given that premise, SLA believed that only a cross-party constitutional convention could achieve its aim and that an inevitable consequence of working with other parties would be an agreement that the parliament be elected by proportional representation (PR).

Just as Labour activists thought things could only get better, the Govan by-election of 1988 took place. The SNP's Jim Sillars wiped the floor with Labour's candidate, Bob Gillespie. Gillespie has gone down in Scottish Labour Party history as one of the worst ever by-election performers. The fact that he was up against the experienced intellectual, Jim Sillars, as well as Bernard Ponsonby, a young Liberal Democrat activist who grabbed the media's attention with his formidable performances, only served to highlight Gillespie's inadequacies. In the party post-mortem that followed, the leadership blamed the humiliating by-election loss entirely on their candidate. This prompted a backlash from SLA whose members argued that it was the party's failure to address the constitutional question which was to blame for the Govan disaster. They claimed that even the best Labour Party candidate would have come unstuck. The by-election result certainly convinced SLA that its arguments were right and it increased pressure on the leadership.

It has often been said that the Labour Party went into the constitutional convention talks as a knee-jerk reaction to Govan but Donald Dewar had hinted at the idea in a speech at Stirling University six weeks before the by-election. Some devolution purists thought at the time that Dewar only agreed to the move to show SLA that an agreement with the other parties would prove impossible. At the time he took his party into the negotiations, it was assumed that the SNP would also be at the table. Perhaps if the Nationalists had taken part, their fundamentalist wing would have made that the case. However, the groundwork done by the CSA proved to be a useful base for the convention.

Bernard Ponsonby, now the political editor of Scottish Television, served on the executive of the CSA. He said:

> It was the activist class who were pushing the idea of cross-party cooperation. Jack McConnell spoke at one of our meetings in Stirling in early 1988 and called for the idea of an electoral arrangement with the Liberal Democrats and the SNP to be closely looked at. He realised that, if the cross-party work was to succeed, we would all have to set aside our sectarianism. Jack was certainly on the ecumenical wing of the Labour Party.

Scottish Labour Action had also won the sympathy of a young party researcher, Wendy Alexander. Although she was not able to join any pressure group within the party because she was employed by Labour, there was no doubt she was on their side and she formed strong friendships with many of its members. The organisation believed that she was an important link to the leadership and helped to persuade Donald Dewar and then General Secretary Murray Elder of some of the merits of their arguments.

SLA targeted most of its work to be released at the time of Scottish party conferences. They produced a series of pamphlets and, in one, there is a chapter written by Jack McConnell in which he calls for PR.

At the 1989 Scottish Labour Party Conference, SLA secured one of its most important victories when it persuaded the party to commit to taking part in the Scottish Constitutional Convention talks. The members of SLA were wise enough to realise that large sections of the party to which they belonged were hostile to proportional representation. Although many members of SLA privately favoured the single transferable vote (STV) system that the Liberal Democrats would have wanted for the Scottish Parliament, they also conceded it would be too big a jump for their party to make. They, therefore, settled on the additional member system, the less proportional system of proportional representation, on which the Scottish Parliament is elected.

SLA was also strongly opposed to any move to have Scottish parliamentary candidates selected from a central list which the leadership could control. As an activist-based organisation, it was determined that party members would be able to determine who got elected to the Scottish Parliament instead of a cabal of party apparatchiks. SLA was also acutely aware that it did not want a parliament full of time-served party hacks and councillors or, as one member put it, 'We didn't want the councillors with the deepest pockets winning.'

In the run up to the '97 election, Ian Smart wrote a private paper that was circulated to a small group of people. In it, he called for membership of the party to be free. His idea was that newspapers could print coupons which readers could fill in to become members. This, he felt, would offer the possibility of massively expanding the party's base. SLA was strongly in favour of a panel of candidates being approved by party HQ before they were allowed to offer themselves for selection in the constituencies.

Ironically, it was SLA members who became the victims of the process when it was eventually set up. Tommy Sheppard was rejected by the panel, as, initially, was Susan Deacon – although she later got on after appealing the decision.

Scottish Labour Action remained a united group that had the respect of the party leadership from the time it was formed until 1992. However, the '92 election shook the beliefs of some of its members. Jack McConnell came out of the election campaign convinced that his party's devolution policy had lost as many votes as it had won for them. He came to the conclusion that the case for a Scottish parliament had to be made in a more accessible way. Instead of it being a row over the constitution, he decided it had to become about how public services could be improved.

Although the election result was another devastating blow for the party, at least, this time, it had come close. McConnell was coming round to the Donald Dewar school of thought that 'one more heave' would deliver devolution. But not all devolution enthusiasts agreed. Others became even more convinced that protest was the only route to change.

At this point, the cross-party Scotland United group was formed and some of the more hard-line members of SLA were attracted to join. This organisation tried to motivate Scots to take part in east-European-style demos on the streets in order to achieve its goal. Pop stars Ricky Ross of Deacon Blue and Pat Kane of Hue and Cry signed up to its aims and a rally was planned for George Square.

McConnell shunned the new organisation. He wanted the same end as they did but never believed they were on the right track and warned that the venture would end in tears. The rally in George Square appeared to prove his point. The SNP's Nicola Sturgeon spoke from the platform and denounced the Labour Party as the obstacle to a Scottish Parliament. Then a Labour Party speaker attacked the SNP for helping to bring down the last Labour government and bringing Thatcher to power.

Meanwhile, McConnell's change of tack won him the respect of the party leadership and paved the way for him to become General Secretary of the party. With one of their own installed in the top job in the party in Scotland, SLA was delighted. After '92, the group slipped from prominence a bit but mainly because they were working with the leadership of the party and not against it. SLA had a hotline to Jack and its members used it to float ideas or to lobby Dewar or Robertson.

The election of John Smith as party leader also caused McConnell to rethink SLA's main argument – the dual mandate. He decided that the idea of Smith going to London to lead the Labour Party, wearing his British hat but refusing to recognise the government because he had stood on a Scottish dual-mandate ticket, was a nonsense. But SLA's plans for cross-party cooperation, a parliament elected by PR and gender balance were all taken by McConnell into party headquarters.

After '92, SLA was badly affected by the steep decline in party activism. Then, in 1994, came another blow with the death of John Smith. Most members of SLA hoped that he would be succeeded by Gordon Brown. Contrary to popular opinion, Ian Smart claims Jack McConnell would have shared that view:

The idea that Jack sided with Blair against Brown does not stand up to any scrutiny. You have to remember that everything was decided in London in the space of seven days.

I can't see why the General Secretary of the Scottish Labour Party would even have been asked his view. And there was no contest – Gordon decided not to run so there was never a case of having to back one over the other.

Scottish Labour Action was further boosted when one of its closest allies, Tommy Sheppard, was appointed as deputy to McConnell at the Labour Party's Scottish headquarters at Keir Hardie House in Lyndoch Place, Glasgow.

With the election of Tony Blair as leader came the party's overriding concern of instilling discipline. New Labour was obsessed by the idea of splits or differences of opinion in its ranks. Interestingly, SLA did not take the view that devolution would die with John Smith but went with the opposite opinion – that it was Smith's legacy and could now never be ditched by the party. When both Brown and Blair described the Scottish Parliament as his 'unfinished business', it allayed any fears they may have had.

As debate within the party was stifled, SLA focused its efforts behind the scenes in negotiations with McConnell and the new Shadow Scottish Secretary, George Robertson. McConnell and Robertson had an excellent working relationship and had formed a firm friendship. As a result, SLA believed they had a new ally in Robertson.

Despite some misgivings about Blair they were also pleased to have a party leader who was receptive to PR and devolution – or so they thought at the time. But then, in June 1996, came the decision that devastated the group and caused its membership to split. Without consultation, the Labour Party announced it was to hold a two-question referendum on devolution. On a Sunday night one week before the decision was announced, McConnell received a call at his home in Stirling from George Robertson. The two men would normally speak over the course of the weekend to discuss issues raised by the Sunday papers and to decide their plans for the week ahead. But, midway through the conversation, Robertson asked McConnell what he thought of the idea of holding a pre-legislative referendum on devolution. It was immediately obvious to the General Secretary that this call was more than their usual Sunday catch-up chat. McConnell gave a warm response to the suggestion.

Twenty-four hours later, Robertson called him again to tell McConnell he must fly to London that night but he couldn't tell him why. On his flight to Heathrow, McConnell read a story by Donald MacIntyre in the *Independent* suggesting a referendum on devolution. MacIntyre is a well-respected lobby correspondent known to have strong links to Number Ten and to Alastair Campbell. McConnell knew immediately why he was on his way to the Commons.

When he arrived at Westminster, McConnell was called to the chief whip's office where Donald Dewar had been in talks with George Robertson. Together, they told McConnell there would be a referendum and that there would be two questions in the poll. Despite the huge row it was set to provoke in the Labour Party, McConnell embraced the idea. He was taken to the Commons office of the leader of the opposition where Tony Blair had been expecting a hostile response from his top official in Scotland. He didn't get one. McConnell told him it was 'a great idea'. However, he warned the future PM that there were key figures in Scotland who would have to be spoken to ahead of any announcement. Interestingly, the people McConnell wanted to reach were not his SLA friends but people like Canon Keynon Wright who chaired the Constitutional Convention, the Lib Dem leader Jim Wallace and Campbell Christie of the STUC.

It was made clear to McConnell that the decision had been taken – the discussion was over – and McConnell promised Blair that he would 'do everything he could' to deliver the result they wanted.

At the time, the party pretended to the media that the idea had come from George Robertson. While he was certainly on board for the plan, it is obvious that the decision was taken by Blair. One senior party figure said:

> The decision was taken by Tony but he had been heavily influenced by Derry Irvine and Gordon Brown. Derry was extremely worried that the legislation would not get through both houses in the form they wanted and Brown was very nervous about the Tories' 'tartan tax' campaign – both he and Alastair Campbell felt something had to be done to kill the argument.

Derry Irvine and Donald Dewar were not on speaking terms following the breakdown of Dewar's marriage when his wife left him for Irvine.

The idea of Derry Irvine devising a mechanism to ensure Dewar's devolution dream survived intact seemed unlikely to many in the party. However, Neil Stewart, a former adviser to Neil Kinnock claims Dewar's experience of the 1979 referendum was enough to convince him that the party had to do everything it could to prevent the settlement from being wrecked. Stewart said:

> Blair and Dewar were fearful – they were looking at the polls in the rest of the UK which weren't good. Remember it was Labour Party MPs, obstructionists from the north of England, who imposed the 40% rule in the 1979 referendum. It wasn't the Tories who wrecked devolution and Dewar was well aware of that.

Like Dewar, McConnell was equally convinced that there was a strong intellectual case in favour of a two-question referendum. But, even before he had left Blair's office to 'fix' the party, Alastair Campbell entered the room to tell them that he had been 'bounced' into confirming the plan to the press. Until that moment, McConnell's view had been that the idea was a great one which could be sold to the party if properly handled. But he instantly realised that, with no time to 'square' members of the Scottish Executive and SLA, he could have a war on his hands. How right he was.

The idea of a vote on devolution had already been discussed informally with key members of SLA. And, while the principle of a referendum posed no problem for SLA and many of its members had been coming round to the view it would be helpful and easily winnable, what did pose a huge problem was raising the spectre of Scots voting for a parliament without tax-raising powers. Since its first meeting, SLA had been clear that the parliament must have the power to vary tax and that the absence of that power was the main reason the 1979 referendum had been lost.

SLA felt betrayed by Blair and let down by McConnell. The organisation, which had spent the best part of a decade working on the devolution proposals, saw their cherished policy begin to unravel. Smart said, 'We thought this was fatal. If people voted "no" on the second question, it would leave Labour in the position that it would be legislating for a parliament based on a model the party had argued was inherently unstable.' Blair flew to Scotland for a showdown meeting with the Scottish Executive of the Labour Party. Since he had become leader, he had developed a habit of ensuring that his party meekly followed wherever he led.

McConnell and Robertson were all too aware that this was one occasion when they could not guarantee to deliver for the leader. After flying up from London, the two men sat in George Robertson's car at Edinburgh Airport, contemplating how they would handle the potentially explosive situation. McConnell had a bundle of that day's newspapers under his arm. The headlines were catastrophic for Labour. Robertson told him they would not be able to face the task that lay ahead if they ploughed through hundreds of column inches warning them of Labour civil war. So the papers were tossed into the back of Robertson's car and they drove off to one of the most difficult political meetings they would ever have to attend.

What happened in the room that day left even Tony Blair shaken and bewildered and would set the tone for relations between the Scottish party and Blair for years to come. One Executive member said:

> He looked us in the eye and said how sorry he was that the news had leaked before he had a chance to speak to us. We knew the story had been briefed by Alastair Campbell – we were finished with Blair.

In an act that antagonised some Executive members even further, the Labour leader's press spokesman Alastair Campbell sat through the meeting. Luckily for Blair there was no vote taken at that meeting – it was postponed until the next meeting to be held several days later. George Robertson describes the meeting as the biggest 'wobble' of his time in Scottish politics. He said:

> It was my highest point and the lowest point. We knew it was the right thing to do but the coverage was so bad we couldn't read it and we said, 'If we read this today, we will never succeed.'

As General Secretary of the party, Jack McConnell knew his job was to deliver for his leader. But his former comrades in SLA took the view that he had gone over to the dark side and betrayed everything they stood for. The scars from this fight have now faded but the relationship between McConnell and his fellow bright young things would never be quite the same. To this day SLA members are split over the motive behind holding the referendum and some even sway from one month to the next in their views.

Ian Smart was always of the view that the tax-raising power would not be used by a Labour administration in the Scottish Parliament because doing so would be pointing up that a Labour government in London was not spending enough on public services. However, he believed that, without the power, the SNP would blame everything on the inability to raise revenue.

SLA's fears of a plot to undermine devolution were exacerbated because the leadership had made it clear their view was that, in the general election, the party could not go to the electorate pledging to raise income tax because it felt it would lose the election. Now the Scottish party was expected to believe that somehow the calculation was different when it came to devolution north of the border. The activists smelt a rat. If Blair thought the threat of higher tax would lose him the election, then surely he thought the possibility of higher tax in the Scottish Parliament would lose him the second question in the referendum. Smart said:

> We thought it was such an obvious error. We were saying to people we won't use this power – only a lunatic government in the future would do that – but vote for the power anyway. Our argument was why would people take the chance of there being a lunatic government in the future when they could just vote no?
>
> We were also steeped in this argument – without being arrogant, we felt we knew more about it than Blair. But it was made clear that New Labour would not tolerate dissent of any kind.

Another of SLA's founding fathers, Bob McLean, was equally angry about the decision. He had fought for the devolution policy as it stood since the 1979 debacle. He, more than most, had forged cross-party support for the idea. He said, 'The thing that angered me most was that this was not the policy one day but suddenly there it was the next day. There was no process which had been gone through – it was just sprung on us.'

Pro-devolution Scots based at Westminster lost patience with their Scottish colleagues over the issue. One claimed:

> It was a case of the referendum would have been a great idea if it had been their idea but, because they hadn't thought of it, they hated it. It was nothing more than a case of 'not made in Scotland, therefore, not something we want'.

Almost a decade on from the row, Bob McLean is prepared to concede there is something in that argument. 'That might have been part of it but I also feared for how things were going to be run if this was how we were starting off.'

Although McLean was furious about the referendum proposal at the time, his reaction was more tempered than that of Smart. Smart wrote a paper in which he made strong criticisms of Blair's style of leadership. Not long afterwards, his local MP, Norman Hogg, stood down from the Cumbernauld and Kilsyth parliamentary seat. Smart had long been regarded as his heir apparent. However, after being interviewed by Labour's National Executive Committee, he was blocked from standing and Rosemary McKenna went on to be selected. The party had exacted its revenge.

Around this time, McConnell and SLA parted company. Unlike many Central-Belt politicians who had fought their battles with the right or the left in the party, McConnell had had more run-ins than most with the Tories. His political homeland was the leafy suburbs of Stirling where, for years, the Tories had controlled the local council and won the parliamentary seat at Westminster and he had had plenty of encounters with the local MP, Michael Forsyth. McConnell and Forsyth have a strong regard for each other's ability – if also a strong contempt for each other's views.

As a result of his political background, McConnell has always been convinced that Labour had to shed its tax and spend image. He was of the view that fears of higher taxes had cost Labour the 1992 election. He believed that tax was a powerful weapon in the Tories' hands – and that the tartan tax was a deadly weapon in Michael Forsyth's hands. To him, the second question on the tax-raising powers for the parliament was not designed to destroy devolution but a way of shooting the Tory fox. McConnell was utterly convinced it was the right tactic but he would never convince his friends in the home-rule pressure group.

However, SLA did not want to be on a collision course with the party leadership. The 1997 general election was just months away and, with it, came the chance to get the parliament they had all devoted their political lives to achieving. No one wanted to put that at risk with a damaging row. In the days that followed, they tried every means imaginable to get the decision reversed. They pushed their case with McConnell. They called George Robertson and Pat McFadden, a Scot who had worked for John Smith and now worked for Blair. They tried to reach Gordon Brown but he was out of the country for most of the crucial period. They then put forward the suggestion of a complex question along the lines of 'We believe a parliament for Scotland needs tax-varying powers. Do you back such a parliament? – yes or no'. But the party was not for turning – the decision had been made, the leader had spoken. SLA was left bitter and disappointed and much of their resentment was taken out on McConnell whom they felt could have done more to stop it.

However, the pro-home-rulers still believed they could vote the referendum policy down. They had done the figures and were convinced that they would defeat the leadership in a vote of the Scottish Executive. They reckoned they had nineteen votes to seventeen. But the leadership targeted those dissenters they believed they had most chance of convincing.

The candidate for the Govan constituency, Mohammed Sarwar, had defeated a sitting Labour MP, Mike Watson, to win the nomination. He had not suffered the usual Labour Party offensive to protect its MP. He felt he owned them and they were not slow to call in the favour. George Robertson spent hours trying to reach an accommodation with Sarwar. In the end, he agreed to support the leadership if they promised to give voters an opportunity to vote for tax powers not once but twice. In essence, the policy became that, if there was a 'no' vote on the second question, there would be a third question, after the parliament was set up, asking the electorate to reconsider. That day, the Scottish Executive voted for what became known as the 'three-question referendum'. It was ridiculed. From a row over whether there would be one question or two, there had come a solution that there should be three. It made sense to nobody.

SLA founder Ian Smart was outside the meeting in Stirling. The doors were locked but he received a call on his mobile, informing him of the decision. He immediately tried to reach fellow SLA members Jackie Baillie and Bob McLean who sat on the Executive. They had opposed the idea, voting instead for a one-question referendum, but their opposition wasn't enough to block the plan. The three-question referendum became the policy of the Scottish Labour Party. The SLA activists immediately realised the three-question referendum policy was farcical and were prepared to drop their opposition but it was too late to convey that news to George Robertson who had already held a press conference announcing it.

After several days of listening to the Shadow Scottish Secretary George Robertson trying to defend the decision and then explain it, the embarrassment became too much – for both sides. The three-question referendum policy was dropped with the agreement of everyone. But the leadership had got its way – there would be a two-question referendum on devolution and there was nothing anyone in the Scottish party could do about it.

# 6

# GENERAL SECRETARY

On 8 April 1992, Labour wheeled out its big guns in Scotland in what the party hoped would be the dying hours of Tory rule in Britain. At the Guild Hall in Stirling, John Smith, Gordon Brown, Robin Cook and Donald Dewar, along with the local candidate Kate Phillips, held a joint press conference. The four heavyweights would be pivotal figures in a Labour government if it were to be elected the following day. Hardened by thirteen years in the electoral wilderness, the senior party figures were not taking victory for granted. They would turn out to be right not to do so. However, given their seniority, they had been forced to make plans for government in the event of Neil Kinnock getting the keys to Number Ten.

Keeping a careful eye on the press conference that day was the General Secretary of the Labour Party in Scotland, Murray Elder. Elder was John Smith's most trusted political ally. If Smith were to become Britain's next Chancellor, he wanted Elder at his side in Number Eleven. That would mean giving up his role as the head of the party organisation in Scotland. Both Smith and Elder were clear who they wanted to succeed him in Keir Hardie House. Their choice was Jack McConnell, then the leader of Stirling District Council. It was in this capacity that McConnell attended the Guild Hall press conference on the eve of poll.

As he walked across the car park after the event, he was stopped by Elder who told him he was leaving his job and that both he and Smith wanted Jack to take over. Until then, it was assumed Elder's successor would be party loyalist Anne McGuire of the Scottish Council for Voluntary Organisations, now the MP for Stirling, or Johann Lamont, a founding member of the Scottish Labour women's caucus. The fact that they were both female reflected the strong belief within the party that the job should go to a woman. However, to the Labour establishment figures of the time, McConnell's leadership of Stirling District had marked him out as a rising star. They had concerns over his strong nationalist leanings and about his leading role within Scottish Labour Action, the pressure group campaigning for home rule.

As Shadow Scottish Secretary, Donald Dewar kept a careful eye on SLA and, while he did not embrace its ideas with great enthusiasm at that stage, he recognised that the young politicians involved in the movement had talent and would be the next generation of Scottish politicians. However, he also saw them as ambitious young men and women in a hurry and he would have liked them to slow down a bit. Of the influential group, the leadership believed that McConnell was the most moderate and they began to see there was merit in having him inside their tent. The election defeat of 1992 scarred McConnell along with every other member of the Labour Party who thought that victory was at last in sight. Although his belief in a Scottish Parliament was unshaken, the '92 defeat left him convinced that the devolution policy as it stood was a turn-off for the voters.

As the hard-line nationalists inside the Labour Party regrouped and formed Scotland United to push for a parliament in Scotland, regardless of the make-up of the new government at Westminster, McConnell went in the opposite direction. He did not blame the Tories but believed Labour had failed to make a convincing case for devolution and that the policy needed to be overhauled. Because McConnell had distanced himself from the hardliners within the home-rule movement, the leadership knew they had found their man – a devolution enthusiast who was also a realist. The decision was made at the party conference in 1992.

Although Kinnock was no longer leader, his former adviser, Neil Stewart, still carried enormous weight in the party. He arrived at the conference to discover that McConnell's appointment was not yet in the bag so he set about speaking to leading trade unionists and members of the National Executive Committee (NEC) to ensure they were aware of McConnell's work in Stirling and telling anyone who would listen that he would have been Kinnock's choice for the job. When the party's National Executive Committee picked McConnell for the job in August 1992, McGuire and Lamont's supporters were stunned. They had no idea that Smith and Elder had been lobbying for the Stirling Council leader.

Most politicians in Mrs McGuire's position would have felt a bitter sense of betrayal after senior party figures had led her to believe the job was hers. In Labour Party circles, many members hold sustained and lifelong vendettas against rivals for what are seen as less serious betrayals. However, McGuire is both a loyalist and a pragmatist – one of the few who genuinely always puts the party's interests ahead of her own. One of McConnell's first acts as General Secretary was to meet Anne McGuire the weekend after his appointment for a meeting to clear the air. The two had been friends before they went for the job and have remained so to this day.

Although Anne McGuire did not bear a grudge against Jack McConnell, others used what they considered the poor treatment of her to take against him. Some women in the party were particularly aggrieved that the popular and highly effective Mrs McGuire had, as they saw it, been cheated out of the job by a man. When she first went to work for the party, Patricia Ferguson, Party Organiser, was one of those who distrusted McConnell most. Ironically, she became his campaign manager when he became Labour leader – thus proving Jack's rare talent for turning political enemies into firm friends. She said:

> He appointed me to the job but I knew that I wasn't really his choice. Although I didn't take to him, I had to respect his ability to do the job. And gradually you see people in vulnerable situations and realise they are human. Even when I disagreed with him, I eventually found it difficult to dislike him.

But, if McConnell was successful in changing the views of those who were against him, he also lost the support of some of those who had initially backed him. Although he had quickly risen through the ranks to make his mark in local government, he arrived in Labour's HQ at Keir Hardie House as a naive outsider. In the Scottish Labour Party, understanding the feuds and vendettas as well as the strong allegiances is vital for survival. McConnell was too trusting and too open for his own good. Not long after he was appointed to the post of General Secretary of the Labour Party in Scotland, Tony Blair and Gordon Brown were standing for election to the NEC and both men approached McConnell for help with their campaigns. McConnell instantly hit it off with Blair, becoming swept along by his enthusiasm and fresh approach, but he found the intense Brown more difficult to warm to. In those early days, McConnell was prone to air his views openly. For someone who did not even realise that Murray Elder and Gordon Brown had been friends since primary school, it was a dangerous habit and it undoubtedly earned him some unnecessary enemies.

Despite being Murray Elder's choice for the job, McConnell had a poor relationship with the Brown camp throughout his tenure. The distrust was mutual and it also extended to some of Brown's allies. When the Chancellor's protégé Douglas

Alexander contested the Perth by-election in 1995, he and McConnell developed a fractious relationship. It had been an open secret that Jack wanted Susan Deacon rather than Alexander to be selected as the candidate for the by-election and, even after he beat her in the selection process, Alexander was left with a sour taste.

Two years later, when McConnell was heading up Labour's election campaign in Scotland, it took a turn for the worse. As is usual in the run-up to important campaigns, extra staff are drafted in from trade unions, MPs' offices and other sympathetic organisations. As part of the '97 influx to Keir Hardie House, Jackie Christian arrived. She was a director with the London-based PR firm Hobsbawm Macaulay Communications which was run by Sarah Macaulay who, in August 2000, was to become Chancellor Gordon Brown's wife. Glamorous and vivacious, as well as hard-working and brimming with ideas, Christian was exactly the kind of addition to the staff who was bound to be welcomed by McConnell and the pair immediately appeared to hit it off. Weary after months of pre-election planning, McConnell was delighted to have a new staff member with a fresh eye and boundless enthusiasm. In addition to that, her upbeat approach and sense of humour meant McConnell also enjoyed her company and considered her an ally. In the intense atmosphere of an election campaign, he believed he had found a like-minded person in whom he could confide about the wrangles and rows which often come to a head during such periods.

He would often call Christian after work to let off steam, laugh off the day's difficulties and discuss how to approach the next one. After one particularly stressful day that left McConnell seething over the actions of Gordon Brown's supporters, he called Christian late at night to vent his anger. Unbeknown to him Christian was at the time with her new boyfriend and he heard every word Jack said. Her boyfriend was Douglas Alexander, one of Gordon Brown's closest lieutenants. Alexander, now the MP for Paisley South, later married Christian in a lavish wedding ceremony attended by hundreds of friends. Jack McConnell was not invited. For a canny political operator, McConnell sometimes gets it badly wrong. This faux pas was not just cringingly embarrassing – it also fuelled the Brown camp's distrust of him.

However, there are other occasions in which McConnell's flirtatious personality has been better appreciated. Some young women in the party say they find McConnell utterly charming. One of his protégés summed him up:

> He is full of mischief which makes him great fun to be with. He is an outrageous flirt – when he turns his attention to you, it is very flattering but you also know it is nothing more than harmless fun. He was equally encouraging to the young guys like Derek Munn and Lee Whitehill – he just wasn't quite as playful with them.

Throughout his time as General Secretary McConnell took pride in increasing party membership and encouraging young activists. As part of his crusade to lower the party's age profile, he came up with the idea of creating a youth cabinet. McConnell hand-picked the brightest up-and-coming young activists and gave them policy portfolios. At the 1997 Scottish party conference, the young cabinet sat on the platform as Tony Blair delivered his speech. The imagery summed up New Labour at its peak. The party looked young, dynamic and exciting. Of that McConnell cabinet of youngsters, Richard Baker is now an MSP, Kirsty O'Brien is a policy expert at Labour's HQ in London, Chris Winslow runs a successful public affairs company and Roseanne Foyer is a senior officer with the STUC. Recent history has shown McConnell has an eye for spotting talent and nurturing it.

By taking such a keen interest in the fortunes of Labour's youth, he has also ensured he has a powerful network of supporters among the next generation of Labour politicians. Following his speech at the 2004 party conference, the First Minister would have had several invitations to spend the evening dining with senior Scottish political editors and their newspaper editors but, instead, he chose to have a meal with twenty of his young Labour protégés including the former NUS President Mandy Telford, Kirsty O'Brien from Labour HQ, Anna McMillan who works for the London Mayor Ken Livingstone, Blair McDougall, an adviser to Party Chairman Ian McCartney, and Lee Whitehill spokesman for the influential Amicus trade union.

During his time as General Secretary, it is generally recognised that McConnell turned the organisation into a modern campaigning machine. He increased membership. He built up relations with the business community, held gala dinners to raise funds for the party and helped to work out a system to deliver a Scottish parliament with the highest calibre of MSPs, many of them women. He won the trust of the party leadership. Tony Blair decided to begin his party battle to scrap Clause 4 in Scotland because he believed he could rely on McConnell to organise things well. People who watched Jack at the Inverness conference where the Clause 4 vote was held say they have rarely seen him so uptight. He knew the stakes were high and that his reputation hinged on him delivering the vote.

Around this time, Blair's entourage would confide in Jack and seek his advice on speeches the leader was making in Scotland. They respected his judgement and Jack had a great deal of admiration for Blair. A friend of Jack explained, 'Jack liked Blair's style. He saw him as a politician who didn't just want to win the vote but more importantly wanted to win the argument. Jack thought that was the right approach and learned from it.' The Clause-4 vote was seen as one of Jack's biggest achievements during his time working for the party but it is the high-profile scrapes that he got into that he is best remembered for.

In 1996, Mohammed Sarwar was selected to contest the Govan parliamentary seat for Labour. The decision came after a bitter two-and-a-half-year battle against a sitting MP, Mike Watson. Watson had been the MP for Glasgow Central for seven years but the constituency was disappearing because of boundary changes and the new Govan constituency offered his only chance of political survival. The party hierarchy had no reason to want to get rid of Watson but nor did it seem to offer the usual protection that it would to a sitting member facing a challenge from a newcomer. The reason was obvious. If Sarwar won the nomination, he would become Britain's first Muslim MP and that was something Labour wanted to be able to boast about. The fact that he was also a millionaire businessman made him all the more attractive to New Labour.

The campaign between the two men was hard fought and mired in allegations of dirty tricks. On 12 December 1995, supporters of the two camps gathered at the City Halls in Glasgow to hear the result. Such was the interest in the outcome there was also a huge media presence. The selection process had been run from Keir Hardie House by the party's senior Scottish organiser, Lesley Quinn, who was effectively Jack McConnell's deputy. Watson supporters say that they believe McConnell was fair in his approach to the contest but that the party in London was working against them. Following the count, Lesley Quinn was forced to announce the result in the midst of a media scrum. Watson had won by literally the narrowest of margins – just one vote. The atmosphere was electric but also poisonous and it was obvious there would be repercussions from such a slender victory.

But McConnell wasn't there to hear the result which had grabbed so much interest. He had picked that afternoon to go Christmas shopping. During the selection process, fifty-two votes were disqualified because of discrepancies over their signatures. Sarwar believed more than half the votes were for him and he threatened to take court action. Glasgow Kelvin MP George Galloway, a Sarwar supporter, described the contest as 'political murder most foul'. Jack McConnell was forced to intervene the following week calling for calm and a halt to the accusation and threats which were flying around. Such was the row that followed, many senior figures in the party concluded that the contest had to be rerun. The National Executive of the Labour Party in London took the same view and ordered the process to be gone through again. Gordon Brown left the meeting and called Mike Watson to break the news that he faced another challenge from Sarwar to him personally.

In June '96, Mike Watson decided he had to take the Labour Party to court over their decision to allow some of Sarwar's supporters to participate in the rerun. It is highly unusual for an MP to take action against his own party because they do so in the knowledge that the party machine will turn against them. Watson's legal bid to delay the rerun of the contest failed. The following week Mohammed Sarwar was selected for the seat, defeating Watson by 279 votes to 197. Watson believed his political career was over. However, he went on to be given a peerage. And, when the list of candidates for the Scottish Parliament was being drawn up, he went to McConnell to ask what his chances would be of being given another chance. Eighteen months after being on opposite sides of a court battle, McConnell urged Watson to put his name forward.

With the Govan selection finally settled, Jack hoped that the party's troubles were over and that he could concentrate on planning a positive election campaign for the forthcoming General Election – it was not to be. The party became extremely disciplined in the run-up to Labour's 1997 landslide victory. Even when they did not agree with it, politicians rarely deviated from the party line, believing that unity was the only way to secure victory. But senior figures worried about problems at local government level which they feared could be used against them by the Tories in the run-up to the election and their concerns were well founded. The Conservatives had tried to damage John Smith by portraying Monklands Council as a rotten borough. In the prevailing jobs-for-the-boys culture, it was alleged that councillors' relatives were all but guaranteed council jobs. John Smith tried his best to stay out of such rows but, under Blair's new leadership, a different view prevailed. After Blair took over, the mantra became 'If there's a problem, we'll attack it before anyone else does'.

Glasgow City Council had long been dominated by two groups – one was comprised of the supporters of Pat Lally and the other backed Jean McFadden. The merger of Strathclyde Region with Glasgow, following local government district reorganisation, sparked infighting between the two groups and the authority was riven by factionalism. The party leadership viewed this situation as unhealthy. Early in 1997, the leader of the council, Bob Gould, lifted the lid on the simmering tensions within the authority. Fearful he was on the verge of losing the leadership of Scotland's biggest council, he decided to expose what he claimed was a 'votes for trips' scandal within the council. The allegations made front-page news. Keir Hardie House was furious and the MPs in London were equally unhappy. They were all too aware that Glasgow Council could become the kind of problem for Donald Dewar and the other Glasgow MPs that Monklands had been for John Smith. The strategy was clear – the party would condemn the council and take firm action.

In March '97, the party announced that six Glasgow councillors would be investigated over the votes-for-junkets row. Before the inquiry had even started, Keir Hardie House was suggesting that there would be 'hangings in George Square'. Although Bob Gould had been one of the people to make the allegations, he was among those suspended when allegations of his involvement in controversial property deals were made. Along with Lord Provost Pat Lally, he was accused of failing to display proper leadership. Deputy Provost Alex Mossan, Baillie James Mutter, Cllr Gordon MacDiarmid and Cllr Deirdre Gaughan were also suspended. They were dubbed 'the Glasgow Six'.

The idea of suspending councillors was devised by Labour HQ as a way of dealing with the militant element which was operating in Liverpool. The so-called 'Liverpool trap' was invented by aides to the former Labour leader Neil Kinnock but, when they came up with the plan, they also added two provisos – the party should stop short of expelling members as this could possibly give rise to legal action and the party should not use emotive language to describe those it was trying to oust. It appeared that, by taking stronger action than was deemed necessary and by briefing the press about the probable outcome, McConnell had broken both golden rules.

However, behind the scenes, Jack was arguing that the party should stop short of expelling the Glasgow councillors but he was overruled. Donald Dewar was facing enormous pressure from the party in London to take the toughest action available and that meant throwing them out of the party. On the day it was announced that the Glasgow Six would face a party trial that was widely expected to end with their expulsion, McConnell said, 'I am delighted the NEC is prepared to take action to secure the highest standards in Glasgow City Council and elsewhere.' But privately he was nervous about the move and warned the party off taking such strong action. He was to be proved right. Lally and Mossan were never going to take their expulsions lying down. They took the party to court and won. If Labour had wanted to look tough, its strategy had backfired badly as Lally and Mossan triumphed over the party machine. Interestingly, they do not appear to blame McConnell for the action taken by the party.

Despite the fact it was McConnell who advised against the move, he was the one left to deal with the humiliating outcome and to suffer the damage for the bad judgement. Another low point in McConnell's time at Keir Hardie House came when the leadership decided they wanted to get rid of his assistant Tommy Sheppard. Sheppard had been a close friend of McConnell since they met in the late '70s while they were both active in student politics. Their mutual interest in environmental issues and in devolution made them natural allies. Sheppard was also an enthusiastic supporter of Scottish Labour Action. As the devolution debate took centre stage, McConnell brought his friend into the party in 1994 to work alongside him. For a time, the alliance worked well. Between them they changed the name of the party to the Scottish Labour Party by constantly referring to it like this. Jack had coined the phrase 'Labour, the real national party of Scotland' in an attempt to halt the rise of nationalism and they both employed it to great effect.

For a couple of years, McConnell and Sheppard were left to their own devices but, as the 1997 election approached, London began to take a greater interest in what was happening north of the border. Every policy proposal had to be sent south to be scrutinised by policy wonks in party HQ at Walworth Road. Peter Mandelson was in charge of the manifesto and he was not going to bow to Tommy Sheppard or Jack McConnell's greater understanding of the Scottish dimension. Sheppard was made responsible for putting general election plans in place and for liaising with the party nationally on policy areas. It was a poisoned chalice. He said:

> They would expect us to put out a policy document they had written about education and I would be left explaining that it was pointless when we don't have A levels in Scotland. I don't recall Jack disagreeing with me on any major issues and

sometimes he would come in behind me in these arguments but word soon got round London that there was trouble at t'mill. I was trying to originate Scottish policy in Scotland and that's what they hated.

However, there were no blazing rows and Sheppard did not realise how much trouble he was in until Robin Cook asked to see him in his room at the Hilton Hotel in Glasgow on the night of the party's gala dinner in November 1996. Days earlier, focus-group findings that had been commissioned by the Labour Party had mysteriously found their way to the SNP. The documents showed that some floating voters thought that Blair was 'smarmy'. The Nats had a field day. They used the evidence to portray Blair as a London Labour invention who played badly in Scotland. It was embarrassing for Labour and for the Prime Minister in particular as he was visiting Scotland during that week. One positive could be taken from the affair – the leaked findings would certainly help anyone trying to make the argument that the Scottish Labour Party should be given greater autonomy.

The finger of suspicion fell on Sheppard but he categorically denies leaking the documents. However, two weeks earlier, his car had been broken into outside his flat in Edinburgh. His briefcase was lying in the back and it was stolen. When news broke that the damaging documents had found their way to SNP headquarters, Sheppard and McConnell drew press attention to the car break-in. According to Sheppard, it was a deliberate attempt to create a diversion rather than answer some hard political questions. Sheppard said:

It is true that my briefcase was stolen – I reported it to the police and it was later recovered near my home. But Jack and I basically tried to create a suspicion in the public mind that there could be an association between the break-in and the obtaining of the documents by the SNP. We never said outright that the SNP condoned breaking into their opponents' cars but it was an example of the political black arts that were practised then – and perhaps more so now – by the highest echelons of New Labour. It is not an episode of which I am proud. I wasn't entirely sure at the time that the documents were in the briefcase. But this is certainly not how the SNP got their hands on them because they were most certainly there when the briefcase was found weeks later, its contents intact if somewhat mildewed, after having spent some of the winter outside at the bottom of a neighbour's garden.

The Labour Party spin may have had the desired effect in some sections of the Scottish press but, when news of the story reached London, it only served to heighten their fears that Sheppard was trouble. The story soon rebounded on him in Scotland too. Robin Cook was dispatched to break the news to Sheppard that he had lost the confidence of senior party figures. Cook told him there was a rising tide of opinion that didn't want him to be at the centre of the election campaign but that the party thought he would have a contribution to make in the post-election period. However, not long afterwards, a meeting of senior politicians in London decided that he should not be allowed to stay. The party scoured Sheppard's mobile phone records and discovered he had been making phone calls during a meeting of the Scottish Executive. He was accused of leaking information from the private meetings and McConnell was told that his friend must go. He refused to break the news to Sheppard and told the party's General Secretary in London, Tom Sawyer, that he wanted Sheppard to leave with a healthy pay-off. The sum he received was a record amount given to a Labour Party staff member at the time and it helped Sheppard to finance the setting-up of two successful comedy clubs.

Although he doesn't blame McConnell for what happened, Sheppard said:

> He could have done more, I'm pretty sure it was George Robertson who really wanted me out and, given that Jack had his ear, he could have reassured Robertson that I was not the problem he thought I was. Ironically I cannot think of a single instance during my years as a party official where I compromised, embarrassed or in any way undermined the leadership. Looking back, I can't help but feel it was a wasted opportunity but such was the discipline of my old broad left political upbringing.

Sheppard left the party in January 1997. Until his departure, he had been charged with organising the election campaign in Scotland. According to some in Keir Hardie House, Sheppard's plans were not advanced and that was another reason for him being pushed out. Whatever the truth, Jack was left with a vacuum and he knew it. He turned to his old mentor, Professor Mike Donnelly, and persuaded him to take a six-month sabbatical from work to help with Labour's election plans.

The landslide election success resulted in a honeymoon period for Labour. In the run-up to the election, there were rumours at Westminster that George Robertson might not, as had been expected, become the Secretary of State for Scotland in Blair's government. The referendum row had damaged Robertson so Blair felt he would benefit from a move to another department and decided to make him the Defence Secretary. That left the way open for the former Shadow Scottish Secretary, Donald Dewar, to move back to the job he loved. Blair was also confident that Dewar would master the detail of the huge constitutional package which had to be delivered.

But Labour's honeymoon was short-lived in Scotland. Two months later, the Paisley South MP Gordon McMaster was found dead in his car. He had gassed himself. The MP had been suffering from ME for some time, he had been the victim of a mugging attack in London and it was clear to colleagues that he was depressed. But it was also claimed that he had been the victim of a smear campaign over his sexuality. McMaster left a suicide note in which he pointed the finger at the Renfrewshire West MP Tommy Graham and the former deputy whip Don Dixon for some of his unhappiness. It read, 'I would rather be dead with my conscience than alive with theirs.'

McMaster's death brought years of faction fighting within the Paisley area out into the open. Two years earlier, McConnell had tried to sort out some of the problems in the area. Much of the bad feeling stemmed from boundary changes that led to part of Graham's constituency moving into Irene Adams' Paisley North seat. In 1995, following the discovery of irregularities in membership records, Jack suspended three constituency parties – the two Paisley seats and Graham's Renfrewshire West. This means they no longer have the right to meet, attend conferences or select candidates. They have, therefore, been deprived of important powers and this has led to the party HQ having greater control over them. There were claims that pensioners had been signed up to the party without their knowledge and subscriptions had been paid for forty-four union members with a single cheque. Party HQ had hoped the action would sort out the faction fighting but the arguments and smears continued.

After McMaster took his own life, the party suspended Tommy Graham and held an internal investigation into his conduct. At the time, Scottish Labour had suffered the embarrassment of threatening tough action against Glasgow's Lord Provost Pat Lally and Deputy Alex Mossan but, when the courts backed the councillors over the party, they had failed to see it through. Following the election, Glasgow Govan MP Mohammed Sarwar had also been suspended as he faced electoral fraud allegations. This time, Labour was determined to get it right and to come up with hard evidence against Graham. He faced five charges. He was cleared of smearing Gordon McMaster but the party found him guilty of bad-mouthing Irene Adams and of offering compromising photographs of a trade union official to two party members in return for information about a rival. Graham claimed that McConnell knew he was innocent of any wrongdoing in connection with recruiting members but that he failed to stand up for him when the party machine decided it wanted to end his career. He said:

> I always got on very well with Jack – I even gave him a researcher's pass to give him access to the House of Commons. He knew I had done nothing wrong so I was shocked when he didn't so much as lift a pinkie to help me. At that time, he was so under threat in his own job that he probably didn't want to be seen to be supporting me.

One of Jack McConnell's final acts as General Secretary was to get the party to agree a system for selecting its candidates for the Scottish Parliament. His experience of rooting out problems in local government had convinced him even further of the need for a new generation of politician to break through the party's ranks. During his time as a member of SLA, he had spoken out about the necessity to prevent the parliament becoming a retirement home for Central-Belt councillors and he was equally convinced of the need to get more women elected. McConnell persuaded the party's ruling national executive to agree to set up a panel system under which those who were interested in standing for the parliament would be interviewed and those deemed not up to scratch could be stopped from putting themselves forward. Ahead of the panel system being set up, McConnell was also seen as being sympathetic to the 'network group'. This was essentially a group of mainly Blairite modernisers who met to discuss how Labour should operate within the new parliament. Its membership included MPs like Rosemary McKenna and Jim Murphy as well as people like Rhona Brankin who were expected to play an important role in the parliament once it was set up.

Most of those who were members of the organisation and who wanted to get on the panel for the Scottish Parliament elections proved to be successful. Others were less fortunate. The MP Dennis Canavan was told he was not a suitable candidate and his Westminster colleague, Ian Davidson, withdrew from the process, fearing he was about to be told the same thing. Given their tendency to speak their minds, it was not altogether unsurprising that they would be stopped by a leadership that, at the time, put loyalty above all other attributes. However, there was shock that the party's former General Secretary, Murray Elder, did not make the grade and prominent activists like Susan Deacon, Mark Lazarovich and Tommy Sheppard also failed to make it through the process – although Deacon was later successful in appealing against the decision.

Despite the fact that McConnell had been instrumental in setting up the process, he was unhappy with the outcome. Many people he had believed would have a strong contribution to make in the parliament, like Jeanne Freeman who was head of the Apex charity at the time and Kaliani Lyle who ran the Citizens Advice Bureau, had failed to get through the panel system that he set up to help them. The process resulted in months of bad publicity for the party.

Although there were one or two concessions made, the position on Dennis Canavan remained and Tony Blair was adamant there should be no place for him in the new legislature. At the height of the row, he ordered Donald

Dewar to go on the offensive and explain why Canavan was being blocked. As a result, Dewar told Labour's gala dinner in November '98 that Canavan 'was not good enough'. McConnell was horrified. Canavan was the first MP he had ever voted for and, no matter what differences they may have had, Jack knew of his record as a local MP and believed the party could not have got it more wrong.

McConnell was also responsible for 'twinning' constituencies. His idea was that seats would be paired up and one would select a man while the other would have to select a woman. The plan suffered a major setback when the party was given legal advice that the plan would fall foul of employment law. The opinion that the party's flagship gender policy would not stand up to scrutiny in the courts was a serious blow. It meant that, if a man challenged the right to stand in any of the seats designated for a woman, there was a good chance he could win. Given how many ambitious men were likely to see their hopes of becoming MSPs dashed by the proposal, there must have been a reasonable chance the twinning plan would end up in court.

However, McConnell decided it was a risk worth taking. He wanted the twinning arrangement to work and he opted to cross his fingers and hope it wasn't subject to a legal challenge. It wasn't and so Jack got away with it. McConnell expected those on the panel to get together and run as pairs. This worked well in many areas. However, two well-known activists and friends of McConnell's fell foul of the system. Bob McLean, who was the best man at McConnell's wedding, would have easily won his own constituency of Midlothian but it had been deemed a woman-only seat and it went to Rhona Brankin. Likewise, Ian Smart would have won Cumbernauld and Kilsyth but that wasn't an option for him either. Friends of McConnell say that the Scottish Parliament could have been a better place in the early days if Labour had had these two men in its team.

During his time as Labour's General Secretary, Jack McConnell enjoyed a high profile and had the ears of senior politicians in London but his last year in the job was not a happy one. When Donald Dewar was appointed Secretary of State for Scotland following Labour's landslide election victory, nobody bothered to inform Jack and he was left to hear of the announcement on the news. Dewar immediately began work with his close team of advisers. It was three days before he spoke to McConnell. Suddenly Jack had gone from having constant communication with George Robertson to feeling like an outsider. Given that the party had just moved from opposition to government, it was largely inevitable that the relationship between Scotland's most senior politician and the General Secretary of the party would change. But McConnell felt frozen out.

His fear that he was no longer part of the 'inner circle' was compounded in the run-up to the 1997 referendum. McConnell began to get the impression that there were two campaigns being run by his party. It seemed there was one set of plans that he knew about and had been involved in and then there were other decisions that were sprung on him at the last minute. There was strong disagreement over his plan to hold a rally in Edinburgh the day after the referendum vote. Some of Dewar's aides believed that, if they planned such an event, news of it would leak out in advance and give the appearance that the party was being too triumphalist. But McConnell dug his heels in, insisting that Dewar and Blair must appear at a big event the following day to take credit for delivering devolution. Around that time, it was one of the few arguments he won and the rally in Parliament Square was a huge success.

On the night of the referendum result, Donald Dewar's aides organised a private party to celebrate the historic vote. Jack wasn't invited. As Scotland voted for the parliament that McConnell had spent twenty years campaigning for, he was left out in the cold. Jack wasn't happy being stripped of the influence he had been used to and he began to realise he needed to find a new job. He was acutely aware that he was on the verge of becoming an MSP – a job he planned to do for many years – but that he had no experience of the private sector. Early in 1998, he spoke to Gordon Beattie of Beattie Media about the possibility of carrying out policy and PR work for his firm on a part-time basis. He was also offered a weekly column in the *Daily Record* newspaper by the then editor Terry Quinn.

Jack felt the newspaper experience would be useful and decided to quit as General Secretary for Scotland. He travelled to London to meet the party's UK General Secretary Tom Sawyer at the party's national headquarters in Millbank Tower to advise him of the decision. Saywer accepted his resignation but asked him to finish off some policy work for the party. After Jack walked out of Millbank Tower to start his life in the private sector, he received a call from a colleague in the party to tell him that Sawyer had left the meeting and boasted, 'I didn't even have to pay him off.' McConnell hadn't realised that he had jumped just minutes before he was about to be pushed and had walked away without his golden handshake.

Then, just days later, the editor of the *Daily Record* changed and he received a letter telling him his services as a columnist were no longer required. He had lost that job before it even started. Then Gordon Beattie informed him that he had decided to change the description of the job he was offering. He wanted to set up a public affairs company and to make McConnell its chief executive. Jack was immediately uncomfortable with the idea but he felt he had no other options left. It was a rare period in Jack's life when he turned out not to be so lucky. Jack was the chief executive of Public Affairs Europe Ltd for just seven months. On paper, he ran the company along with a former newspaper editor, George McKechnie but, in effect, he did very little over that time. McKechnie pledged to protect him from getting involved in any situations which could be seen as a conflict of interest, a promise he fulfilled. The job was all about going out and winning new business for the firm – something McConnell did not enjoy doing. He stuck it out but resigned in November 1998 after he won the selection contest for Motherwell and Wishaw. He had not brought in a single new client in the time he was employed.

# 7

# THE BATTLE FOR HOLYROOD

The Motherwell and Wishaw parliamentary seat was to be Jack McConnell's springboard to leading his country. The area was battling to recover from the loss of the Ravenscraig steel works and some of its housing schemes area had become crippled by drug problems. It is a place where poverty is rife. The problems of the constituency were not familiar ones for someone who grew up in the rural idyll of the island of Arran and who had spent most of his adult life in the leafy suburbs of Stirling. McConnell had initially thought about going for the seat of Ochil, near his Stirling home. He was committed to that area and his plans to stand there were well advanced when he came under pressure to change his mind. The Motherwell and Wishaw MP Frank Roy was instrumental in persuading him to think again and Bridget was also convinced he would enjoy representing the area.

Even before leaving his post as General Secretary, McConnell had set his sights on winning Motherwell and Wishaw. He expected an easy ride. After all, Frank Roy was a close ally who commanded widespread support in the local constituency party which would prove invaluable. Roy had lived in the constituency all his life and knew its people and problems well. McConnell left Roy in no doubt that he wanted to serve those same people and would be committed to solving their problems. Jack and Bridget discussed moving to the area and, although they did not announce their intention to do so, they were clear that, if he was to become the MSP for the area, then he should live in it. The McConnells sold their Victorian conversion in a quiet area of Stirling and moved the family to Wishaw. His son Mark was in his final year at school and this could have been used as the perfect excuse to delay such a move had they wanted to do so. But Mark had been unhappy at school in Stirling and he moved from Stirling High to Wishaw's Coltness High School – a switch that his parents think transformed him.

Under the system that the Labour Party had devised to ensure gender balance, the seat was twinned with the Airdrie and Shotts constituency, which meant party members in that area would also have a vote on who would become the candidate for Motherwell and Wishaw. Unfortunately for McConnell, many in the area despised him. They saw him as the party hatchet man who had expelled their local councillors following the Monklands inquiry into nepotism. His last visit to the constituency was when he tried to persuade the CLP of the merits of all-women shortlists before the '97 election. McConnell spoke passionately of the need to get more women into politics to a smoke-filled Lanarkshire hall. The membership was deeply divided between supporters of Frank Roy and those of influential local party figure Hugh Mulholland. McConnell's plea, which had worked so well in Stirling, Ayr and Aberdeen, went down like a lead balloon in the heart of Lanarkshire.

During the process of electing candidates to the Scottish Parliament, party members in Airdrie and Shotts had no option but to select a woman. Long before any votes were cast, local party member Karen Whitefield, a second cousin of Peggy Herbison, the formidable Pensions Minister in Harold Wilson's government, was regarded as a dead cert to win that seat. She too was not only backing McConnell's candidacy for Motherwell and Wishaw but, like Roy, was pulling out all the stops to ensure her supporters also voted for Jack. It is not unusual for politicians to favour their allies or those they feel they could work with during selection battles but the sheer dedication and downright hard work which Roy and Whitefield poured into McConnell's campaign is extremely rare. Roy and Whitefield would spend all their days and most of their nights chapping on the doors of those they thought they could influence and often those who they knew they couldn't.

Jack also had the backing of other influential Lanarkshire MPs like George Robertson and John Reid. But, just as they thought McConnell was home and dry, a Lanarkshire-based trade unionist decided he would enter the fight to win the seat. At the time, Bill Tynan, who later became the MP for Hamilton South, was the political officer for the engineering union the AEEU (later to become Amicus). Schooled in the ways of Lanarkshire politics, Hamilton-born Tynan has a fearsome reputation as a political fixer and McConnell had every right to worry about his entry into the race. Tynan's union had a strong base in the area and it was to come close to delivering for its man. On one night, Tynan won three of the five party branches in Shotts and later four out of five in Motherwell.

He also had the backing of Hugh Mulholland. Jack's close friend Frank Roy beat Mulholland for the Westminster parliamentary seat in 1997 and relations between the two are poor. Mulholland was unhappy at what he saw as an attempt by Roy to parachute McConnell into the safe seat. Mulholland said:

> I judge a man by his friends and McConnell is a friend of Roy's. I wanted someone local for the seat and I felt I didn't know what McConnell stood for politically. I still don't. In my opinion Bill Tynan would have been a better MSP. I was also concerned by some of the rumours I heard about the way McConnell operated while he was General Secretary.

McConnell was under intense pressure as he contemplated the fact his career in the Scottish Parliament might not even get off the ground. Then came one of the biggest crises of his career. McConnell's chances of success suffered a major blow after he decided to publish his memoirs about his time as the party's General Secretary in the *Scotland on Sunday* newspaper. As Karen Whitefield drove over the Forth Road Bridge on her way home from work in the office of the Dunfermline West MP Rachel Squire, she heard a radio advert featuring McConnell's voice promising to spill the beans on his time as General Secretary. Whitefield was livid at what she saw as McConnell's betrayal of the Labour Party. She had been on course to win Airdrie and Shotts comfortably and, since teaming up with McConnell, had already suffered a backlash from some in her constituency who loathed McConnell over the Monklands debacle. She had been prepared to defend her running mate but this was a step too far. Whitefield called McConnell, told him he was a 'disloyal bastard' and that her deal to run with him was off. McConnell realised that, without Whitefield, he could be sunk.

Although McConnell believed his memoirs would not damage the party, he immediately accepted that Whitefield had every right to be concerned. He used every ounce of charm to win her back round. She eventually relented because she became convinced that they had more in common than they disagreed over. She said:

> He can make you very angry but he can bring you back from that anger. I think it's because you know that, even if he does something you profoundly disagree with, he will have done it with the best of intentions.

If Whitefield's anger panicked McConnell, it was mild compared to the fallout at the party's HQ. As was often the case, the BBC's political correspondent, the late Kenny McIntyre, was first on the phone to Keir Hardie House, looking for a reaction to a story they didn't even realise was about to hit them. McIntyre, a colourful character and a likeable rogue, took much delighted in springing his surprise. He used several expletives as part of his analysis of the potential damage he believed the party could be about to suffer. The 1999 Scottish election campaign was a hard-fought battle. Labour had been badly rattled by an increase in support for the SNP in the early part of 1998. The Prime Minister personally took charge of the strategy and sent trusted allies like Matthew Taylor, now in the Number Ten policy unit, north to put the party back on track.

Although McConnell had warned the party he was considering writing an account of his time as General Secretary, the only person he had trusted to look at his memoirs was Frank Roy. On the day news of his impending serialisation broke, Labour was moving out of its Keir Hardie House HQ in Glasgow's Park Circus to Delta House, a soulless, modern city-centre office block. Party staff sat in their cars parked in the street liaising with Downing Street over how to handle the affair. Journalists had told the party the memoirs would include an account of the bullying that the late Paisley South MP, Gordon McMaster, had encountered before he committed suicide and an assessment that the party could have done more to help him. That weekend was the anniversary of McMaster's death. Party chiefs were furious that the episode was to be raked over again and feared the impact it would have on the late MP's elderly parents. It is now largely accepted that there was little information in McConnell's memoirs for the Labour Party to worry about but, at the time, there was some concern that Labour's Scottish leader, Donald Dewar, would not come out of the account well given that he had been in charge of the whips' office at the time of McMaster's death.

The memoirs were expected to criticise the party for not having done more to protect McMaster from party infighting. McConnell's loyalty to Blair over the years counted for nothing as the serialisation row engulfed McConnell. The Prime Minister's Official Spokesman, Alastair Campbell, called the party's press office and suggested they issue a statement along the lines that this was a man who knew very little while he was General Secretary and was now trying to cash in on his limited knowledge of the party. The suggested wording brutally dismissed McConnell's work with the party and would have left his credibility in tatters, thereby handing ammunition to the SNP. Staff at the party's Scottish HQ thanked Campbell for his thoughts but pointed out that, despite McConnell's lapse of judgement as they saw it, he was still one of their candidates and, therefore, could not be thrown to the wolves. That was based on the assumption that McConnell would remain on Labour's approved panel of candidates – something that was far from certain for a time.

McConnell spent forty-eight hours wheeling and dealing as never before in a bid to save his political career. The politician in charge of the Scottish election campaign was Helen Liddell – no great fan of McConnell's. As a former General Secretary herself, she was critical of his handling of the Monklands by-election which she eventually won after one of the dirtiest and most bitter campaigns in recent Scottish history. And Helen was aware that Jack had been critical of her performance as Education Minister. When the row broke, she insisted that she be given copy approval of the memoirs before they were printed. As she went through McConnell's account of his time as General Secretary, huge chunks of the manuscript were cut out.

McConnell was forced to plead for his political life with the newspaper executives who had suggested the idea. The deal between *Scotland on Sunday* and McConnell had been struck over a dinner at the Crowne Plaza Hotel on Edinburgh's Royal Mile. The paper's deputy editor, Alan Cochrane, a fun-loving bon viveur, his wife Jenny, their ten-month-old daughter and the paper's political editor Iain Martin persuaded McConnell the profile would benefit him in the run-up to the election. They offered just £6,000 for McConnell to spill the beans, a move which could have ended his career. They say he was flattered by the interest and the money would have given him the option of buying a new car. Jack's friends say he made the decision because he had been frozen out by the party leadership and felt that many of the things which the party had achieved during his time as General Secretary, like increasing the membership, getting the finances in order and modernising the party machine, had been overlooked. As the claret flowed McConnell signed up to the idea that almost destroyed him. Cochrane recalls the biggest stumbling block to persuading him. He said, 'Bridget was not happy – she just kept saying, "Don't do it, Jack."' It was advice that he would come to wish he had listened to.

McConnell spent two days holed up in a hotel room in Edinburgh with Iain Martin, giving his account of controversial events in the Labour Party. Martin left the hotel with piles of tapes on which McConnell told his story – tapes he still has in his possession. At the end of the interviews, Martin gave McConnell a final chance to back out but McConnell assured him everything would be OK and that he had no intention of backing out. To this day, Jack believes that the biggest mistake was to promote his story by taking part in a high-profile advertising campaign on the radio. Through a combination of displaying huge remorse to the party hierarchy and appealing to the newspaper that held the taped conversations in which he had detailed some of Labour's most difficult episodes, McConnell managed to save his skin. *Scotland on Sunday* agreed to let him drop significant portions of his account so that he could appease Helen Liddell and keep his place as a potential candidate for the Scottish Parliament.

Legally, the newspaper could have told him it was too late to renege on the deal but, instead, the executives sat in their offices in North Bridge, watching their scoop disappear, as Mrs Liddell scored off their best lines. In desperation, Alan Cochrane rang Alastair Campbell on his mobile in a bid to assure him that the McConnell interview was not damaging and to ask him to 'call off the dogs'. 'He's on your side,' Cochrane told him. Campbell was not impressed but the call from Cochrane probably helped to persuade him it was an error of judgement rather than an act of disloyalty. Jack had struck it lucky once again. However, he knew he had a lot of ground to make up if the episode was not going to do him lasting damage.

It's estimated that McConnell personally knocked on the doors of 900 party members in a bid to secure the nomination. Whitefield said, 'He never expected anyone else to deliver a single vote for him. He went out there and he did the work.' It was a hard-fought campaign in which every vote counted. Unbelievably, one elderly woman who had been won over by his charm and voted for him using a postal vote died just hours after casting it, not living long enough to hear the result.

Inevitably, in a clash between two such experienced election hands, the campaign became mired in allegations of dirty tricks. In a dig at Tynan's age, McConnell and Whitefield adopted The Corrs' hit 'So Young' as their campaign song. Tynan's camp claimed McConnell supporters played the sectarian card. They said Tynan's Catholic religion was used against him on the doorsteps. McConnell's supporters claimed Jack's Protestant background was used against him. If McConnell supporters did resort to such tactics, it was out of desperation and without his consent. He has often spoken out about the need to eradicate bigotry and sectarianism in Scotland. It was also alleged that Tynan's supporters had tried to influence postal votes. The party's senior Scottish officer at the time, Lesley Quinn, now General Secretary, wrote to Sam Love, one of Bill Tynan's supporters, warning him that she had been told he had personally collected applications for postal votes which is against the party code of conduct – the votes must be collected by a neutral party official from party HQ. The letter also pointed out any breach of rules could lead to disciplinary action for 'bringing the party into disrepute' – a thinly veiled threat of expulsion. In accordance with party rules, the letter was also copied to the CLP secretary, Michael Ross.

Tynan's supporters vehemently denied any wrongdoing but his campaign was derailed after a copy of the letter was leaked to the *Sunday Mail's* political editor Angus MacLeod and *Scotland on Sunday's* political editor Iain Martin. On 22 November 1998, the papers ran front-page stories of a 'votes scandal' surrounding the fight for the seat. Tynan's camp believe that the accusations becoming public cost them the election. Just how the letter from Lesley Quinn to Sam Love found its way into the public domain is not clear but the leak probably saved McConnell's political neck. Despite there being no evidence that the Tynan camp had broken party rules, party members were left with the impression that McConnell had been the victim of a dirty tricks campaign.

It is interesting to note that the party did not take any action against Bill Tynan's supporters following the vote. Tynan allies believe that, without the newspaper stories, Bill Tynan would have become the MSP for Motherwell and Shotts. They believe Tynan was the victim of every dirty trick in the book during the campaign. Tynan's camp was also unhappy that the ballot boxes were overseen by Jack's supporters before the votes were counted. That Sunday, after three recounts and four disqualified votes, Jack McConnell was declared the Labour candidate for the Motherwell and Wishaw constituency in the forthcoming Scottish Parliament elections. Like so many of McConnell's victories, it was by the skin of his teeth. He won selection by just two votes but his passage to Holyrood was assured.

## 1999 Election Campaign

Despite being one of the most experienced politicians on Labour's list of candidates for the 1999 elections to the Scottish Parliament, Jack McConnell's services were not in big demand from the party. He was still largely considered an outsider by the party hierarchy and he was out of favour for trying to serialise his story of his time as General Secretary. Although he had a vast wealth of experience running election campaigns, it was clear that he would not be called upon to assist with the election plans. As the election approached, Donald Dewar and his advisers put together a team of spokespeople who would take part in the campaign. It was, in effect, a shadow government although on a large scale so that Dewar could include as many of the candidates as possible.

One Sunday night, Dewar called Jack at home to tell him he wanted to include him in his campaign team. Given Jack's experience of handling Stirling Council's revenues and his years of teaching, finance or education would have been obvious portfolios to hand him and, now that he was standing for a Lanarkshire seat, social justice or enterprise would also have been apt. However, Dewar told Jack he wanted him to speak for the party on issues affecting the environment and rural affairs. Many politicians of McConnell's experience could have taken the offer as a major sleight but, instead, Jack thanked him and said he was delighted before putting the phone down and springing into action.

Rather than spending the campaign sulking over the fact that less experienced people had been handed what appeared to be more important campaign roles, Jack threw himself into his new 'brief'. He toured Scotland, meeting up with other Labour candidates and using his press skills to get photo opportunities in local papers up and down the country. Jack was pictured visiting dolphins in the Moray Firth and examining soil erosion in Fife. At the time he gave him the job,

Dewar probably did not realise that Jack actually has a real passion for environmental issues and he spent the campaign trying to portray Labour as the party of the environment.

Whether it was deliberate or not, by meeting up with so many candidates and boosting their local campaigns, Jack ensured that many of the Labour MSPs who were elected to Holyrood in 1999 were immediately on his side. When it came to challenging for the leadership, many MSPs remembered that he took the time to come to their constituencies and that he had freely offered them advice before they were elected.

Jack took the very fact that he had been given a campaign post at all as a signal that he was, at last, being brought back in from the wilderness. For the first time, he dared to hope that he was not only about to become an MSP but also to become a cabinet minister. He felt he was having a good election campaign and he was given a massive boost in the final days running up to the election. Donald Dewar had fallen foul of Gordon Brown for hinting that he might do a deal in government over the abolition of tuition fees. Dewar was due to appear on one of the final TV debates of the campaign and Brown was furious over what he saw as a gaffe. Brown wanted Dewar to stay off the airwaves and sent one of his aides to ask Jack if he would appear instead. Jack said he would do the programme on two conditions – that Brown asked him to do it personally and that Dewar was happy for him to do it. Both conditions were met. After being hounded out of the party's top job in Scotland and coming close to not getting a seat, Jack's confidence was restored. When the new government of Scotland was formed he was delighted but not altogether surprised to be asked to take a cabinet place as Finance Minister.

# 8

# SURVIVING SCANDAL

It is difficult to describe any one incident in Jack McConnell's career as the one that made him or the one that threatened to break him. He survived the criticisms levelled at him by his critics over his handling of the allegations made against Monklands Council, the suspension of councillors in Glasgow, the running of the Govan selection process and the row over a hoax letter bomb. He fended off the enemies who tried to smear him over his personal life, he saw off the party machine when it turned against him over his decision to serialise his memoirs and he won the Motherwell and Wishaw selection against the odds.

Bruising as all these incidents had been, they were, to all intents and purposes, just internal battles that he fought and won. But, shortly after winning his coveted cabinet place in Scotland's first government to be formed for three hundred years, Jack McConnell faced one of the toughest fights of his political life. In September 1999, the *Observer* newspaper ran a front-page story declaring it had uncovered 'Scotland's Lobbygate'. Reporters, posing as businessmen, set up a fake meeting with two Beattie Media lobbyists to investigate whether the firm, which had previously employed Jack McConnell, had privileged access to the new government of Scotland. An *Observer* journalist claimed to be Anthony James, a businessman representing American investors. He said his clients were hoping to land lucrative government contracts to finance new schools and hospitals in Scotland. In a secretly taped and filmed meeting at the Balmoral Hotel in Edinburgh, the lobbyists Kevin Reid, son of then Scottish Secretary John Reid, and his boss Alex Barr spoke of their contacts in and knowledge of Scottish politics.

Although Reid was careful to tell the fake businessman that he would not 'promise access to people', Alex Barr was more forthcoming. Barr boasted that Beattie Media had been able to place an appointment in McConnell's diary because he was a former employee of the firm, as was Jack's new diary secretary Christina Marshall. Barr said he had wanted the then Finance Minister to make a keynote speech at the Financial Director of the Year Award and that Christina had told him he should 'consider it done'. Barr also told the 'client' that he had arranged events at which he had secured the appearance of government ministers, including Sam Galbraith, Henry McLeish and Jackie Baillie. His boast was not untrue. As a PR executive, Barr handled publicity for agencies such as the Scottish Premier League and Scottish Enterprise. It was not unusual or wrong for ministers to attend the launch of key investments by such bodies. However, Barr was clearly making out that he could lift the phone to key government ministers and to Jack McConnell in particular, pointing out that he had his home phone number.

The subsequent investigation by the Standards Committee of the Scottish Parliament into the allegations stopped a long way short of proving any wrongdoing or that any minister had breached government rules. However, the combination of a new political institution, journalists desperate to uncover a potential scandal and inexperienced politicians led to what could have been Jack McConnell's downfall. First Minister Donald Dewar was irritated by the newspaper report which had the potential to shake public confidence in the fledgling institution.

Perhaps because of his years of experience and partly because of his disdain for the press, Dewar was not inclined to call for investigations that he believed would give the reports more credence than they deserved. Almost a week after the story broke, Dewar was still insisting that there was no need for a probe into the affair. He claimed his own private inquiries had shown that ministers had done nothing wrong and he pointed to a statement issued by Beattie Media in which the firm apologised and admitted that no politician or member of their staff had acted improperly in any dealings with the firm but the response was not what the story-hungry press-pack was looking for.

Confronted by journalists angry over what they saw as a possible cover-up, Dewar's media spokesman David Whitton said the First Minister had examined the diaries of those involved and concluded they were innocent, adding, 'I would have thought that his word was good enough for most people in Scotland.' Whitton was using the fact that Dewar had a significant trust rating with the public. However, the Lobbygate row ignited because the accusations went to the heart of what Scotland's new democracy was meant to stand for – openness and transparency. The idea that the Labour First Minister could investigate allegations being levelled against his own ministerial team and conclude everything was in order did not wash.

By contrast, Jack McConnell was not on the defensive but on the offensive. He was quick to tell the press that he would co-operate with any inquiry set up to deal with the accusations, insisting that his diaries contained nothing that he would want to hide. He even wrote to the Convenor of the Standards Committee calling for an investigation. Although Dewar was confident that the Lobbygate affair would not claim the scalp of any of his ministers, he backed an investigation into the claims by the parliament's Standards Committee. The First Minister had long championed the power of the committees which were to be set up in the new parliament and could not possibly be seen to undermine them so early into the life of the devolved government.

Scottish Secretary John Reid saw the situation differently. He was furious that his son had been dragged into the scandal, which he saw as a newspaper sting without foundation. Reid wanted the story to be 'closed down' and felt that Dewar and his advisers were only prolonging the life of the story. There followed heated discussions between the two sides at Labour's party conference in Bournemouth the weekend that the story broke. The falling-out became so serious that Scotland's two most senior politicians almost came to blows. Tony Blair's aide at Number Ten, Anji Hunter, was forced to intervene in a bid to take the heat out of the situation. The bitter row between Dewar and Reid captured the press headlines for most of that week and the focus of the story became their disagreement rather than the substance of the claims made by the lobbyists.

This meant that attention shifted away from Jack McConnell's role in the affair. Having been in the public spotlight for just four months, some of the ministers in the new Executive were barely known to the press. However, McConnell was different – he had been in the public eye since becoming General Secretary seven years earlier. Journalists who had covered his role in controversial decisions – like expelling councillors, the hoax bomb row or having been on the receiving end of a briefing against a party figure who had fallen out of favour – leapt on McConnell's latest trouble. A new nickname for McConnell began to circulate around the press corps – 'Guilty Jack'. It was probably because of this that the then Finance Minister realised that, if he was going to be able to emerge from the affair with his reputation intact, it was in his interests to have a full public inquiry into the Lobbygate allegations.

He immediately offered to give the inquiry, which was set up by the parliament's Standards Committee, access to his diaries and office files. One month after the story broke, the

Scottish Parliament's first Standards Committee investigation into allegations of impropriety at Holyrood began. McConnell turned to his old friend Neil Stewart, who runs an events company in London, for help. Stewart had watched similar accusations unfold in London and he gave McConnell some valuable advice on how to handle the accusations. Witnesses were summoned and their evidence was given in public and under oath.

Once again, Jack McConnell was being forced to fight for his political life and his reputation. Declaring an interest, his close ally Patricia Ferguson resigned from the committee. She had worked closely with McConnell at Labour's HQ and felt she could not sit in judgement of her former colleague and friend – a show trial this was not. Two important decisions were taken which were to help Jack McConnell. The first was to call the lobbyists Kevin Reid and Alex Barr before the committee. Barr in particular was given a roasting by the MSPs who appeared to have decided in advance that he was guilty of showing off in front of clients and, in doing so and getting caught, threatened to tarnish the image of the new parliament. One committee member admitted, 'It was a clear strategy – if we could discredit Barr, then the accusations would, in turn, be discredited because they were based on boasts made by him.'

Although he was an experienced PR professional, Barr was unaccustomed to the rough and tumble of politics and he was quickly marked down as the 'fall guy' by some of the MSPs. Committee members also decided which MSP would take the lead in grilling the various witnesses. Barr had the unenviable task of facing down Labour MSP Karen Gillon, who was seen as the most able and combative of the MSPs. She showed little mercy for the PR man as she shot down some of the boasts he had made in the fake meeting. She highlighted that fact that the ministers he claimed he had access to were turning up to key events organised by public bodies and were merely doing their job – not responding to a request by Beattie Media.

With Barr's claims thrown into doubt, the committee decided to call McConnell's constituency diary secretary Christina Marshall to give evidence ahead of her boss. By putting Marshall in the firing line ahead of McConnell, the committee took pressure off the Finance Minister. His twenty-two-year-old secretary/researcher had to fend off all the difficult questions and because of her youth and relatively unimportant position, compared to that of a minister, some of the committee members felt they should 'go easy'. One said:

> I just didn't think it was fair to go for Christina – she was a young girl doing her job and [she] suddenly found herself at the centre of a massive political row. She was under enormous pressure and I didn't see it as our place to add to that.

But Marshall's performance before the committee would have been a credit to someone twice her age and experience. She gave the impression of a confident young woman who ran a highly efficient office for McConnell. As the daughter of Labour MP David Marshall, she clearly understood the world of Scottish politics and how to avoid bear traps. She had been one of many applicants for the job of constituency secretary to Jack McConnell and the interviews for the post were carried out by Professor Mike Donnelly. One of the questions he had asked all of the applicants was, 'If Jack got involved in something dodgy and you found out about it what would you do?' Christina didn't hesitate in her answer. 'I'd blow the whistle,' she said. It was that answer more than any other that landed her the job.

Ahead of the Lobbygate grilling, Marshall was put through her paces – as was McConnell – by a team of special advisers from Donald Dewar's office, as well as Prof. Mike Donnelly and Neil Stewart. There is no doubt that this meant they were far better prepared for the hearing than the MSPs who were to cross-examine them were. However, if there was a problem with Marshall's evidence, it lay in the fact that it was seen to be too smooth. It was clear that she had anticipated the line of questioning and she never faltered in her answers.

In his evidence to the committee, Alex Barr had claimed that he called Christina to ask her if McConnell would attend the financial awards dinner and she said, 'I'll pencil it in. If you have not heard back from me in a couple of days, consider it done.' This was the central allegation now left hanging over McConnell. Accepting such an invitation would not, in itself, have been wrong but, set against the background of Lobbygate, it would certainly have done him damage had it been proven to be true.

With great skill, Marshall turned the claim on its head by telling the committee that her understanding of the conversation was exactly the opposite of what Barr had taken from it. According to Christina, she would not have confirmed McConnell's attendance without consulting him. She admitted she had written a note about the dinner in the forward-planner section of McConnell's diary for 2000. She told the committee that, when she asked McConnell about the dinner, he said she should not agree to it as there had been no formal invitation. Christina then told the MSPs that she erased the entry using Tipp-Ex. The committee was told that, when the diary was held up to the light, the words 'Alex's dinner' could be clearly read under the white band of Tipp-Ex.

Ms Marshall was described as 'meticulous' in her work yet the MSPs accepted that, despite McConnell rejecting the request to speak at the dinner, she did not think it was her job to relay that message back to her former colleague at Beattie Media, Alex Barr, who had been left with the clear impression that the minister would turn up. It was clear that only one version of events was correct – either Barr's or Christina's – and that one of them was either lying or suffering from a severe case of confusion. Despite the fact both gave evidence under oath, the committee did not recall Barr to try to reconcile the two versions of events.

The MSPs were also told that Christina routinely destroyed notebooks in the office. When asked if this was not an extreme measure, she replied that they often contained information about drug dealers given to the office by constituents and that the information had to be erased to protect the informants. This they also accepted to be the case. Marshall appeared to make just one slip when she mentioned that McConnell had been invited to a football match by Beattie Media – a fact which had not come to light – yet astonishingly the MSPs on the committee did not bother to follow up the information to find out whether or not he went and nor did they ask about the circumstances surrounding this invitation.

By the time Jack McConnell was called to give evidence, all the difficult issues had been dealt with. Within minutes, he was laughing and joking and jousting with the committee members – all on first-name terms of course. Tory MSP Lord James Douglas Hamilton led the questioning of McConnell. Lord James is no fool but he is certainly a gentleman so there were no low blows and McConnell coasted through his evidence. During his evidence, he said he wished the job with Beattie-owned Public Affairs Europe Ltd had never existed. It was evident shortly after taking on the role that McConnell had some regrets. Although he was paid around £15,000 for six months' work, the firm never had any clients on its books. As soon as Jack was selected for the Motherwell and Wishaw constituency, he gave the job up and spent all his time getting to know the constituency he was about to serve.

When the Standards Committee issued its findings, which exonerated all the ministers accused of having improper links to Beattie Media, it came as no surprise. However, the committee did come in for some harsh criticism over the weak questioning and their failure to examine inconsistencies in evidence. Its reputation took a battering as a result of Lobbygate and Jack McConnell went from being dubbed 'Guilty Jack' to 'Lucky Jack'. It wasn't the first time he had come through a potentially career-ending scrape with his reputation intact and it wasn't to be the last.

# 9

# JOCKEYING FOR POSITION

The battle to succeed Scotland's first First Minister Donald Dewar began the day he was elected. His ambitious, young cabinet ministers never believed he would serve more than one term at Holyrood – if that. From the moment they took their seats round the cabinet table, several of them began to jockey for his job. The Scottish Parliament's rocky start saw the new institution ridiculed after MSPs were seen to award themselves medals on their first day at work. Essentially this was a gift from the parliament to the 129 men and women who took up their places in the new legislature as a way of commemorating that it was open for business. But the tabloids didn't see it that way – or didn't want to – and it didn't help when the first vote in the new parliament was on MSPs' pay and holidays.

Much work had been done by the all-party steering group on housekeeping matters before the parliament was set up but the group decided to leave it up to MSPs to agree a pay package for themselves and their staff and this resulted in an early PR blunder. After getting off to a bad beginning, Donald Dewar's leadership was later to be dogged by the sharply rising bill for the new parliament building at Holyrood – so much so, it was dubbed 'Donald's Dome', a reference to the exorbitant cost of London's Millennium Dome. Dewar was much criticised on the policy front too. A series of astonishing mistakes within the Scottish Qualifications Agency (SQA) resulted in the exams crisis of the summer of 2000 when thousands of youngsters either didn't get their results or received the wrong ones.

An attempt to repeal the discriminatory law Section 28 was the focus of an aggressive campaign by the businessman Brian Souter. With the help of PR guru Jack Irvine, the idea was lampooned. Lurid press headlines, particularly in the *Daily Record*, warned that young kids would be subjected to gay sex lessons in schools as a result of the change in the law.

The Executive failed to counter the public relations offensive being waged against it. As Dewar's Executive lurched from one problem to the next, most of the senior ministers were reluctant to go into battle for him. Privately, Jack told people that he felt there had been too little policy preparation carried out in advance of the Parliament opening for business. While McConnell had praised Dewar and his team for the way they worked to deliver the Scotland Act, he believed that not enough thought had been given to what they would do in the parliament once it was there. Several ministers even began to seriously doubt Donald Dewar's ability to carry on. At least one was concerned about the way that cabinet meetings were being run. Dewar's senior aide Brian Fitzpatrick would attend cabinet meetings and, unlike the ministers, would leave his mobile phone switched on. On one occasion, Chancellor Gordon Brown called him on it and Fitzpatrick interrupted the cabinet proceedings to relay Brown's views to Dewar. One cabinet minister said, 'It was farcical. I began to wonder if I was at a community council meeting rather than a meeting of Scotland's new government.'

Around this time, only the then Education Minister, Sam Galbraith, and the Communities Minister, Wendy Alexander, remained fiercely loyal but, like Dewar, they had both suffered from severe criticism as a result of their roles in the SQA crisis and the repeal of Section 28 respectively. The then Industry Minister, Henry McLeish, and Jack McConnell, who was Finance Minister at the time, were seen as the most likely contenders to succeed Dewar as the pressure on him intensified. This led to the pair being dubbed the 'Big Macs' in some sections of the media. Friends of Donald Dewar's believe that he would like to have seen Wendy Alexander take over from him but that he felt she was far from ready. It is likely it would have been several years before Dewar would willingly have handed over the reins of power to his young protégé.

It is believed that Dewar held McConnell in some regard mainly because of his background as a maths teacher. When introducing his first cabinet to the Queen and Prince Philip at Holyrood Palace, he told Her Majesty, 'This is Jack McConnell – he was a sums teacher, you know, and now he does the sums for us.' The Queen's reaction to this bizarre introduction is not known. But, prior to this, Dewar had been suspicious of McConnell during his time as General Secretary of the party. An old-fashioned politician, Dewar hated the idea of spin and reacted against the importance New Labour attached to presentation – be it of policy or of himself.

The first First Minister had worked closely with Henry McLeish at Westminster in pushing the devolution bill through the Commons. However, he probably trusted him the least. The speculation on Dewar's succession tended to focus on McLeish because he was seen as the most experienced politician in the cabinet. The perceived wisdom at the time of Dewar's leadership was that, if the First Minister did stand down early, the mantle would fall to McLeish and, if he saw out a full first term or more, then McConnell would be well placed but, if he completed two full terms, then Wendy Alexander would move into pole position as McLeish's time would have passed.

The jostling for position in the cabinet intensified in the spring of 2000 when Donald Dewar made the surprise announcement that he was going into hospital to have major heart surgery. His supporters tried to play down the significance of the operation, claiming that he would quickly be back to full fitness and, if anything, he would be a more effective leader than before because he would not be struggling with a heart condition. But Dewar's enemies saw the health setback as an opportunity to undermine him further. His cabinet ministers were careful not to question his ability to make a speedy return to office but, when the father-like Dewar went into hospital to have his operation, there ensued some of the most bitter infighting the cabinet had experienced.

Henry McLeish was annoyed that the constitutional arrangements of the parliament meant that the Deputy First Minister, Liberal Democrat Jim Wallace, took over as acting First Minister in Dewar's absence. However, it did fall to McLeish to stand in for Dewar on Labour Party matters and this served to confirm his seniority in the cabinet. Dewar was all too aware of the ambitions of his fellow ministers and, although he did not hold that against them, it was his view that none of them was ready to take on the demands of his job. His critics would say that such a view showed some arrogance on his part. However, with the benefit of hindsight, it is likely that both Dewar's successors would now think that he had a point at that stage.

Most of the time, Dewar did not mind the jockeying for position within his team because he felt secure in the post. However, he did become angry when the spats between ministers harmed his government. Just eleven days after Donald Dewar was released from hospital, following his life-saving operation, came the worst row to hit his cabinet. Jack McConnell held a press conference to unveil the new accountancy procedures he was using in the Scottish Executive budget. Each year there is an underspend in all of the spending departments. Under McConnell's plan, each department, instead of rolling the money over, would be told to hand over one quarter of its underspend at the end of every year. That cash would go into a central reserve from which money would be reallocated for special projects and it would also be there as emergency fund for the Executive. The Finance Minister had believed the new budgetary measure would be welcomed.

However, when the BBC's political correspondent, John Morrison, asked if Health Department money would also be included in the reserve fund, the answer sparked an enormous row. It emerged that the Health Department had an underspend of £135 million at the end of 1999. Under McConnell's new rule, £34 million of that had been ploughed into the central reserve. When journalists then discovered that the contingency fund would be used to give money to forestry projects and to Historic Scotland, the next day's headlines screamed of money being taken from health to be spent on trees and old buildings. McConnell, who had hoped to win some praise for his initiative, found himself dubbed 'Lumber Jack'.

The press pack on The Mound were left in no doubt about the feelings of the Health Minister Susan Deacon – she was livid. It was clear that relations between the Health Minister and the Finance Minister were appalling. The story ran for days. Donald Dewar was forced to read about his squabbling ministers from his sick bed. One Sunday, Susan Deacon even turned up at his home in a bid to get him to take her side in the dispute. Dewar was incensed, telling one friend, 'At least Jack was one of the few people who managed to leave me alone while I was ill.' The row damaged both ministers. The opposition demanded to know why Deacon had such a large underspend in her department when the previous winter had seen a flu crisis and waiting lists needed to be tackled and McConnell was considered guilty of showing poor political judgement.

The spat also provided evidence of a damaging split in Dewar's cabinet which he had wanted to keep under wraps. Within a week of McConnell's policy statement, he was forced to do a U-turn and announced that he would be handing back the £34 million to the Health Department. Deacon had won her money back but, the following day, the First Minister issued a statement from his home warning that any minister found briefing against a cabinet colleague would face the sack. The rebuke, which was extremely harsh and unusual for Dewar, was seen as being directed at Deacon over the way she had handled the affair and she faced taunts in the chamber which took the gloss off her apparent cabinet victory.

Donald Dewar's heart operation took place at Glasgow Royal Infirmary on 8 May 2000. Although the procedure was a success, he was under orders to rest, take his medication on a regular basis and get as much gentle exercise as possible. Anyone recuperating from a serious operation is also advised to avoid stress and, although there is no conclusive evidence that Dewar's condition was aggravated by stress, he certainly had plenty of stressful situations to contend with that summer. He complained to friends that he was being badgered by his colleagues who were worried about their positions and power – or lack of it – in his absence. Dewar loved his work and would not have taken any longer than necessary to recuperate from his operation. Meanwhile, his beloved Holyrood building plan had suffered a severe setback with the death of its architect Enric Miralles in July 2000. However, Dewar's friends claim it was his concern over the failure of the Scottish Qualifications Agency to get the exam results out which made him determined to get back – perhaps sooner than he should have.

One of his closest cabinet allies was the Education Minister, Sam Galbraith, and he was in the eye of the storm. Dewar believed that, by returning to work, he could bring some stability back to the cabinet. It was little over a month after he made his return to the parliament chamber that he tripped outside his official residence Bute House and sparked renewed fears over his health. The Scottish Executive press office issued a statement on the afternoon of 10 October 2000 revealing that the First Minister had been taken to hospital as a 'precaution'.

The news prompted a flurry of reports speculating that the First Minister had returned to work too soon. It was only later that evening that the First Minister's official spokesman, David Whitton, revealed just how seriously ill Donald Dewar really was. Shortly after 9 p.m. that night, he admitted that Dewar was critically ill and on a life-support machine. The next morning's newspapers reported that the First Minister was in fact dying.

The cabinet ministers were all called to St Andrew's House early the following morning. It was apparent that all but McConnell had been kept well informed of developments the previous evening. Jack later told friends he was taken aback by the lack of visible upset in the room that morning. However, according to Sam Galbraith, Jack wasted no time in planning his campaign and, in doing so, he further alienated several cabinet members. Galbraith said, 'Jack left the room and was straight on the phone to Andy Kerr, the East Kilbride MSP, and people didn't like that.' At 12.18 p.m. on 11 October 2000, it was announced that the First Minister Donald Dewar had died from a brain haemorrhage. The ministers who had all been eyeing up his job were being given the chance to go for it in circumstances none of them could have predicted and none of them wanted. Immediately following Dewar's death, it is fair to say that nobody wanted to talk about the succession. Scotland was a nation in mourning. But the Scotland Act, which Dewar had drafted himself, did not allow for a prolonged period of grieving. The law stated that a new First Minister must be in place within twenty-eight days, which meant a successor had to be in place by 7 November.

The Labour Party decided that the tight timescale meant its normal rules for electing a First Minster would have to be abandoned – there simply was not enough time to ask party members to vote. Instead of taking a vote among MSPs, MPs, MEPs, trade unions, affiliates and party members, the party

HQ ruled that the contest would have to be judged by Labour's fifty-four MSPs and the twenty-seven members of the party's ruling executive only. This fast-tracked procedure was bound to help any candidate favoured by the leadership because, in effect, it controlled the party's Scottish Executive.

On the day of Dewar's death, Murray Elder spoke to Jack McConnell and told him that Henry McLeish was putting himself forward for the post of First Minister and that everyone else was happy to stand aside for him. Jack's first instinct was that, in avoiding a leadership contest, the party was making the wrong decision. He did not think that the Labour Party or the public would like the idea of another First Minister simply being anointed by the leadership rather than being elected – at least by party members if not the voters. McConnell told Elder that he needed more time to consider what was the right thing to do. Jack then faced making a horrendous choice. Either he accepted the decision to appoint Henry or he made a challenge. The latter would force what he considered to be a much-needed policy debate but it also ran the risk of making him appear disloyal. He was to decide that it was no more disloyal to stand for the position than it was to organise the succession without a challenge.

Donald Dewar's funeral took place on Wednesday 18 October 2000 at Glasgow Cathedral. The Prime Minister and the Chancellor were there, as were all the members of the Scottish cabinet. Although all the possible contenders for the Labour leadership had been careful not to speak about their ambitions ahead of the funeral, privately they were taking soundings and making preparations. After the funeral service, the mourners gathered at the Kelvingrove Art Gallery and Museum in Glasgow. Henry McLeish was seen speaking to the Prime Minister, albeit briefly. Jack McConnell's close ally, Frank Roy, advised him not to be seen to be looking for support in the midst of such grief. Even before Dewar's funeral, the 'line' among leadership loyalists had been that, following Dewar's death, a contest for his job would be unseemly. The clear implication, which continued to be made, was that anything other than the annointing of Henry McLeish would be an insult to Dewar's memory.

It was a pressure that McConnell refused to give in to. Among the many people he consulted before deciding to run was his close ally from his Stirling Council days, Mike Donnelly. Donnelly told him that the party machine would move behind McLeish because he was seen as the 'safe pair of hands'. McConnell reacted with despair, exclaiming that, if they wanted a safe pair of hands, then it was him they should be backing. He also called his close friend, Alan Clements, who gave him a similar message but also urged him to stand, telling him of the importance of 'putting down a marker' for the future. That night McConnell called Sally Morgan, Tony Blair's political adviser in Downing Street. As a courtesy, he wanted to let Number Ten know that he intended to stand for the leadership of the Scottish party. Jack's phone call went unreturned.

After Donald's funeral, Henry McLeish and his wife Julie went out for dinner in Glasgow before heading home to St Andrews. During the evening, Henry received a phone call from his close ally in the cabinet, Angus McKay, who advised him that Jack McConnell had decided against challenging for the leadership. McLeish was relieved, believing that the only person who could stand in his way was not going to do so. This misinformation was put out by the McConnell camp to lull McLeish into a false sense of security. As McLeish relaxed, McConnell was already hard at work planning his leadership campaign. He stayed up all night and, by 9 a.m. the next morning, all the Labour MSPs had an e-mail from McConnell informing them of his intention to stand for the position of Labour Leader in the Scottish Parliament.

By 10 a.m., McConnell's campaign HQ in Wishaw was full of MSPs and party workers determined that he should succeed. His campaign co-ordinator Patricia Ferguson said, 'In making my decision, I thought, if I was a candidate in a key seat, which of the two would l like to walk down the street with and the answer was Jack. That decided it for me.' The Labour Party had decided that it must select a new leader following a campaign lasting just forty-eight hours. There was an outcry from the McConnell camp. His supporters believed that, with a bit more time, they could convince enough of the electorate to back their man. However, such a short timescale would inevitably help McLeish, who was seen as the favourite and who had the backing of most of the unions. Jack McConnell knew that the odds were stacked against him but his political past told him that it doesn't automatically spell failure. From talking to those closest to him, it appears that, deep down, he thought McLeish would win but he would, at least, come close and might possibly even win against all the odds.

McConnell left behind a team of experienced politicians in his campaign office at the ISTC trade union base in Motherwell and they spent the day contacting MSPs to canvass their support. They included the Motherwell and Wishaw MP Frank Roy and the MSPs Patricia Ferguson, Scott Barrie, Cathy Craigie, Andy Kerr, Karen Whitefield, Cathy Peattie and Andy Kerr. Meanwhile, he headed out to take his leadership campaign message to the country and the eighty-one people who would take part in the vote – wherever they were. The North Lanarkshire Councillor, John Pentlands, spent two days driving McConnell round the country. They were joined by one of McConnell's young Labour protégées, Kirsty O'Brien, who had flown back from California when Jack told her of Dewar's death. Although McConnell would not tell O'Brien if he would stand for the leadership when he called her, she believed there was a chance and caught a flight home to help with any bid he launched.

The day after Donald's funeral, McConnell toured round the Borders, stopping in Ayr on the way home where he did an interview for BBC Radio. He had an early success when the Edinburgh *Evening News* decided to back his candidacy. That evening, he told his campaign team that he wanted Henry McLeish to turn on his radio the next morning to hear him speaking from Aberdeen. At 4 a.m. the next morning, McConnell left his home in Wishaw to make his way to Aberdeen. He did early morning interviews for local radio and his wish was granted when, at 8.10 a.m., he was interviewed live on *Good Morning Scotland* from the north-east of Scotland. McConnell was delighted and believed that his campaign had more momentum than that of McLeish. Frank Roy had dampened his enthusiasm following his early interviews by telling him that his campaign message sounded too similar to that of his rival's and that they must act quickly to mark him as offering something different and radical. McConnell upped the ante by the time he was questioned on *GMS*, declaring that he would not be dictated to by Gordon Brown. There was no subtlety in the attack. It was well known that Henry McLeish had the powerful backing of Brown and McConnell had decided to turn his opponent's biggest strength into a weakness. Although Brown was careful not to be seen to be meddling in the leadership vote behind the scenes, he was using his influence with the unions to ensure they delivered for his man. Brown and McLeish have always been close and the Chancellor's desire to see McLeish become the next First Minister would have been increased by the thought of the alternative. Throughout the contest, Gordon Brown was giving advice to McLeish and using his influence, albeit carefully – he took the decision that he could not speak directly to MSPs.

Despite McConnell's loyal support for Tony Blair, it was never reciprocated. The best he could hope for was that Number

LUCKY JACK

Ten would not interfere in the selection. Anyway, having attacked McLeish for his London-based support, McConnell could hardly be seen to be asking for help from Downing Street himself. He had already calculated he would be unlikely to get it. As Parliamentary Press Secretary to John Reid, Frank Roy was giving regular updates to the Scottish Secretary from the McConnell camp. He informed Reid that the result was too close to call. Reid was sceptical and asked Roy several times if he was sure of his numbers. Roy assured him he was and advised Reid to tell Number Ten to remain neutral in the contest.

McConnell was also keen to attract the support of the *Daily Record* newspaper. Frank Roy spent much of his time trying to persuade the paper's political editor, Paul Sinclair, that they should back Jack. However, the McConnell camp would have been pleased enough if they could even persuade the paper to stay neutral. Jack and his closest advisers held a meeting with executives from the paper and, while they accepted that the *Record* would want to take a view on the contest, they asked if they would hold off doing so until the day of the vote. The newspaper agreed, saying that it would first examine the views of the contenders before reaching a conclusion in its Saturday edition. However, on the Thursday night, Paul Sinclair called Roy to give him the bad news – the paper had decided. Jack was told, 'It has to be Henry.' and that would be their headline on the Friday morning. Because that was only the midway point of the two-day campaign, the McConnell camp believed the newspaper's backing for McLeish could still influence the outcome of the vote.

Despite this perceived setback, McConnell's campaign team in Wishaw had been pleasantly surprised by the level of support they were receiving and they still thought they had every chance of winning. However, out on the road, Jack McConnell was refusing to get carried away. He was fighting to win but, according to O'Brien, he never gave the impression that he thought he had pulled it off and urged those around him not to get carried away by thinking that he might have. Although at least twenty-five MSPs had pledged their support for McConnell, he fared less well among the 'payroll' vote. These were the ministers, many of whom were desperate to back the winner to enable them to keep their jobs in government. McConnell was buoyant after his friend and Deputy Minister, Frank McAveety, broke ranks to offer his support. He believed that, if one minister was brave enough to put their head above the parapet, others might follow. He was to be sorely disappointed. When McAveety was leant on by the other side, he caved in and withdrew his support. By instinctively wanting to help McConnell but not having the courage of his conviction, he had damaged his ally more than if he had simply said nothing. With the ministerial vote and the votes of the Scottish Executive of the party mainly behind him, McLeish needed fewer than a dozen backbenchers to secure victory.

On 21 October, just ten days after the death of Donald Dewar, Labour's electorate met in Stirling to decide on their new leader. Jack's supporters met for coffee at the Bannockburn service station on the outskirts of Stirling ahead of the meeting. Patricia Ferguson told McConnell she thought that McLeish had won by forty-four votes to thirty-six and the biggest problem they faced was persuading people that the contest was close. As a last-ditch attempt to wrestle the job from Henry, she proposed they raise a point of order at the meeting so Kate McLean asked party officials what would happen in the event of a tie. It was a ploy to impress upon people that it was a tight contest. Jack's team believed that many people were voting for Henry for no reason other than they thought that he was the clear winner. But the tactic came too late – some people in the room even laughed at the suggestion of a tie.

During the meeting, both candidates made speeches about what they would offer. Unusually for McConnell, he spoke from notes rather than from the heart. He later told friends that he was disappointed by his own performance. After the meeting, the party's General Secretary, Lesley Quinn, took both Henry McLeish and Jack McConnell into a side room to tell them the result. Jack then asked Quinn to leave the room for a couple of minutes. During that time, he told McLeish that he wanted to be included in his team and given the respect he was entitled to as a result of the support he had demonstrated that he had. He also demanded that there be no retribution against those people who had supported him. If those conditions were met, then McLeish would have his full support, he told him. Henry agreed that would be the case and the two men shook hands before going out to face the press.

It had come as no great surprise that Henry McLeish was the victor. What did shock many people was the small margin of victory. Despite McLeish having the backing of Gordon Brown, all the Scottish ministers and the Scottish Executive of the party, Jack McConnell had come to within eight votes of defeating him. Patricia Ferguson had predicted the outcome accurately. The former General Secretary had lost the vote but was seen to have won the campaign. As the result was announced, McConnell was grinning but McLeish looked shaken as if he realised instantly that his leadership was damaged before it had even begun. Following the vote Gordon Brown called McLeish, demanding to know what went wrong.

The year that followed was one of mixed fortunes for McConnell. He excelled at the education brief handed to him by McLeish, his support on the backbenches if anything increased, and he had secured his position as the heir apparent. But the leadership contest had resulted in already-strained relationships becoming even more difficult and some colleagues coming under even greater pressure. McLeish viewed McConnell as a rival who could not be trusted. Ministers who valued their positions within McLeish's cabinet went out of their way to distance themselves from Jack. They did this partly because they wanted to be seen as loyal to the First Minister and also because they harboured feelings of distrust themselves.

Ahead of the weekly cabinet meetings at Bute House, ministers would gather in the room next to the cabinet room for a coffee and a croissant as well as a quick chat with colleagues before getting down to the week's business. Jack didn't join them. He would go straight to the cabinet room to take his seat for the meeting as he saw little point in having coffee with a group of people, some of whom would turn their backs on him when he entered the room. For almost a year, Jack was shunned by all but one or two of his cabinet colleagues and, for the last nine months of his leadership, Henry McLeish did not have a single direct conversation with McConnell such was the state of their relationship. A civil servant who observed those cabinet meetings said, 'Particularly towards the end, the cabinet had become quite fractured. It did not work particularly effectively.'

One cabinet minister at the time recalled how Jack would be the target of political attacks by his own colleagues. 'I used to sit there and watch the arrows flying. They were mainly coming from Jackie Baillie's direction but Angus McKay would also join in and Jack certainly gave as good as he got.' The situation became so bad that Jack rarely tried to raise serious issues at cabinet meetings, believing any idea he put forward would be blocked because it had come from him. He even devised a bizarre strategy to get round the problems he had working with his own colleagues. On a couple of occasions, when he wanted to raise something important he went to the Liberal Democrat Junior Minister, Nicol Stephen, to ask him to get Jim Wallace to raise the issue so that Jack's Labour colleagues would be more inclined to listen. There is no evidence that Wallace knew he was acting as a conduit between McConnell and the rest of the cabinet but the ploy worked.

The former Education Minister, Sam Galbraith, who resigned shortly after McLeish came to power, argues that McConnell was not a 'team player' and confirms that the reason he was not trusted by the rest of the cabinet was because they believed he was constantly briefing the press. During his time as Education Minister, Jack waged a campaign to have his own special adviser. This was partly because he did not trust the advisers whom McLeish had appointed and also because of his strong instinct to install his own people around him. It was a request that would never be granted. McLeish immediately saw it as Jack attempting to increase his power base and he also suspected that any adviser of McConnell's would automatically be against him and would, therefore, brief against him.

The stand-off over this issue led to one of the biggest rows of that year. In his memoirs, McLeish tells of his fury after a badly wrapped parcel was sent to his home and intercepted by the police as a suspicious package, only to find it contained McConnell's latest demand to have his own adviser. McLeish made it very clear to him that it would never happen during his leadership. But, if Henry thought Jack would use advisers to work against him, then the feeling was mutual. McConnell's view that McLeish's people were operating against him was reinforced when he was sent an anonymous note from someone claiming they had been dining in an Edinburgh restaurant at a table next to two of McLeish's advisers and were appalled by the terms in which they were describing Jack. McConnell was also furious when an invitation to speak at a fundraising dinner at the Edinburgh Central constituency was mysteriously withdrawn after McLeish had learned about it. The constituency is a particularly important one for any politician trying to build a power base and is not one that McLeish would have wanted his rival to address.

If Jack felt cut off from the centre of power during McLeish's reign in the sense that he was shunned by colleagues, he was literally cut off too. Most of McLeish's ministers were based in offices in the parliament buildings on George IV Bridge, off the Royal Mile, in the heart of Edinburgh. McConnell's department was based at Victoria Quay in Leith and this also added to the sense of isolation. Former special adviser to Henry McLeish, Tom Little, said:

> I would go to his office once or twice a week to have a meeting about the weekly grid of events and announcements coming up. It was like entering another government. Jack conducted things differently. He was certainly very focused. But he worked in a bubble – no one trusted him.

Of all McLeish's advisers, Little was probably the only one Jack did not view with distrust and he was one of the few to be asked to stay on in the job when McConnell took over as First Minister. It is unclear whether McConnell's suspicion of the other advisers was justified. Little said, 'I was never asked to brief against Jack during my time working with Henry and nor would I have done it.' However, he does reinforce the view that McLeish was paranoid about McConnell. He said, 'Henry thought about sacking him. I think he would like to have been in a strong enough position to do it but he realised that he couldn't because Jack represented a strong faction within the group.' Little also revealed that, instead, the former First Minister decided he would like to move McConnell from the role he loved at Education to Health – a real poisoned chalice. But McLeish was to be hounded from office before he had a chance to reshuffle his cabinet. Rather than finding himself sacked, the next ministerial line-up was to be decided by Jack himself.

# 10

# SECOND LEADERSHIP

In the autumn of 2001, the Scottish Parliament was engulfed by scandal. First Minister Henry McLeish was accused of misusing his office expenses. When the story first broke in the *Mail on Sunday* some months earlier, it was largely ignored. It centred on a claim that the legal firm Digby Brown had been subletting part of McLeish's office for £4,000 a year. The rest of the press corps put it down to a disgruntled constituent making allegations they didn't much care about but 'Officegate', as it became known, continued to dog the First Minister. Every few weeks, there would be a new allegation to answer. McLeish understandably tried to keep the issue out of the newspapers.

In April of 2001, he registered the sublets with the parliamentary authorities in Edinburgh and London. When he discovered that sublets were not allowed under Commons' rules, he paid back £9,000 and thought that would be the end of the matter. However, when the press eventually discovered that McLeish had paid money back, they smelled blood. As often happens when journalists suddenly think they might have missed a story, they go into overdrive to compensate for the stories they failed to cover earlier. McLeish was insisting he had done nothing wrong yet he had paid back money from his own pocket – the inconsistency was glaring. From that moment on, it was open season on McLeish.

It is now accepted by all but the most sceptical that Officegate should never have been a resignation issue. The allegations the First Minister faced were not in themselves serious. He made no personal gain from his office arrangements. The money he made from the sublets was used to run his office. Despite that, he had used his own money to refund the House of Commons for the cash he had mistakenly taken in sublets. What McLeish was guilty of was failing to give a clear explanation of the situation. For months, the opposition parties had a field day and Labour backbenchers squirmed with embarrassment as they had to endure their leader being humiliated week after week.

Jack had run McLeish so close in the leadership contest and now Labour MSPs who had not supported him in his bid began to think they might have made a mistake. And, as they watched McLeish try and fail to draw a line under the Officegate saga, some of McConnell's supporters started to think his time may have come. McLeish's lowest point came during a long-planned appearance on the BBC's *Question Time* programme during which David Dimbleby asked him how much money was involved and he replied, 'I don't know what the sum was.' After months of questions about the running of his office, it seemed an astonishing admission and the pressure on McLeish intensified again.

Despite this, Jack never believed that the story was going to end McLeish's political career. Under Labour Party rules, there was no mechanism for forcing him out and it never crossed McConnell's mind that McLeish would simply walk. Jack's reading of the situation seemed to be compounded on the evening of 6 November 2001. Along with his Labour colleagues, he attended a meeting of the Scottish MSPs. Henry McLeish addressed the meeting for an hour and a half in an attempt to convince his backbenchers that he was being unfairly pursued. Earlier that day, he had called a press conference in the First Minister's official residence, Bute House, to set out the facts. McLeish memorably described the affair as a 'muddle not a fiddle'. By and large, the details he gave that morning satisfied his critics but, having revealed all, McLeish could not afford any further revelations. That night MSPs on the Labour benches gave the First Minister their unanimous backing and Jack left the meeting convinced that McLeish would weather the storm.

Throughout McLeish's Officegate troubles, McConnell's allies claim he resisted the temptation to brief against his rival in order to damage him. But then he didn't have to. Henry McLeish appeared to be digging holes for himself and his 'come clean' press conference was to be another self-laid trap. As McLeish became a target of hounding by the opposition Jack was approached and asked if he would issue a statement in support of the First Minister. Although McConnell had decided not to add to the First Minister's problems, he balked at the idea of going that far. However, after he realised McLeish still had the support of the group of Labour MPs in the Scottish Parliament, he spent that night pondering if he should go to the rescue of his leader.

As McConnell weighed up his options McLeish left the meeting to attend a sports gala dinner at the Palace of Holyroodhouse. McLeish was exhausted after suffering a difficult few days and he was apprehensive about a no-confidence motion he would have to face in the parliament the next day. It was while McLeish was at that dinner that he received the message that was to end his political career. The papers had discovered another office let that McLeish had failed to declare at his 'come clean' press conference. The office space was rented to the old people's charity Third Age who paid £25 a week for it. The revelation was hardly the kind of information that would make or break a political leader but it was the last straw for McLeish.

The First Minister had simply had enough. He had no fight left in him and he was coming to the conclusion that any good work he tried to do on behalf of the Executive was being overshadowed by his inability to deal with Officegate. That night, he decided he would have to quit. Ironically, during those same hours, Jack McConnell came to the decision that he would have to publicly back McLeish. McConnell called close friend, Neil Stewart, at 8 a.m. the following morning, to tell him he was set to put out a statement in support of the First Minister. Stewart replied, 'Don't – do absolutely nothing.' That advice could have been nothing more than political gut instinct – he could not have known anything of the events that were about to unfold.

Three hours later, McConnell's mobile rang. It was Tom McCabe, the parliament minister and a close ally of McLeish. He told McConnell that the First Minister was about to resign but that he was concerned about the way his resignation was to be handled. He asked Jack to take a taxi with him to see McLeish to ensure the First Minister was spared any further trauma. It was an odd request, given that McConnell and McLeish had not spoken to each other for about nine months, but McConnell agreed to it. Some of McLeish's advisers wanted him to stand up in parliament to announce his resignation but, bizarrely, it was left up to Jack McConnell, the man who challenged him for the job in the first place, to persuade him of the best way to leave with dignity.

As McConnell arrived he was initially blocked from seeing McLeish by the then Communities Minister, Jackie Baillie, who wanted to try one more time to get McLeish to change his mind. She did not succeed and Jack began to plan the handover of power. One friend of McConnell said:

> Henry was in a terrible state but he had made his decision to go and Jack had nothing to gain from Henry breaking down in public. Jack has got kids and he did not want Henry's kids to see him upset. If Henry had been forced to make that statement, that would have been the likely outcome.

With McLeish's unexpected resignation Jack McConnell was close to realising his dream of becoming Scotland's First Minister.

Despite the fact that he had been networking from the moment he got elected to make sure that he would have enough support to secure the job when his time came, Jack was remarkably unprepared for the challenge which lay ahead of him. The MSP who masterminded McConnell's first leadership election was quick off the mark. Patricia Ferguson organised a meeting of key supporters that evening. Mike Watson, Cathy Peattie, Andy Kerr, Janis Hughes and Karen Whitefield all met at the home of the Stirling MSP, Sylvia Jackson, that evening. Watson said:

> Although we didn't see Henry McLeish as a long-term option for First Minister, everyone was taken aback by what happened. Jack was doing a good job at Education but we still believed his time was some way off. We thought the party machine would still try to stop him and the *Daily Record* was still unconvinced by him.

It had only been a year since McConnell had staged a bid for the leadership and many of the same tactics used the first time around were employed again. Ferguson shored up his support on the backbenches, Kerr began work on a press strategy and the others canvassed for support, making hundreds of phone calls to contacts in the party and in the trade unions. Jack knew how to run a leadership campaign and there was never any doubt it would be a slick operation. However, there were two things bothering him. One was that he had had an affair some years earlier and he believed this would be used against him. The other was whether or not a challenger would appear and, if one did, who it might be. How McConnell reacted to the first issue is dealt with in the chapter about his relations with the press. He took the initiative and held a pre-emptive press conference in order to do what he thought his enemies would do for him. By doing so, Jack believed he would then be free to concentrate on the campaign and run the contest on his terms.

However, a split developed in Jack's camp between those who did not want there to be a leadership contest and those who believed it would actually be beneficial to Jack if there was one. I understand he was of the opinion that he should face a challenge. Two potential rivals emerged. One was the then Deputy Health Minister, Malcolm Chisholm, who was portrayed as the left-wing choice, and the other was the then Communities Minister, Wendy Alexander.

Alexander both benefited from her strong links to the Chancellor Gordon Brown and suffered from them. The McConnell camp were all too aware that Brown could deliver the unions for Alexander in the same way he had for McLeish but they were also conscious of a resentment building up among MSPs over his influence in any contest. It was, therefore, decided that, if they pitched their message correctly, Alexander's biggest strength could be turned into a weakness. From the outset, any time she was mentioned in the papers, the words 'Brown's choice' or 'Brown's preferred candidate' accompanied her name.

Jack's supporters, by contrast, made much of McConnell being his own man free from Westminster interference. They knew that some sections of the party blamed Brown for making the wrong choice when he persuaded them to back McLeish and they would be reluctant to take his word again. Although the main union leaders were expected to back Alexander, McConnell's supporters were confident that, this time, the union barons would not be able to persuade their membership to back Alexander and they set about speaking to hundreds of ordinary members.

The party's ruling executive also decided that unions should not be allowed to use block votes in the contest but would have to ballot their membership and distribute their votes accordingly. This was effectively a death blow to the Alexander campaign. Although Wendy would have been able to count on the support of many of her cabinet colleagues, she would not have been able to come anywhere near getting the same level of support as Jack McConnell could among backbenchers. Without a guarantee of union block votes, she faced humiliation. Alexander had also suffered criticism in the press over her handling of the decision to repeal Section 28, over allegations that she treated her staff badly and over her attitude when McLeish tried to pile more work on to her – all of which could be used to claim she was not ready for high office.

After she announced her interest in the job, a newspaper poll asked its readers which candidate they would prefer to see as the future First Minister. Just 22% opted for Wendy Alexander with McConnell getting 50%. It looked as if she was still suffering a public backlash over her mistakes while McConnell had managed to put the Lobbygate affair behind him. When McConnell had challenged McLeish the year before, polls put them neck and neck. On the day the poll was published, Alexander announced she was withdrawing from the race. Alexander claimed she had simply decided, at the age of thirty-eight, that there were other things she wanted to do with her life. But, in quitting, she suffered further political damage. She had persuaded many in the ministerial team to back her and they had gone public in their support of her, risking their careers in the event she didn't win. They were furious she had led them to believe she would stand and now she was walking away.

Jack had been at a remembrance service in Wishaw and was returning home along with the MP Frank Roy when he was told of Alexander's intention to stand down. Roy said, 'He was very pleased – nobody had underestimated Wendy.' Alexander's withdrawal left just Jack and Malcolm Chisholm in the race. Jack's supporters did not dismiss him either but they did see him as much less of a threat. They were right to do so. He didn't even manage to secure enough support among his colleagues to get himself nominated in the race. When Jack's camp realised that Chisholm did not have the required backing to stand, they held a meeting at which they considered having several of Jack's supporters sign his nomination papers, just to ensure that a contest did take place. Jack could see a great deal of merit in the plan but, in the end, he was persuaded that a free run at the leadership was not to be looked upon as a problem.

The absence of a challenger took the pressure off McConnell but it also created a vacuum in the campaign. Alexander had been promising to stand as a 'left-of-centre, modernising' candidate. A policy debate between her and McConnell would, without doubt, have produced some interesting ideas but, because there was no debate, the attention focused solely on Jack. As a result of the press conference he held about his personal life, the press went off in search not of policies but 'smoking bimbos'. They didn't find any.

But nor did the leadership campaign shed much light on what McConnell would do once in a position of power. Years later, he would look back and regret not having had the platform of a leadership contest to explain what he stood for but, at the time, that was of little importance to the McConnell camp. What mattered was that they had won. It may have taken the death of one First Minister and the unexpected resignation of another but the way was now clear for Jack McConnell to become the third First Minister of Scotland. Lucky Jack.

# 11

# THE SCOTTISH MEDIA
# A LOVE-HATE RELATIONSHIP

Most Scottish Labour politicians are in awe of the *Daily Record* newspaper. They believe it can make or break them. Rightly or wrongly, they think it has massive influence over their constituents and is, therefore, revered and feared in equal measure. When the paper failed to back Jack McConnell for the Labour leadership, plumping instead for Henry McLeish, it was a psychological body blow to the McConnell camp. As his second leadership challenge loomed, McConnell was determined to get Scotland's biggest-selling daily newspaper on side. On the evening of 9 November 2001, a McConnell ally called to tell him that Douglas Alexander, brother of Wendy Alexander (his rival for the leadership), had been to the paper's Central Quay offices to speak to the editor about the forthcoming battle. McConnell was extremely nervous. He was all too aware that the then editor, Peter Cox, was prone to taking the line he believed the Chancellor wanted him to take. And Douglas Alexander, who often wrote speeches for Brown and was one of the Chancellor's strongest supporters, would be seen as relaying Gordon Brown's message.

The following day the *Daily Record* ran an editorial in which it said the candidates for the leadership must be able to withstand the sort of media scrutiny that Henry McLeish could not withstand. The *Record* 'View' warned, 'Each candidate's background will be examined in the most minute detail by our investigative reporters. If there are skeletons there, we will find them. We simply cannot afford to lose another First Minister to scandal.' To the average reader, it was a fairly innocuous leader but, to McConnell, the gauntlet had been thrown down and he felt he had to pick it up.

For many years, it had been the biggest open secret in Scottish politics that McConnell had an affair with a Labour Party press officer while he was General Secretary of the party. Every newspaper editor in Scotland knew about it, every political journalist knew about it and McConnell's wife and family also knew about it at the time. However, the affair took place in 1994 when McConnell was merely a Labour Party official. The story was not covered because no editor felt it was of sufficient interest to readers. Many years earlier, the *Daily Record* had learned that the *Sun* was thinking about running the story. The then editor Terry Quinn asked his political staff if there were children who would be affected by the story emerging. When he learned that McConnell had two children, he told his staff to warn McConnell and help him to cover up.

But, as McConnell stood on the brink of becoming First Minister, newspaper offices suddenly became nervous that a rival paper would do the story. One or two papers took the decision that, although a rival may decide to cover the story, they would not run it. Most politicians have spent sleepless nights worrying about the possibility of press intrusion into their private lives and it is almost certain that the story of McConnell's affair with Maureen Smith would have been written about. So, when he read the *Daily Record* editorial, he made a decision to take on the gossip and the slurs and stand up and announce his indiscretion to the people of Scotland.

He went to visit the home of the Motherwell and Wishaw MP Frank Roy and told him of the decision. Although Roy agreed with the strategy, he refused to give McConnell his support for the plan, fearing he would act too hastily. He told him to sleep on it. The following day, after he had explained to Bridget that he felt he had to come clean, McConnell asked Roy to come to his house. McConnell's allies say, even if the story hadn't come out during the leadership campaign, he would have spent his time as First Minister always looking over his shoulder, worrying about when it might come out and fearing, when it did, that he would lose the trust of the voters. After a tense weekend of discussions, Bridget announced to his campaign team that she also wanted there to be a press conference and that she wanted to speak at it. The decision to go public had been Jack's but Bridget decided the way in which it would happen. Some of the couple's friends were worried by the idea of her going through such a public ordeal but, as one put it, 'None of us were in a position to argue with Bridget.' As McConnell was cruising to victory, it was a high-risk strategy to hold such a press conference – but McConnell has always been a high-risk politician.

Although he ran a slick campaign for the leadership when he stood against Henry McLeish, his supporters said the second time round they felt they had to do all that and more. Frank Roy said, 'We had to think the unthinkable. We thought of every possible area where things could go wrong.' After the decision to speak publicly about his affair had been taken, the campaign temporarily ground to a halt as Jack switched off from electioneering and tried to give his wife and family some support ahead of the press conference. On Tuesday 13 November, the press pack were called to a press conference at the Holyrood Hotel in Edinburgh. But, even before the press pack gathered, McConnell's plan appeared to come unstuck. The event, which had been shrouded in secrecy, was revealed in the *Sun* newspaper that morning. The paper had wrecked McConnell's hopes of making his revelation to all of the papers at the same time. There is no evidence that anyone from McConnell's inner circle deliberately briefed the paper. It is more likely the *Sun* got the scoop through a combination of old-fashioned digging around and a bit of putting two and two together. However, the *Sun* splash infuriated *Daily Record* bosses at Central Quay who were convinced that McConnell had done the dirty on them.

Although the *Sun* story was outwith his control, McConnell's desire to build a good relationship with the press was to suffer yet another setback. In the main, the rest of the press corps gave the McConnells a sympathetic hearing. With Bridget at his side, Jack did what no other high-profile elected politician has ever done and proactively announced a part of his personal life he had hoped would never be uncovered. Bridget also made her own statement. After enduring years of her husband being smeared by his opponents over his indiscretion, she wanted to explain to people that her husband's portrayal by some as a cheating, untrustworthy philanderer was inaccurate and unfair. However, Bridget's carefully crafted message of support for her husband was largely overlooked in the next day's papers as they chose to focus on her words that he 'betrayed her trust' rather than the real thrust of what she was saying. She believed that, despite his mistake, her husband was a good man and people could trust him to run the country.

During the carefully stage-managed press conference, the McConnells refused to name the woman at the centre of the story and agreed to answer just a handful of questions from the press pack. McConnell was asked if there had been any other affairs and he replied that there had not. Paul Sinclair, the political editor of the *Daily Record,* went on to ask McConnell whether he would resign if any others did come to light. By now, the tension of the occasion was beginning to tell and McConnell's reply that the situation would not arise was not as free flowing as his earlier answers had been. With the ordeal behind them, the McConnells left the room. They felt they had robbed his enemies of their best ammunition. The boil was lanced – for now.

However, the right-wing *Daily Mail* later went into overdrive. If McConnell had any others secrets, the paper was determined it would be the one to unearth them. One woman in Stirling was offered £10,000 by a paper to tell about her affair with Jack McConnell while he was leader of Stirling Council. She had never actually dated him. McConnell's enemies continued to brief journalists that they knew of other women in his life. One senior Labour politician called a tabloid journalist to his office so that he could 'dish the dirt on McConnell'. He provided the name of a woman he alleged had been involved with McConnell weeks earlier. He named a location where a rendezvous had taken place in front of many witnesses. His account amounted to nothing more than a pack of lies aimed at destabilising the Jack. However, the incident also showed that, even after revealing all, McConnell would continue to suffer hugely personal smears.

His personal life aside, the press were inclined to be kind to McConnell. All newspapers had increased staff to cover the growing interest in politics following devolution. The first First Minister, Donald Dewar, had no time for the press and they, in turn, were quick to criticise him. During his year in power, the media savaged Dewar. It was only after his death that they came to regard him as a saint. While he was in the job, he was savaged over such issues as: the decision to repeal Section 28; the design of the new parliament building and its escalating costs; and even the state of his own health.

The political staff of the main newspapers installed their correspondents in a dingy building on the capital's Lawnmarket. Desperate to produce front-page stories, the 'Lawnmarket men', as these journalists became known (very few woman were employed there), leapt on every announcement and decision and often ridiculed it. As deadlines approached, it was not uncommon to hear a frustrated journalist demand his colleagues provide an alternative word for 'fiasco', only to shout back, when other suggestions were offered, that he had already used the words 'farce', 'disaster', 'ridiculous' and 'bungled'. This showed how quickly the Scottish press and public had become disillusioned with the new institution. However, if the press were hostile to Dewar while he was alive, they performed a remarkable volte-face when he died. Almost overnight, he became the father of the nation, the best First Minister Scotland would ever have and a true statesman. Dewar's sudden elevation in the eyes of the press made it impossible for the next First Minister Henry McLeish to win good headlines.

Unlike Dewar, McLeish loved the press and he thought he knew how to work it. He would brief those he liked and cut off those he didn't. It is a tactic that can work well for politicians in opposition or those seeking to undermine their rivals. However, once McLeish was in government, it backfired badly for him. McLeish's tongue-tied performances at First Minster's questions became a source of vicious comment. The malapropisms he used were dubbed 'McLeishees' by the press. A list of his worst efforts hung on the wall in the Lawnmarket offices so journalists could easily refer to them when writing their next vitriolic article.

By the time Jack McConnell became First Minister, he had carefully watched the way the press had made his predecessors suffer and was determined not to fall victim to the same fate. One of his first moves was to sack Henry McLeish's press spokesman, Peter MacMahon, who, ironically, had been a close friend of McConnell during his General Secretary days. However, he believed MacMahon had a poor relationship with the press and it needed to be fixed. Douglas Campbell, a press spokesman for East Ayrshire Council was brought in to liaise with the media. A less confrontational figure than the spin doctors for the previous First Ministers, he tried to work with the press rather than against them. He also had the benefit of knowing his master extremely well. The reason Blair's former press secretary, Alastair Campbell, had been so influential among the press was that Campbell was believed to know Blair's mind. In much the same way, Douglas Campbell knows Jack's. The two have known each other since University, even sharing a flat together at one point. As has often been the hallmark of McConnell's success, he also struck it lucky with this choice.

There was a realisation among newspaper editors that the Scottish Parliament had been badly damaged by the instability and the rows of the first two years. They instinctively wanted McConnell to make a go of it and he was given a chance that his predecessors were denied. The dogs at the Lawnmarket were called off for a time. Alan Cochrane, the Scottish editor of the *Daily Telegraph*, said:

I was much more pro-Jack because I thought Henry had become a laughing stock and I believed Jack would do things differently. I was delighted that he got rid of the spin doctors and handed the briefings over to the civil service. He had a very good first two years.

However, three years on, Cochrane is livid over the way the First Minister runs his press operation:

The civil servants come to brief us but they rarely know what is going on. Meanwhile, Douglas Campbell hands out lollipops behind the bike sheds to his favourites – normally *The Herald* or the *Record*. I now think what we have is worse that the dark depths of the lobby system at Westminster.

Cochrane claims that, after McConnell was ridiculed wearing a kilt to the Tartan Day celebrations in New York and then savaged by the press over his initial decision not to attend the D-Day service in France, he has fallen out with the press. Cochrane said, 'He has been in a bad mood ever since we gave him a mauling and has become very cynical about the way he operates the press, doing favours for those he likes and shutting out those who criticise him.'

However, Angus MacLeod, the political editor of *The Times* in Scotland, believes McConnell's media strategy on coming to power was a smart one:

> He went out of his way to put distance between himself and the media. He realised Henry had been too familiar with the press and the media monster stopped being cuddly and decided to bite him. Instead, Jack McConnell dealt with the media at arm's length. He knew the febrile atmosphere at the time had to be cooled down and very cleverly got the neutral civil servants to do the briefings. McConnell has maintained the instinct he had while he was General Secretary. He can be friendly to the media but tends to talk off the record so that the media cannot exploit what he said at a later date.

Like Cochrane, MacLeod thinks McConnell's approach to the press is slowly changing. He said:

> His strategy worked for a while but the media always finds new ways to attack and McConnell was criticised for being boring and lacking vision. I think that hurt him so we are seeing more in the way of announcements and, as he grows in confidence, he is tending to be less cautious in his dealings with us.

The Holyrood press pack is alerted to government announcements and given an idea of the First Minister's views of current events at press briefings that are held twice a day.

These are normally taken by Fiona Wilson, a civil servant who, by the nature of her job, must remain impartial and not give political spin. The First Minister's personal spokesman, Douglas Campbell, operates under more relaxed rules and can politicise the government's message.

Retired journalist Bill Clark was a political correspondent on the *Glasgow Herald* and the *Daily Mail*. He had dealings with Jack McConnell over twenty-five years from the time he was a young student activist. Clark said, 'He was a smart operator and always knew how to get what he wanted. Many people saw him as just a party fixer but he was much more than that. I always felt he was underrated.'

It wasn't just the press that McConnell worked well. Some news staff at BBC Scotland complained that, as General Secretary of the party, he would often phone up to complain about the way a story was being covered, only for the executives to give in to the pressure and change it for later bulletins. While some journalists vividly remember being on the end of a tongue lashing from McConnell, others formed firm friendships. Kenny McIntyre, BBC Scotland's late political correspondent, was a close pal. Despite being highly valued by Radio Scotland, Kenny was useless when it came to the technical part of the job. His inability to work a tape recorder forced the BBC to send the station's travel reporter, the late Ali Abbasi, to stories along with McIntyre to make sure his interviews got recorded and then sent back to the studio via the radio car. Abbasi also became a close friend of the entire McConnell family. He even went to the family home to cook curries for them on special occasions like their son's eighteenth birthday. When BBC staff held a remembrance service for Abbassi in 2004, McConnell made a moving speech during which he was forced to pause, choked by tears.

# 12

# POLITICAL PASSION

Even after almost four years as First Minister, there are still many in the Labour Party and beyond who say they do not know what Jack McConnell stands for. Sam Galbraith believes that McConnell is too afraid of making unpopular decisions to be a bold leader. He points to the Glasgow housing stock transfer and the land reform bill put through by Donald Dewar as examples of real vision. But he claims that, since Dewar's death, there has been no big picture and says, 'The last election was like a sweetie shop – it came down to a choice between one party saying, "I'll give you 100 extra police officers." and another saying, "I'll give you 200." It was safe and easy.'

However, in researching this book, I have found there are key policy areas in which Jack has shown a strong and consistent interest over the last twenty years or more. There are certain areas of government that he claims to be his top priorities – the economy, health, education, crime, transport and Europe – but, of these, there are three fields in particular which stand out as attracting his personal interest the most – education, crime and Europe. It is perhaps because of his passion in these three areas that his policies relating to them are where he has made the greatest impact.

**Education**
Tony Blair may have invented the mantra 'education, education, education' but, for Jack McConnell, it has been a lifelong crusade. Even as a kid, Jack loved going to school and helping other youngsters with their lessons and, although his initial plan

was to study accountancy, it really surprised no one when he left Arran to study maths with a view to teaching the subject. When it came to teaching, he was a natural. For someone who was so politically motivated, it seems odd that McConnell opted to stay out of the politics of teaching during his time in the classroom. While other teachers his age were active in the EIS teaching union, Jack showed little interest in it – his politics were wider than those of the EIS.

When Henry McLeish took over as First Minister, Jack acted quickly to let it be known that he wanted to remain in his job at Finance. Given his strong showing in the leadership contest, he calculated that McLeish would probably be too scared to take him on. The managerial skills that had been so evident during McConnell's time at Stirling Council made him well suited to the Finance brief. It also has the advantage of being one of the safest portfolios in the Scottish government. With no immediate prospect of the tax powers becoming devolved, it is simply a case of taking the block grant from Westminster and distributing it to the Scottish spending departments. McConnell knew it was the kind of job he could do standing on his head.

But McLeish had other ideas. Sam Galbraith was locked in talks with Scotland's teachers in an attempt to get a package agreed which would give them more pay in return for changes in their conditions of work. The negotiations had stalled. Teachers had been unhappy with their lot for the last twenty years. The government wanted to give them a better deal – but not at any cost. The months before McLeish came to power had also seen one of the biggest disasters in Scottish education – thousands of schoolkids had been given the wrong exam results or received none at all. The Scottish Qualifications Agency (SQA) was in crisis and the public were furious at their failure. A deal on teachers' pay had to be delivered and the SQA had to be sorted. Neither task would be easy. McLeish knew it was vital for his leadership that both problems were fixed and he knew that McConnell had the ability to do the job. He reckoned that, if McConnell succeeded, it would look good for his leadership and, if he failed, it would damage him as much as it would damage himself. For McLeish, it was a win-win situation.

McConnell, on the other hand, had different plans. He had been keen to stay on in his role at Finance and let someone else tackle the hard issues on McLeish's behalf. Initially, McLeish gave in and told McConnell he could remain at Finance but he later reneged, putting pressure on Jack to move. When it was put to him for a second time that he should become the next Education Minister, it was hard to resist. The stakes were high – if he failed to deliver, he knew it would be a major setback to his ambitions. It would have been far safer to sit on the sidelines of the McLeish administration and wait for it to implode, as he suspected it would in time. But the temptation to get his teeth into the Education portfolio was great. Jack had been frustrated watching the work of the Scottish Labour Education Ministers who had gone before him. He felt that Brian Wilson, Helen Liddell and Sam Galbraith had all been too timid in their approaches and he believed he could make a real difference.

As usual, before coming to a decision McConnell took soundings from people whose opinions he values. One friend told him that the calculation had to be whether or not the problems could actually be fixed. In his view, he told McConnell, they were not insurmountable. That was it. If it could be done, he wanted to be the one to do it. The friend said, 'If Jack was a careerist, he would have stayed at Finance and waited for Henry McLeish's administration to fall.'

In one of his first acts as Education Minister, Jack McConnell called for the resignation of the twenty-strong board of the SQA because they had failed to act on warning signs that exam chaos was looming. Part of the problem with the SQA was that it was an agency that operated at arm's length and that meant McConnell did not actually have the power to fire the board members. The day he was made Education Minister, he held a meeting with John Elvidge, the official who headed the department, and he told him he wanted a clean start. Instead of ordering the board members out of their jobs, they phoned each one individually and asked them to quit. In every case, the pressure to stand down was enough to force the board out. Although some were later reappointed, McConnell had got his way – the board were out by the end of his first week in office.

By effectively sacking the board and appointing a civil servant to the role of national exams co-ordinator, McConnell had regained an element of control. He also put more money into funding more exam markers to try to prevent a repeat of the fiasco that had left 17,000 young people not knowing if they had passed or failed their exams and unable to prepare for going to university or finding themselves jobs. McConnell was also personally touched by the exams crisis as his own son, Mark, was one of those caught up in the chaos.

The SQA was forced to send monthly progress reports to the Education Minister and a new Chief Executive was appointed to draw up a recovery plan. The former CBI Scotland Chairman John Ward agreed to take on the task, giving his services for free. A state-of-the-art computer system was bought in the United States to try to ensure that the process would go smoothly. That summer Jack took his family to Arran on holiday ahead of the exam results coming out. While he was there, he got a call to inform him that the computer system on which the exam results depended had suffered a major malfunction. It was just a couple of weeks before the results were due out.

Although Jack is accustomed to being under pressure, this was one of the most stressful incidents of his political career. It turned out that an electrician had wired the computer

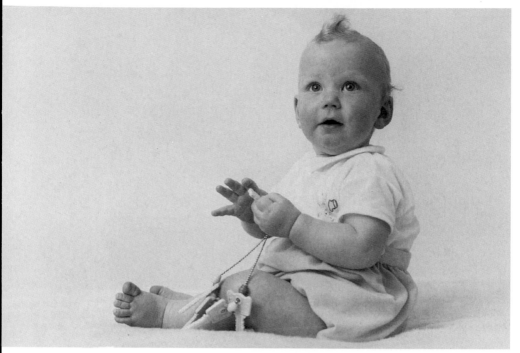

Jack Wilson McConnell was born on 30.06.60 in Irvine. Jack was his mother's maiden name.

The McConnells at a family wedding in 1969 – his mother, Elizabeth,
his father, Willie, his younger brothers, Iain (left) and Calum, and his sister, Anne.

Stirling District Council Labour Group, 1984.

Jack welcomes the Labour leader, Neil Kinnock, to the Scottish Party Conference in Perth, 1987.

Jack and the moustachioed Mike Donnelly, also a member of the Stirling District Council Labour Group, after a fundraising run for the Special Olympics, 1990.

Jack and Bridget's wedding at the Seafield Hydro in Ayrshire, 1990. Also in the picture are Jack's grandparents and Hannah and Mark, Bridget's children from her previous marriage.

Jack with the late leader of the Labour Party,
John Smith, during the General Election campaign of 1992.

Jack, as General Secretary of the Scottish Labour Party,
speaking at the party's conference in Dundee in 1994.

Jack with Scotland's first First Minister, Donald Dewar, 1999.

Jack with his daughter, Hannah, at her graduation from the University of Stirling, 2001.

Jack visits Soweto in 2002, part of his trip to South Africa
to the World Summit on Sustainable Development.

Jack and Bridget on the steps of Bute House after his re-election as First Minister in 2003.

Jack and Bridget at the MTV awards in Edinburgh, 2003.

Jack gets some tips on playing golf in the snow
from Scotland's top golfer, Colin Montgomerie, 2004.

Jack with US President George Bush who has just stepped off *Air Force One*.
Bush was on his way to attend the G8 Scotland Summit at Gleneagles, 2005.

up wrongly but, luckily for Jack, the problem was resolved. That summer 99.7% of Scotland's 135,000 candidates received their correct exam results on time. But, as Jack toured radio and TV studios giving interviews about the success of the process, he received a phone call from Mark, giving him the news he dreaded. His own son didn't have his results and he had been told they could not be traced. As a parent, Jack was livid – as Education Minister, he was panic stricken and he wondered how many other youngsters could be in the same position. It later transpired that Mark's results had been sent to the wrong address. However, one of his results remained lost. The practical part of his music exam had gone missing – one of the very small number of practical tests which, unfortunately, do get lost every year. At the time, Mark wanted to be a musician and that exam result was the most important one to him. Unbelievably, Jack McConnell had delivered for 99.7% of Scotland's young people but not his own son.

He expected a phone call from the First Minister to discuss the success but it never came. It was his second triumph of the year. In February 2001, Scotland's teachers backed a pay and conditions deal. In return for giving up thirty-five hours of their own time over the year for extra training, they got rises of 21% over three years in their pay. Teachers were also promised added help in the classroom with the appointment of more classroom assistants. Although there has since been criticism that the package was underfunded, at the time, even teachers viewed it as a generous settlement. The deal also made them the envy of teaching colleagues in England.

So how did McConnell pull it off? Until he took over, the talks had mostly been taking place with the unions, the local authorities and officials from the Executive. The negotiations were well under way – new teaching grades and pay scales had been agreed. In fact, it should be pointed out that critics of McConnell argue that the SQA situation had been fixed by Sam Galbraith but it was McConnell who grabbed the credit for it. Believing the situation was under control, McConnell was horrified to discover that the deal had not been costed. It was clear that any agreement was going to go over the budget the Executive had set for the package but the new Education Minister was determined to put a figure on it so that he could then argue for it. In November 2001, he held a meeting with the unions and the local authorities to try to hammer out a deal. He immediately realised that the Executive would have to stump up far more money than it had previously been prepared to acknowledge. He told the local authorities they would have to cost the package properly and give him an assurance in writing of what their top figures would be. McConnell said he would not agree a deal on paying teachers a higher percentage only to find out that, in years to come, it was costing more than anyone imagined. The local authorities realised they would not be able to return to the Executive in a year's time to demand more money. This was their only chance.

The councils came back with costed proposals and believed they were about to get the package they wanted when McConnell sprang a surprise on the teachers. He said he would agree to higher pay but, in return, he wanted one more concession from them. McConnell said that, unless they agreed to make it easier for bad teachers to be sacked, there would be no deal. From his own time as a teacher, McConnell had despaired of colleagues who could not control their pupils or who consistently failed to work their way through the syllabus. Everyone in the school knew the teachers who couldn't hack it but nobody could do anything about it and the children's education suffered as a result. When his own children went to school, there were two or three bad teachers McConnell felt were not up to the job. He believed there were similar teachers in schools all over Scotland and their poor performances meant thousands of kids were not getting the chance to achieve the grades they might otherwise have reached with better tuition.

Under the rules devised in 1918, teachers could not be removed from post unless two thirds of the education committee on the local authority voted in open session to remove them. McConnell told the unions that, unless they were prepared to shift on this issue, there would be no deal. With the bumper pay offer on the table, the deal had become impossible to resist. McConnell had got his way. However, he still had another hurdle to clear. Although he knew he could get an agreement from the teachers, he didn't yet know if he could get the Scottish Executive to fund it.

Since being defeated for the leadership, he was all too aware that his relations with his cabinet colleagues were at rock bottom. The situation was so bad that McConnell suspected one or two of them would try to block the deal from going through for no reason other than wanting to prevent him scoring a victory. McConnell believed he would only be able to end the teachers' pay deadlock if he out-manoeuvred his cabinet rivals. In one of the rare one-to-one meetings Jack McConnell had with Henry McLeish during the latter's time as First Minister, he reminded McLeish that he had assured him he would have his full support if he took on the role of Education Minister. He made it clear he was calling on that support in order to conclude the negotiations. McLeish was true to his word and told him he had his full backing – the money was on the table. When Finance Minister Angus McKay discovered what McConnell wanted, he was furious but it was too late – McLeish had already promised to stump up and one of the longest-running disputes in Scottish Education was settled.

Jack's reputation as a minister was greatly enhanced. Even his political opponents give him credit for pulling off the deal on teachers' pay, acknowledging he had had the courage to negotiate in a way that his predecessor, Sam Galbraith, would not have done. The SNP's Michael Russell shadowed him as Education Minister. He said, 'It was fun opposing him – he knew far more about education than Sam Galbraith or Cathy Jamieson. He was always a good performer in front of the committee – he enjoyed the debate and jousted with the committee.'

However, McConnell did not always get things his own way. The idea of a children's commissioner was one the education committee was keen to drive through. Jack was also in favour of the idea but he thought he could wrest it from the committee and take the credit for implementing it. He had a dinner with key members of the committee in a restaurant in New Lanark on the night of the September 11th terrorist atrocity in New York. He put up a convincing argument – but lost.

During his time at Education, there were also some changes he made that did not attract big headlines. He made significant alterations to the way children in care are looked after. One supporter said, 'He tightened up legislation in that area – not to get votes but because he does really care about kids who have had a crap life and risk falling through the net.' His determination to make children in care a priority came from his days as a teacher at Lornshill. Children from a nearby home who attended the school were the thinnest, poorest looking, most dysfunctional pupils. When he tried to discover what lay behind some of their problems, Jack discovered, among other things, that the kids had no facilities to do homework. Jack was appalled that the children in care had started out in life with such a disadvantage and, as he saw it, the system continued to fail them so much that he could actually pick out which children lived in the care home. As one way of assisting them, local authorities now employ people to help them with their work after school.

As an educationalist, Jack McConnell knew the Education brief and the problems inside out. Instead of adopting the attitude of his colleagues in London who ran down comprehensive schools as 'bog standard' (a description Alastair Campbell originally applied to them at a press conference), he pursued his own agenda. There are plenty of friends and enemies who will criticise McConnell's work as First Minister but critics of his time as Education Minister proved nonexistent and, since becoming First Minister, Jack has described his time as Education Minister as the happiest year of his life. He had been looking forward to carrying on in the job for another three or four years when Henry McLeish decided to resign and unexpectedly gave him the chance to lead his country.

## Crime

The seat of Motherwell and Wishaw lies in the heart of Scotland's Central Belt. More than most communities, it has suffered from economic hardship and the problems that brings. The closure of the Ravenscraig steel works was perhaps the most devastating blow for the area. Like many other areas, it is also blighted by drug-taking and many live in fear of the violence waged by feuding gangs. In the late '90s, two gangs were vying for control of an area in Motherwell. The Jerviston scheme had become a no-go area. Decent people were terrified to leave their homes and sometimes even scared when they were in them.

One elderly woman who was nursing her dying husband witnessed an attack on the house across the road. Her immediately reaction was the call the police. It was the action most law-abiding people would take but she was to pay a heavy price for trying to stop the violence in her street. Six days later, three masked men burst into her house at 3 a.m. Her nephew, a man in his early twenties, ran down the stairs to confront the intruders. As he tried to shut the door on them they raised a machete and took off the tops of his fingers. In desperation, the woman called her local MP, Frank Roy, who immediately got in his car and headed to her house. The following day he went to

Jack's house to tell him what he had witnessed in the early hours of the morning and suggested they both go back to the house to visit the woman.

It was just two months before the Scottish Parliament elections and Roy told his friend that, if he wanted to represent the area, he had to understand its people and their problems. When they arrived at the house, the woman was weeping uncontrollably, her husband lay dying upstairs and blood from the vicious knife attack was still splattered across the walls. Roy says Jack turned a ghostly shade of white as they sat in the house listening to the woman speak about her fears of living in the area. That night, she was to lose her husband from the cancer he had been fighting. Politicians can see hundreds of constituents with problems every year but that woman's suffering was to affect McConnell greatly.

Having grown up on the island of Arran, feuding drug gangs were not something he had ever come across and, until that day, his adult life had been spent in a quiet suburb in Stirling. But this was his new community and he was learning fast what a big job he had taken on if he was to help to address its problems. The chopping off of an innocent man's fingers was just one of several incidents which brought home to McConnell the need to tackle crime and the kind of antisocial behaviour that makes people scared to walk the streets or spoils their enjoyment of their local community.

He was aware that private polling by the Labour Party consistently showed that the voters most loyal to the party were the ones most affected by crime. When questioned, a high percentage of Labour voters said the single biggest factor that would improve the quality of their lives was tackling antisocial behaviour. Middle-aged people living in working-class areas were the most fed up with things like graffiti sprayed in the local area, their bus shelter being vandalised and threatening youths hanging about street corners. Shortly after moving to

Wishaw in the autumn of 1999, the McConnell family fell victim to vandalism and sectarianism. Believing the entire family to be Catholic, the local vandals daubed offensive slogans referring to their religion on their house.

On becoming First Minister, Jack McConnell wanted to give something back to hard-working people who looked to his party to improve their areas. From his constituency cases, he understood the anti-social behaviour many people were having to put up with and he realised that most of them had lost faith in the justice system. Jack was also aware that delivering safer communities would mean making serious reforms to the criminal justice system. Too many people were afraid to report crimes or, when they did, they felt let down by the lack of support they received. One report showed that 70% of witnesses who have gone through the Scottish criminal justice system said they would not like to repeat the experience. It was clear witnesses were disappointed by the high proportion of accused people who were not prosecuted or who were handed light sentences.

Witnesses were also treated badly by the system as they were rarely kept informed of developments in the cases they were involved in. Jack was on their side and, if that meant taking on the legal establishment, he was prepared to do it. Until McConnell became First Minister, the Scottish law officers had been political appointees. Jack's priority was to find the people who could deliver the changes he wanted to see in the justice system. He decided he would oust the Solicitor General, Neil Davidson – even though he was a big donor to the Labour Party – because he thought Davidson had been too keen to maintain the status quo. Jack spoke to the Lord Advocate, Colin Boyd, and told him he needed a new Solicitor General who would be capable of pushing through the reforms he wanted to see.

One name sprang to mind – that of Elish Angiolini. She had risen through the ranks of the procurator fiscal service. At the time, she was working as the chief prosecutor in Grampian region where she had succeeded in forging strong links with the local police force thereby ensuring detectives delivered what was required to stage a successful prosecution. The number of successful convictions in the area shot up. The police were pleased that their inquiries were more likely to end in a satisfactory outcome and fewer witnesses suffered the frustration of enduring a court ordeal for no apparent outcome.

At forty-one, Angiolini was seen as a high-flyer. However, she was qualified only as a solicitor, not as a QC, and this meant she was unable to practise at the bar. The Executive could not have a Solicitor General who was not qualified to appear at the Court of Session. Although McConnell had never met Angiolini, he insisted on a meeting being set up. Following this, he was determined she was the right person for the job and he asked for the rules on the appointment of a Solicitor General to be carefully checked. The Lord Advocate, Colin Boyd, then came up with the suggestion that the Executive could get a special warrant that would enable Angiolini to practise at the bar. Such a warrant was granted and the problem was solved.

Neil Davidson was called in and was asked to resign but to tell nobody of his departure. After the meeting, Davidson immediately cleared his desk. Word was out that McConnell, fresh from axing half his cabinet colleagues, had just taken another scalp. The new First Minister had hoped to keep news of Angiolini's appointment secret until the furore over his cabinet reshuffle had died down. He thought it would give him the kind of good-news appointment he needed to take attention away from his 'night of the long knives'. It wasn't to be. News of Davidson's departure leaked immediately and McConnell was forced to bring forward the news of the announcement that Scotland was to get its first-ever women

Solicitor General. The move also made Angiolini the first solicitor to be appointed to the post since 1604. It was a high-risk decision and one which raised eyebrows among members of the legal establishment at the time. Of all the appointments Jack McConnell has made since he became First Minister, it is probably the one he is the most proud of.

The Scottish legal system was once the envy of the world but McConnell felt its reputation could be lost unless it was modernised. He was furious about the amount of police time being taken up as officers waited around courts for hours on end and about the number of decent people who suffered crimes in silence, believing reporting them would not achieve anything – such was their lack of confidence in the police and the courts. Shortly after taking over as First Minister, Jack McConnell made it clear to the civil service that he intended to push through reforms to the criminal justice system to restore public faith. The reaction among civil servants at the time was one of surprise as the official statistics did not back up much of what McConnell was saying.

However, a Scottish crime survey which was taken a year after McConnell came to office did show exactly the kind of issues Jack had picked up on at his local surgery. It revealed the depth of despair people felt, particularly over low-level crime which they felt went ignored. After becoming First Minister, McConnell announced a 40% increase in funding by 2006 to help the Crown Office and the courts work more effectively. In a speech in September 2003, McConnell spelt out why tackling crime must be one of the Executive's highest priorities. He said, 'The manner by which we as a society both protect our citizens and deal with those who offend against them, is a measure of our civilisation, our maturity and our humanity.'

McConnell's approach is somewhere between the right-wing view that prison is the only effective deterrent and the left-wing view that crime is a consequence of poverty. The First

Minister believes offenders should be given a second chance but only when they have earned the right to it by taking their punishment and changing their behaviour. Electronic tagging has now been introduced for the under-sixteens, parenting orders have been introduced to put more pressure on parents to discipline their kids and those youngsters who commit crimes can now be dealt with through the new youth courts. Prior to this, seventeen- and eighteen-year-olds had to face the ordeal of appearing in adult courts. The police have greater powers. They can split up gangs of young people causing a nuisance in a neighbourhood, close down premises that have turned into drinking or drug dens and issue fixed-penalty notices to punish minor acts of antisocial behaviour instead of clogging up the courts. The First Minister has also openly condemned the legal establishment's 'vested interests' which encourage offenders to plead not guilty until the last minute and hinder the rolling up of all outstanding charges so that they could be dealt with at a single hearing. These things waste the courts' time, cause victims unnecessarily prolonged distress and engender income for lawyers. Jack's views on this have been interpreted as an attack on lawyers and civil liberties campaigners have also been unhappy with some of his ideas. But the First Minister has vowed to build a criminal justice system that is clearly 'on the side of victims, witnesses and ordinary families'.

**Europe**
Jack McConnell never tires of telling audiences that 'Scotland is the greatest small country in the world' – a view that has sustained his efforts to create a distinct Scottish approach on two subjects that are reserved for Westminster. He has managed to put a kilt on Europe and immigration by ploughing a different furrow in both these areas to that taken by the London government. His interest in Europe appears to go back a long

way and seems to be the product of a variety of influences. Staying with a French family as a teenager no doubt gave him an interest in and a thirst for foreign parts but it was the political atmosphere of the late '80s and early '90s that really spurred his political interest in Europe.

His involvement with Scottish Labour Action led him to look at ways Scotland might constructively engage with Europe at a time when the Thatcher government was openly in contempt of our nearest neighbours. The notion of a 'Europe of the Regions' had a superficial attraction as a way of engineering a Westminster bypass that would allow Scotland to engage in Europe without having to rely on the government in London. He was drawn to the idea that Europe's autonomous regions could provide an alternative source of power and influence to that wielded by the member states' governments in the European Union. He backed calls to create a 'Committee of the Regions', a body that was eventually set up by the Maastricht Treaty and on which McConnell now serves.

The notion of a Europe of the Regions also appeared to offer the perfect antidote to the SNP's Jim Sillars' inspired 'Independence in Europe' slogan. The nationalists underwent something of a revival on the back of their campaign which claimed that an independent Scotland could have a seat at Europe's top table (the Council of Ministers), with its own Commissioner and double the number of MEPs Scotland had as part of the UK. With Europe looking very much like where the future lay, Labour was in something of a panic as to how to respond. All its old tactics for dealing with nationalist surges were rendered obsolete by Sillars' ingenious strategy. If Scotland and England were to be part of the same single European market with its free movement of goods, services and capital, Labour would no longer be able to talk about passports at the border or the flight of jobs to the South. McConnell embraced the idea of a devolved Scotland working with other powerful regions across Europe as a way of giving Scotland visibility and clout at the European level without the pain of having to break up the United Kingdom. Less than a decade later, he would be able to put his ideas into practice.

As Finance Minister in Donald Dewar's first cabinet, he was asked by the first First Minister to take responsibility for European Structural Funds – then worth about £250 million a year to Scotland. An eager McConnell not only grabbed the reins of the structural funds but also took to calling himself Europe Minister as well as Finance Minister. Donald Dewar did nothing to discourage McConnell from this course and Jack threw himself into the role with great enthusiasm. McConnell created a Structural Funds steering group to monitor the use of funds, to examine any proposals for reform and generally to be a lobby for Scotland in the distribution and allocation of funds from Brussels. For the first time, local authorities, business people, trade unionists and representatives of NGOs sat down with ministers and officials from the Executive to discuss how Scotland could maximise its take and its benefits from Europe's largesse. To many involved, it was just the sort of cooperation and partnership devolution was meant to bring.

McConnell, though, felt Europe had to be more than just about money. He decided he wanted to try, wherever possible, to create a 'team Scotland' approach to European legislation and policy. The Tories had established an office in Brussels, known as Scotland House, to give a single door for the various Scottish lobbies in Brussels. McConnell added a Scottish Executive presence to those already there and generally beefed up the organisation and visibility of Scotland House. Having ensured there was an effective vehicle for identifying Scotland's interests and concerns in Brussels, he then wanted to ensure an effective method for making Scotland's various representatives in Brussels aware of these concerns and encouraging them to work together regardless of which political party or institution they were in. He established a forum known as the European Elected Members Information Liaison and Exchange (EMILE). Its remit was to bring together Scotland's MEPs, Scottish representatives on the Committee of the Regions, Scottish representatives on the European Economic and Social Committee (ECOSOC), the European Commission's representative in Edinburgh and the ministers and officials of the Scottish Executive who deal with Europe. McConnell himself chaired the forum and generally encouraged participants to take a Scottish view of Brussels' policy initiatives.

Improving and enhancing Scotland's domestic structures for dealing with Europe was, to McConnell's mind, only half the picture. Returning to the Europe of the Regions idea that first sparked his interest in matters European, he started looking around for European networks he could involve himself, the Scottish Executive or the Scottish Parliament in. Europe has no shortage of self-creating and self-aggrandising networks – the trick was to find the right one. As Presiding Officer of the Parliament, Sir David Steel had engaged himself in a network called Conference of European Regional Legislative Assemblies (CALRE). This was founded in 1997 with the aim of consolidating the representation of European regions and nations with legislative power within the new framework of the European union. CALRE was led by the Catalan Parliament and brought together the parliaments of the regions that had devolved power. While in no way hostile to this grouping, McConnell's view was that it just did not seem to possess sufficient clout. Other networks that Scots were engaged in, such as the one bringing together representatives of countries surrounding the North Sea, seemed equally worthy but they lacked the prestige that Jack was looking for.

Perhaps ironically, it was McConnell's predecessor, Henry McLeish, who was the one to find the most appropriate body and that was REGLEG. On its website, REGLEG describes itself as 'an informal co-operative venture of the regions with legislative powers within the European Union'. REGLEG brings together the leaders of the regions of Europe that have devolved legislative powers. In this body, Scotland's First Minister could sit side by side with regional prime ministers and politicians who have real power in their own countries. The leaders of large German *Länder* and Spanish autonomous regions are big hitters in their own countries and cannot be ignored by national leaders and politicians. On becoming First Minister, Jack McConnell threw himself enthusiastically into the work of REGLEG and this culminated in him becoming its President and hosting a powerful gathering, in late 2004 in Edinburgh, of leaders representing over 150 million European Union citizens.

REGLEG, unlike many such bodies, is no mere talking shop. During the negotiations leading to the drawing-up of a European constitution, REGLEG was a powerful advocate of the rights of legislative regions and managed to secure acknowledgement of their position in the constitution. REGLEG was successful in giving the Regions (under certain limited conditions) the right to go the European Court to protect their prerogatives from encroachment by the European Union. The draft constitution contains a clear commitment to what is known in Brussels jargon as subsidiarity – the idea that neither Europe nor its member states should do anything that could be done better at a lower (that is, regional) level. This is an issue that has concerned Scotland's First Minister for some time. Having made an influential speech in Scotland House on this subject in front of members of the European Convention, McConnell can take some personal credit for its inclusion in the text of the constitution for the future of Europe. The Convention spent over a year drafting the constitution, only for France and Holland to reject it.

There can be no doubt that the success of the regions in getting some of their key concerns addressed by the Convention was a major factor in McConnell's decision, in December 2004, to call publicly for a 'yes' vote in the forthcoming referendum on the ratification of the constitution. At the time, the national leadership of Labour Party had taken a collective vow of silence on the issue, to last until after the 2005 General Election. As a rule, McConnell has pursued Scotland's line on Europe in a low-key fashion, eschewing public rows with Whitehall and Westminster in favour of backroom influencing of EU decisions. Much to the frustration of the Nationalists, he has refused to engage in open conflict with the UK government on such issues as fishing policy or Scotland's future share of EU Structural Funds in favour of quiet advocacy of the country's interests at both the UK and EU level of the decision-making process.

On immigration, McConnell's line has been much more openly distinct from the prevailing line in London. At a time when Labour in London appears to be ready to respond to shrill tabloid headlines on asylum seekers and refugees, McConnell has been prepared to stand up and call for increased immigration into Scotland. This approach is based on a mixture of genuine principles and pragmatism. The First Minister knows that Scotland's falling and aging population means it desperately needs to attract new settlers into the country. Some estimates reckon Scotland needs 100,000 new faces a year just to stand still. Scotland is facing a demographic time bomb which, if not defused, will lead to a massive shortage of labour and a shrinking tax base to fund the health care and pensions of an increasingly elderly population.

As Professor Bernard Crick, the well-known professor of politics at the University of London and author of many political books, has put it, 'the question of immigration has brought out a clear difference between the Scottish and English Executives. To England, the question seems a problem but to

Scotland an opportunity.' In February 2003, McConnell's political advisor, Rachel McEwen, persuaded him to take a risk in advance of the election and speak out on the issue. Jack values her judgement and went ahead and did so. One way in which McConnell has grasped that opportunity is through the Fresh Talent Initiative which allows overseas students who have studied in Scotland to stay for two years after graduation. Launching the initiative, McConnell declared that:

> tackling our declining population is a priority for the Scottish government which is why I want Scotland to be the most welcoming country in the world. Scots are renowned for being friendly, welcoming people. Scotland has a great quality of life, a fantastic environment, a first-class education system.

It is difficult to imagine any minister in Westminster speaking like that as they would be too afraid of the backlash from anti-immigrationists. Those at Westminster would be only too aware of how the Tories can whip up feelings about the subject and most of them would be more likely to talk about stopping the flow of immigrants rather then discussing how to attract them, as Jack has done.

# 13

# THE FIRST MINISTER
# AS A POLITICAL OPPONENT

There are strongly conflicting views over McConnell's approach
to opposition politicians. Those who remember him as a teenage
activist are the most likely to say that he is inclusive. They claim
he would happily wheel and deal with those of differing political
views if it meant he would be more likely to achieve his objective.
The descriptions of McConnell's early political behaviour are
also echoed by those who worked alongside him in some of
the cross-party home-rule groups and even by those who took
part in the negotiations which formed the partnership
agreement with the Liberal Democrats in 2003. However, one
Tory in Stirling recalled how McConnell would often put his
hand in his pocket to buy drinks for opposition politicians in
the council but, not wanting to be seen to be owing anyone
anything, would never accept one back.

Most of McConnell's recent political battles have either
been fought within the Labour Party or against the SNP. The
Nationalists are the most likely to accuse McConnell of being a
partisan figure. Senior SNP figures believe that the combination
of George Robertson as Shadow Scottish Secretary and
McConnell as General Secretary of the Labour Party was a
damaging one. One source said, '[McConnell and Robertson]
would wind each other up. Before our party conference, you
always knew there would be a stunt aimed at portraying the
SNP as having been involved in something illegal, racist or
terrorist-related.' The SNP always believed that the report of a

letter bomb being received at Keir Hardie House in September 1995 was one such stunt. Some Nats believed it was designed to show that they were behind the bomb and, as such, the SNP was essentially just a bunch of dangerous extremists.

Ahead of the SNP conference, *The Scotsman*'s political editor Peter MacMahon obtained a leaked memo, written by George Robertson to senior Labour figures, warning them of the 'darker side of nationalism'. Several days later, on the closing day of the SNP conference in Perth, Jack McConnell reportedly discovered a hoax bomb at Labour's HQ. The padded envelope contained pieces of metal, cuttings from SNP pamphlets and a death threat directed at George Robertson which stated, 'Stop making trouble George or you're dead.' The bomb squad were called in and the Sunday newspapers had a great story that weekend.

The incident eclipsed news of the Nationalists' conference and a bitter row followed between George Robertson and the SNP leader, Alex Salmond, over the way the hoax was publicised. The two party leaders wrote articles in *The    rald* attacking each other. Robertson claimed the failure of the SNP leadership to disown emotive language directed at Labour politicians by senior figures in the party, including the use of 'quisling', 'Uncle Tom' and 'traitor', would 'fuel the fevered fires of those who want separation by any means'. Salmond hit back and told Robertson he should take follow the nineteenth-century journalist and politician Horace Greeley's advice to 'grow up with your country'. Salmond wrote, 'It does not take the biggest cynic in the world to suspect something is rotten in the state of Labour politics in Scotland.'

Salmond's counter-attack enraged McConnell who was Labour Party General secretary at the time. He wrote a letter to *The Herald* accusing the Nationalist leader of 'blatant untruths' and he attempted to spell out the facts about the affair. In the letter, he claimed that he arrived at his office at 1.30 p.m. on

Saturday 23 September 1995 to discover the suspect package and that he immediately telephoned the police. This was not the first time he had had to take such action. An hour later, after the police had conducted an X-ray examination of the package and decided it was suspicious, they called in the Navy's Bomb Disposal Unit from Faslane. In an attempt to quash SNP claims that he had contacted the press before the bomb squad, McConnell speculated that a newspaper, whose offices were sited in a building across the road from Keir Hardie House, must have seen what was happening. McConnell went on to urge Salmond to 'express sympathy' for the people who have to deal with the mail of Labour Party figures.

However, instead of clearing up the bizarre affair, McConnell's letter only served to reignite it. An academic, who had attended a seminar at Glasgow's Central Hotel the Saturday of the bomb hoax, contacted *The Herald* to point out what he claimed were inaccuracies in the letter. On 30 September the paper's political correspondent, Robbie Dinwoodie, wrote an article casting fresh doubt on the bomb-hoax allegation. In his story, he quoted the seminar-goer who claimed that McConnell had arrived late to a meeting, organised by the Labour think tank at the John Wheatley Centre at around 10.30 a.m., and, during his speech, Jack had remarked, 'I am sorry I was late this morning but there was another suspect package in the office – surprise, surprise, after this week's publicity.' This version of events appeared to contradict McConnell's and provided evidence that he knew of the hoax bomb at least three hours before he claimed to have discovered it.

The bomb-hoax incident threatened the credibility of both McConnell and George Robertson but, in the face of much goading from the SNP, they stuck to their story. By way of explanation, McConnell claimed he went to his office on the way to the seminar and 'spotted the Jiffy bag, put it to one side and went back to it after attending the conference'. Robertson also defended his senior official, pointing out, 'You have to remember there is a vast amount of mail. It was something going round in his mind and I think it suddenly struck him how suspicious it looked.'

By now, it was Labour's account of the bomb hoax that was looking extremely suspicious. The SNP was so convinced that the story was unravelling that they called for McConnell's resignation. The incident had the potential to destroy McConnell but, as it threatened to spiral out of control, he went to ground while Robertson reiterated his attack, speaking of the 'recent upsurge in extreme nationalist violence, including the death threat [that] weekend'. As a result of the episode, the already bitter relationship between the two rival parties hit rock bottom. The continual warfare between the two main opposition parties was partly because the political stakes at the end of the Tories' rule were so high. It was also because of the personalities involved at the top of the two parties. Robertson was Shadow Scottish Secretary at the time and he and McConnell were a highly combative team – as were Alex Salmond and his Chief Executive, Michael Russell. The combination was always going to create fireworks in the small world of Scottish politics.

As far back as 1992, the SNP were aware that Labour had stolen a march on them by appointing McConnell to the post of General Secretary. Two years later, they responded by creating the post of Chief Executive and brought in the formidable Michael Russell to counter McConnell's efforts. In the run up to devolution, the main parties in Scotland often worked together on home-rule issues and campaigns, believing that their combined force would have a greater chance of destroying the Tories' case for the status quo. McConnell and Russell first worked together on the plans for an event that was to be known as 'The Great Debate'. It was held in the Usher Hall in Edinburgh in 1995 and was the brainchild of *The*

*Scotsman* newspaper. Offering the main parties the chance to set out their stalls, it was to be televised and all the parties realised it was an opportunity they had to make the most of.

During the discussions about the event, Russell thought he had covered every base to ensure his party leader, Alex Salmond, would win through. However, as he made an impassioned plea for Scotland's independence, TV viewers could see some in the audience shaking their heads in disagreement. McConnell had ensured that he had placed his party members directly behind the SNP leader to make it look as if his argument was going down badly. Although Russell had previously run a TV production company, the strategic placing of his party members in the audience was something he had overlooked. Russell said:

> He was good at that type of partisan politics. I realised that he
> was experienced and able and I learned a lot from him in the
> early days. It is always good to measure up to someone who is
> skilled.

The SNP also believe they were on the receiving end of McConnell's dirty tricks operation in the Monklands East by-election in July 1994 when, following the death of the Labour leader, John Smith, they almost took the rock-solid Labour seat. The Nationalists claim that Labour campaigners went into Catholic areas and told voters that, if the SNP were to win, their constituency would soon become bitterly divided along religious lines just like Northern Ireland was. Labour supporters claim that the Catholic religion of their candidate, Helen Liddell, was used against them by Nationalists who wanted to fuel the perception that it was the Catholic areas of the constituency that benefited from the Labour-controlled council. Labour wanted to counter the SNP's claims by giving the impression that it was actually the Nats who were using sectarian tactics by trying to put people off voting for a

Catholic. On the eve of the poll, posters appeared around the constituency featuring Mrs Liddell and the words 'mafia sponsored' beneath her. That was suspected to have been the work of a sectarian group in the area but, according to Labour, both the SNP and the Tories were happy to stand back and watch the mud-slinging. One senior Labour activist, who worked on the campaign, said:

> There were some pretty disgusting things being said and the other parties were happy to repeat them on the doorstep. The sad thing is that, after that by-election, they all walked away but they left behind a very bruised area and it was Helen who had to pick up the pieces.

The Monklands East by-election was held during a particularly intense period in Scottish politics. John Major's government looked to be in terminal decline and Labour was expected to form the next Westminster administration. The Tories were fighting to protect the constitutional make-up of Britain as it stood. Labour was offering devolution – as were the Liberal Democrats – but the SNP was strongly anti-devolution and continually derided the idea of a parliament in Edinburgh if it was to be set up along the lines suggested by Labour and the Lib Dems.

While he was leader of the opposition, John Smith suffered taunts from the Tories over the way Labour, at local government level, was running his own constituency of Monklands East. Several local councillors also picketed his surgery to complain about jobs being given to the relatives of prominent councillors and the tendency to spend more money in predominantly Catholic Coatbridge rather than in the more Protestant Airdrie. The building of a showpiece leisure centre, called the Time Capsule, which was sited in Coatbridge, was at the root of much of the tension in the area. John Smith insisted there was nothing wrong and the council was being smeared by political opponents.

So, following his death in May 1994, Labour faced a by-election in an area that was rife with accusations of Labour corruption. In the fevered political atmosphere of the time, the stage was set for one of the most bitter political battles Scotland has ever seen. During the campaign, Helen Liddell performed an astonishing U-turn on John Smith's stance over the council by declaring that the party would show 'no mercy' if allegations of corruption within the council were discovered to have any foundations. Her decision to go on the offensive was aimed at persuading voters that Labour would not tolerate any wrongdoing. However, her course of action also served to infuriate the Monklands West MP, Tom Clarke, who accused Mrs Liddell and other critics of the council of indulging in the promotion of 'smears and mythology'.

Clarke was backed by Jimmy Wray, the chairman of the Scottish group of MPs, and their combined intervention came close to sending Labour's by-election campaign into meltdown. As she contemplated losing the seat held by her friend John Smith, Liddell was furious and she ordered McConnell to sort it. There ensued a race to track down Jimmy Wray who, by now, had the press pack as well as McConnell in pursuit of him. McConnell got there first and, whatever was said or threatened, Mr Wray was to change his mind and come round to supporting Mrs Liddell's approach to the council.

The media saw getting the party out of this dismal situation as McConnell's greatest achievement of the campaign. Some campaigners within Labour claim that McConnell was well warned at the start of the by-election of what was likely to follow but that he did not take their advice seriously and failed to grasp the full extent of the nastiness of Lanarkshire sectarianism. He was blamed by many in the party for running a shambolic campaign. Helen Liddell, herself a former General Secretary of the party, was understood to be far from impressed by his handling of the campaign. The SNP blame him for not being in control of his activists. The press, by the admission of several of the pack that covered the by-election, were 'out of control'.

The SNP leader Alex Salmond drafted in a former senior office-bearer of the party, Michael Russell, to help. Russell's campaigning skills were well known and he can be a bruiser when required. A close ally of Salmond, Russell watched one of the morning press conferences hosted by Andrew Welsh and was aghast at what he saw. Journalists who covered the contest admit that party speakers were variously told to 'shut up', 'stop pissing about' and generally shouted at and abused by the press pack. Although this applied to all the parties, the SNP was not helped by its own weak central organisation. Nonetheless, Russell tried to pull the SNP's by-election efforts together in the last few days and went on to become the party's Chief Executive charged with undertaking the same job on a national level.

Monklands East should have been a simple victory for Labour – the by-election had been caused by the death of one of the party's most loved figures, John Smith. But Smith's majority was cut from 16,000 to 1,600. Labour called on the Tory government to hold a public inquiry and the party also set up its own investigation into the council which was chaired by Anne McGuire. Both found no evidence of wrongdoing. Had Labour lost the Monklands East by-election, many believe McConnell would have paid with his job. The fact that it scraped home meant he lived to fight another day.

The Perth and Kinross by-election in 1995 was equally hard fought between the SNP and Labour. The SNP held the seat but Michael Russell recalls Jack McConnell launching an immediate spin operation against them. He said:

Jack was running around the hall telling journalists that the SNP got less votes than at the general election. He would always try to spot the gap and then exploit it in any way he could. On that occasion it was a weak spin and he would have been better not to attempt it. I suspect he doesn't always ask himself if his answer is a good one or a bad one – as long as he's got one he would get excited.

Some SNP figures point to McConnell's nationalist credentials within the Labour party and claim that, because he is a nationalist with a small 'n', this just makes him all the more determined to present Labour as a party sympathetic to those Scots who want a greater say in the running of their own affairs. In doing so, he believes Labour can capture the votes of people with nationalist leanings but who want to stop short of independence. Relations between McConnell and the SNP took a further turn for the worse when the main opposition parties tried to stop a BBC *Panorama* programme about the Tory Prime Minister, John Major, being broadcast on the eve of Scotland's local elections in the spring of 1995. The SNP were negotiating with McConnell over making a legal attempt to block the programme being shown but the party claim that Jack went behind their backs and launched a joint effort with the Liberal Democrats instead, cutting them out of the process. Labour claim that it was the SNP who backed out of the fight.

When it became clear there was no longer an all-party challenge, McConnell had to decide if his party should also back down. He called Blair's Press Spokesman, Alastair Campbell, for advice. Between them, they decided they should go for it regardless. Jack called the Labour Party's solicitors, Drummond Miller in Edinburgh, and they hired three of their experts: Andrew Hardie, who went on to became the Lord Advocate under Donald Dewar; Colin Boyd, who succeeded Hardie in that role and who was working his first day as a QC at the time he was contacted; and Des Browne, who went on to become a government minister at Westminster. Labour's legal team won the argument and the courts ruled the programme should not be shown north of the border because of the influence it could have on the elections.

But McConnell's delight was to be short-lived. Within hours, the BBC, fearing that a precedent had been set whereby a political party could dictate their programme scheduling, launched an appeal. Three appeal judges were taken from their homes at 8.30 in the evening to the court to hear the BBC's case. The corporation was defeated yet again but it was determined to fight on and requested permission to appeal to the House of Lords. Jack panicked, realising the costs of the action were spiralling out of control. Once again, he called Campbell, looking for reassurance. He got it – 'in for a penny in for a pound' was Campbell's response. In the end, there was no need to panic. The BBC was refused leave to appeal and the programme was stopped. It was one of the greatest highs of McConnell's time as General Secretary. He felt he had taken on the establishment and had beaten it. However, as a result of the mistrust that developed between Labour and the SNP during McConnell's time at party HQ, the Nationalists found it difficult to work with him on the cross-party referendum campaign. According to the Nats, McConnell was sidelined because the party hierarchy realised that he would not be seen as playing fair.

The SNP's portrayal of McConnell as a back-stabbing plotter who is only interested in quick fixes is totally at odds with how he is described by the Liberal Democrats. According to senior Lib Dems, the First Minister is a modern politician who understands the need for cross-party cooperation. The Liberal Democrats appointed their Chief Executive, Andy Myles, at the same time as McConnell took over at Keir Hardie House. The two men shadowed each other for the next five years. Although Michael Russell got on with McConnell at a personal level, it is clear there was little trust in their professional relationship. Myles, on the other hand, refutes any suggestion that McConnell was sidelined during the 1997 referendum campaign, dismissing such claims as 'nonsense'. While he claims his party worked well with Labour, he says relations between Labour and the SNP threatened to mar the campaign.

All the parties had agreed to suspend campaigning immediately following the death of Diana, Princess of Wales. The decision meant that the campaign to persuade Scots to back the idea of a parliament with tax-raising powers had to be won in just a hundred hours of campaigning over the final days ahead of the vote. The pro-devolution parties met to discuss how they would proceed and Myles claims McConnell and Russell were behaving like schoolchildren. He said:

> There were a couple of times that I was almost left holding the jackets – it was pathetic. Mike Russell was sitting there, saying, 'We've got Sean Connery and he is the greatest living Scot!' and Jack McConnell was shouting, 'But I've got Tony Blair and he is the greatest living campaigner!'

The row resulted in Myles losing his temper with both men and a compromise deal was eventually struck under which Sean Connery sailed across the Forth in a boat along with Gordon Brown – it was the photo opportunity to relaunch the campaign.

The view within the SNP is that McConnell cannot work with them as well as he appears to work with the other parties because he sees them as the greatest threat to Labour losing power. One senior Nationalist said, 'Jack is not against the whole world – he is just against us.' Certainly his history with the Liberal Democrats has proved that to be a more constructive relationship.

Another reason for his ability to work better with the Lib Dems could date back to the constitutional convention. The cross-party discussions which led to a blueprint being drawn up which formed the basis for how the Scottish Parliament would work was dominated by the two parties. The SNP decided that they would be better fighting their own corner and walked out of the talks. Both McConnell and Myles were key figures in the discussions, along with their leaders George Robertson (who held the post from 1993 to 1997) and Jim Wallace.

Although sections of the Labour Party were strongly against the idea of proportional representation, McConnell and Robertson realised they would have to give a concession and the Lib Dems believe it was done as part of a genuine attempt to modernise the way Scotland is run. Myles said:

> Great credit must go to George Robertson. I remember a journalist saying to him, 'But the PR deal means that Labour won't be in control.' and he said, frustratedly, 'But I'm not trying to create a Labour parliament – I'm trying to create a parliament for Scotland.' I could hear Jack McConnell saying the same thing.

Myles thinks that McConnell's upbringing in Arran and his experience of local government in Stirling taught him that, although Labour might be the biggest tribe in Scotland, the country is not in reality dominated by Labour. McConnell's former opposite number credits him with being a politician with some vision and one who has a reasonably clear idea of where he wants to take Scotland.

While it is probably true that the Liberal Democrat leader, Jim Wallace, enjoyed working most with the first First Minister, Donald Dewar – the pair shared a legal background and many experiences at Westminster – it is also safe to assume that the thought of a Labour group led by McConnell would have been an attractive prospect, given their dealings on the constitutional convention. Dewar and Wallace formed Scotland's first coalition government following the 1999 elections. The late First Minister came to the negotiations to form a partnership agreement between Labour and the Lib Dems with his team of advisers and half a sheet of A4 paper on which to base his plan. The Liberal Democrat leader arrived with a larger negotiating team and fifteen pages of notes.

The Lib Dem negotiators claim that, in 1999, Labour simply assumed that the Lib Dems would just sign up to Labour's manifesto in return for a couple of cabinet posts. In contrast, by the time McConnell was elected First Minister, there was a greater understanding of how coalition government worked. Also, the Lib Dems had no reason to fear a Labour group led by McConnell. During the meetings of Dewar's cabinet in 1999, there were several occasions when Jim Wallace and the other Liberal Democrat cabinet minister, Ross Finnie, had agreed they wanted to raise an issue, only to find that Jack got in with it first. This only served to reinforce their belief that he was someone they could do business with.

When it came to putting together the partnership agreement with the new First Minister, instead of sitting down as he had done with Dewar and thrashing out the details, Wallace sat in one room with McConnell. Their negotiating teams were in another room and they went through the two parties' policies, one by one, to discuss areas of agreement and disagreement. The sticking points were highlighted. Only those were passed through to McConnell and Wallace in the other room – and there weren't many of them. The relationship between McConnell and his coalition partners is probably helped by the fact they think that privately he shares their view that PR for local government will improve the governance of

Scotland. However, they appreciate his reluctance to trumpet it in his own party. Myles said:

> Jack is a politician of the new school in Scotland. That in no way makes him inferior to Gordon Brown, Robin Cook or George Robertson but the key to his success is that he understood there had to be changes in the way Scotland was run.

The Deputy First Minister Jim Wallace describes Jack as a 'pragmatic politician'. Of the partnership negotiations, he said:

> I knew that Jack was on our side on PR – we did not have to convince him of the argument – but we realised he had some sensitive handling issues in his own party. It was also made clear that he expected a trade-off in return for PR – he wanted to make sure we would agree to some of the stronger antisocial-behaviour measures which he wanted to introduce.

The Liberal Democrats also believe that the coalition is functioning far more effectively than it ever has done. They put this down to the greater experience that now exists on both sides and the lessening resentment between the two political groups on the backbenches. While Wallace and McConnell clearly have a good working relationship, they would make unusual best friends. However, when Jim Wallace had a private party to celebrate his fiftieth birthday in 2004, Jack was one of only a handful of politicians to be invited.

The relationship the First Minister also has with the Tory leader, David McLetchie, is one that verges on friendship. It has been reported that the two men frequently meet up for a round of golf – although David McLetchie is keen to play down the extent of their friendship. According to McLetchie, his social dealings with the First Minister have been much exaggerated. He owns up to having played around five games of golf with McConnell, over a five-year period, rather than the weekly round which his enemies in the Tory party and the press hint at.

In the run-up to the demise of McConnell's predecessor, Henry McLeish, the friendship between the two men led to much speculation that there might have been plotting on the golf course. McLetchie was seen as McLeish's chief interrogator in the parliament. He certainly landed some serious blows on the then First Minister as he struggled to defend himself against allegations that he had misused his office expenses. But McLetchie says he merely asked the questions of McLeish that any opposition leader should have asked. And he claims that, despite liking McConnell, if a similar situation arose with him, he would have no hesitation in adopting the same approach again. He says, 'If the situation replicated itself, absolutely I would do exactly the same.'

McLetchie, who has a golf handicap of ten, is no great admirer of the First Minister's ability with a golf club. He likens his approach to the game to his approach to politics. McLetchie says, 'He takes it very seriously. Technically, he is not great but he is extremely enthusiastic and, as you would expect, very determined.' As an opponent at First Minister's Questions (FMQ), McLetchie clearly rates his debating skills more highly than his golfing ability. He admits McConnell has a good grasp of his brief but accuses him of being garrulous and unfocused at times. On one occasion in the chamber, McConnell even admitted that he was waffling before sitting down. McConnell's long-time mentor, the Independent MSP Margo McDonald, says she has also advised him to deliver sharper, more succinct answers if he wants to wrong-foot his opponents. McDonald has also told the First Minister he needs to be bolder in the job. She believes McConnell has the ability to deliver more than he has so far if only he would strike out and do it.

The greatest criticism of McConnell's leadership has been that he lacks vision. However, McLetchie takes the view that the First Minister should not strike out with headline-grabbing measures but should concentrate on running departments properly. The Tory leader is scathing of the Executive's handling of the NHS in Scotland and claims that, whenever McConnell tries to be bold, he comes unstuck. He says:

> If the Executive could point to the hospital waiting lists coming down, that would be a real achievement – instead, they have gone up. The Executive has tried to be bolder than John Reid on the smoking ban and I'm sure it will lead to problems. Jack also said, at the start of the year, that he had reservations about it. Then we are expected to believe he had a weekend in Dublin and underwent some sort of Damascene conversion, when, in fact, he just felt under pressure to come up with something innovative. And we are constantly being told the Fresh Talent Initiative is a great idea which has come from the Executive, when it is only a Scottish pilot of a UK initiative.

McLetchie claims that the smoking-ban policy has become for McConnell what free personal care for the elderly was for his predecessor, Henry McLeish. He says, 'It's all about defining their First Ministership but, actually, getting the basics right is what is important.'

The former leader of the Scottish Socialist Party, Tommy Sheridan, first met McConnell while he was studying at Stirling University. When Sheridan arrived as an undergraduate, McConnell was beginning his second year as President of the Student Association. But, unlike McConnell, Sheridan, at that time, had little time for student politics, spending most of his spare time playing in the university football team. He did, however, attend a couple of meetings of the left alliance in which McConnell was an important player. In those days, the alliance was a group that took in all students with left-of-centre views, from the more moderate to the communists. But it was only much later that the two politicians crossed swords.

Like McLetchie, Sheridan also confesses to a degree of warmth towards the First Minister. Sheridan said:

> I find him warmer and more personable than Donald Dewar or Henry McLeish ever were. Some people say that Dewar was a statesman while Jack is nothing more than an apparatchik – I certainly don't buy that. Dewar was over-rated – remember he was the guy who got out of his sick bed to persuade his backbenchers to vote against the abolition of warrant sales in 2000.

The Scottish Socialist also believes that McConnell's more nationalist leanings have been a great asset to the Scottish Parliament. According to Sheridan, McConnell has shown signs of taking on vested interests where issues like the smoking ban are concerned and he believes the previous First Ministers would not have done the same. He said, 'To me, that was the first example of a bit of bottle being shown – although I think it's too early to say if that will continue.' He added:

> Jack McConnell also has a greater recognition that Scotland is a country. Although I don't think he has gone far enough, at least he will refer to it as a great small country. Henry McLeish might have done that – although I don't think he would have meant it – and Dewar would never have done it.

# 14

## DOING LESS, BETTER

Deacon Brodie's pub at the top of Edinburgh's Royal Mile was a favourite drinking hole for MSPs, journalists and tourists when the parliament sat on the Mound. On Thursday nights in particular, when the week's parliamentary business was over, dozens of Scotland's political elite would gather to gossip about recent events. Many of the conversations held there on a Thursday night would form the basis of the headline-grabbing stories in the following Sunday's newspapers. Deacon Brodie's became an obvious meeting place because of its close proximity to the parliament. It has a restaurant upstairs which serves fairly ordinary pub food. It's the kind of place you would grab lunch if you were in a hurry, but not somewhere you would want to take an important contact. Yet, on the night of 22 November 2001, Jack McConnell had booked a table for twenty people there. Hours after becoming Scotland's third First Minister, he chose to celebrate in Deacon Brodie's rather than one of Edinburgh's many upmarket eateries. Instead of his usual table of loyal political supporters, he had opted to spend the evening with his wife, kids, mum, dad, nieces, nephews and cousins.

After years of climbing his way through the ranks of the Labour Party and two decades of fighting for a parliament for Scotland, he was now leading it. Through a combination of his own talent, the tragedy of Donald Dewar's death and his luck that Henry McLeish decided to unexpectedly quit, Jack McConnell had been elected First Minister of Scotland. A salary of £120,000 a year comes with the job – as does a chauffer-driven car, a large private office staff, a team of special advisers and the palatial official residence of Bute House in the capital's Charlotte Square. Yet it was into the rather ordinary surroundings of Deacon Brodie's pub that Scotland's new First Lady, Bridget McConnell, walked to meet her husband that night. One family member who attended the meal said:

> It was great night – Jack was so relaxed. I think he is at his happiest when he is surrounded by people who care about him but not about politics. We didn't discuss politics at all that night and he was able to let his hair down.

Jack McConnell may have taken that evening to savour his success but, when he woke up to his first full day in the most powerful job in Scottish politics, he was far from relaxed. He was handed the keys to Bute House by a civil servant and told to go there. When he arrived, there were no staff and the heating was turned off. It was far from welcoming but the most pressing issue on his mind was the cabinet reshuffle. Jack knew he would have to sack former colleagues, axe special advisers – some of whom had been friends in the past – and, most importantly, restore the public's confidence in devolution.

McConnell was acutely aware that the job had placed enormous strains on the late Donald Dewar and had destroyed the confidence of his predecessor Henry McLeish. He had learned a lot watching from the sidelines but now there was no place to hide. McConnell had the job he had always wanted. However, it had come to him much sooner than he had expected and he must have harboured doubts as to whether he was quite ready for it. As a way of countering the instability and the petty rows that had dominated the first two years of devolution, McConnell decided his administration should launch fewer initiatives and focus on the policies they had made a priority.

He used a phrase that had been employed by the former European Commission President, Jacques Santer – 'do less, better'. It didn't work for Santer, whose commission was forced from office several years later amid allegations of corruption.

Given the chaotic running of the administration over the previous two years, there is little doubt that McConnell had the right idea. The Executive had been dogged by cabinet infighting – a huge public row over the repeal of Section 28, the soaring cost of the parliament building, the Lobbygate investigation, the SQA exams fiasco and Officegate (which had ended in Henry McLeish's downfall). Jack McConnell wanted his government to deliver on health, education and the economy. Addressing the parliament on the day of his election, he spoke about the people's priorities:

> They want action to speed up important operations. They want action to improve our schools and motivate our young people. They want action to lock up the dealers and the thugs. They want action on transport, with railways and roads which serve their purpose.

It sounded like the new beginning that the parliament desperately needed. If McConnell could deliver in his new job the way he had done in his previous job as Education Minister, there was little doubt the public would have noticed significant improvements in a short time.

The loyalty that the new First Minister had within his cabinet helped to create an impression of unity among the Labour team. His vow to do less also bought him some time to steady the administration and take stock of what it should be doing. The media frenzy that engulfed the parliament in its early years also subsided. After the loss of two First Ministers, even media figures were beginning to fear for the future of the parliament. These factors came together to ensure that Jack

McConnell enjoyed a honeymoon period that had not been granted to either of his two predecessors.

From the outside, the early months of his leadership looked like plain sailing but, behind the scenes, McConnell was struggling with a battle to regain his self-confidence. In two short years, he had gone from being a public affairs consultant to holder of the most powerful job in the country. He used the same techniques as he had used while he was Education Minister but they failed to produce the same results. As soon as he became First Minister, he told senior civil servants his top priority was to deliver stability. He ordered an end to the blizzard of initiatives which were being unveiled every month. His chief of staff, Mike Donnelly, devised a programme for the first one hundred days that was similar to the one used by Tony Blair when he took office. The difference was that, while Blair wanted to create the impression that he had hit the ground running, Jack wanted to give the impression that he had, in his own words, 'stopped the madness'.

Another decision he took early on was to continue the major initiatives that had been started by Henry McLeish. Despite its unpopularity with many sections of the Labour Party, McConnell adopted McLeish's flagship policy of free personal care for the elderly. Many of his colleagues were of the view that it was a costly promise which would mainly benefit the middle classes. McConnell could easily have ditched it but he could see merit in it and he wasn't going to throw the idea out just because it had been Henry's. He also decided to water down the plans to ban the smacking of children, fearing it could result in a public backlash.

Behind the scenes, the government of Scotland began to run more smoothly but, although Jack gave the appearance of being in control, he probably didn't feel it. It is more than likely he felt overwhelmed by the responsibility he had always craved. Jack had always thought McLeish suffered a poor image in part because his performance at First Minister's Questions (FMQ) was lacklustre. McConnell always thought he could do much better. But now that he had centre stage he began to feel he wasn't performing as well as he knew he could or as well as he thought he needed to. He spent hours trying to absorb the detail of every portfolio in his government and he lashed out at civil servants who gave him what he thought were inadequate briefing papers. But, in those early weeks, he still returned to his office and kicked himself for not doing better.

The media were giving him a relatively easy ride but the SNP believed they could get under his skin. Despite being criticised for his tongue-tied performances, Henry McLeish did not fall into many of the SNP's traps that were laid at First Minister's Questions. The Nationalist leader, John Swinney, found it difficult to land a blow on McLeish because of the evasive nature of his answers. Jack McConnell's approach to FMQ was the opposite – he tried to answer the specifics of every question and was desperate to look as if he was on top of his massive portfolio. McConnell's directness played into Swinney's hands. The SNP leader picked the issue of 'closed' hospital waiting lists with which to beat McConnell. The new First Minister began by denying that there was such a concept within the NHS. When Swinney then produced a letter from a health board stating there was, McConnell was forced to announce an investigation.

On several occasions following his appearances at FMQ, Jack McConnell would write to the SNP leader to 'clarify' answers he had given. This meant that, after leaving the chamber, the First Minister had discovered that he had given either wrong or misleading information. His political opponents believe much of the problem lay with poor civil service briefings. John Swinney said:

Trying to nail Henry McLeish through the fog of information he created was very difficult. When Jack took over, he tried to engage with the question and wanted to give the impression that he was the guy who was running Scotland perfectly. He learned the hard way that he couldn't control everything.

John Swinney also picked his subject well. For any new First Minister, the Health portfolio will always be the most difficult to get to grips with. Perhaps because he was acutely aware of the image problem his predecessor had as a result of his performances at FMQ, McConnell put a lot of time into preparing for these weekly bouts. He would start to pore over the morning's papers as he sat in his dressing gown in Bute House. McConnell would arrive in his office between 7.30 and 8.00 a.m. and would expect his civil servants to be ready to brief him on the issues of the week. Later in the morning, he would sit round a large table with civil servants, political advisers and press officers in an attempt to work out what he would be asked and to have his answers prepared.

Throughout his career, McConnell has wanted to surround himself with people he can trust and people in whom he has confidence. On becoming First Minister his relations with some parts of the civil service were not good. McConnell believes that during Henry McLeish's time as First Minister civil servants were instructed to keep information from him. While the vast majority of civil servants are able to work with politicians of any party and across various factions, McConnell had singled out one or two for being too enthusiastic in their support of McLeish. Those he blamed for 'taking sides' were quietly moved to parts of the civil service where they would have less direct contact with him. Jack likes to pick his own people but, even as First Minister, there are limits on the control he has over the civil service.

His relationship with the former Permanent Secretary, Sir Muir Russell, was reportedly very poor. However, senior civil servants say relations between the two were never as bad as reports made them out to be. As in any walk of life, the best ministerial–civil service relationships occur when the two people involved hit it off and think along the same wavelength. Although they did not find it impossible to work together, Jack McConnell and Sir Muir Russell certainly had very little in common and did not get on particularly well. Relations between the two hit a low in the spring of 2002 when Sir Muir advertised for forty policy advisers without informing the First Minister. Although McConnell eventually agreed to the recruitment drive, he was furious over the way it had been handled. However, civil servants stress that the relationship was far from dysfunctional. That said, McConnell was not upset when Sir Muir left his post at the top of the civil service in 2003 to become the Principal and Vice Chancellor of Glasgow University.

Government rules state that the head of the civil service in Scotland has to be someone put forward after a rigorous selection procedure and the decision is ratified by the Prime Minister in consultation with the First Minister. The fact that the civil service suggested John Elvidge, who had been in charge of the Education Department while Jack was First Minister, delighted him. Elvidge is closer to Jack in age and approach. The two built up a strong working relationship during McConnell's time at Education. The First Minister both rated Elvidge and, crucially for Jack, trusted him. Civil servants tend to be happy working for ministers they can 'run' – that is, ministers without strong views on the portfolio who rely on the civil servants for help. They can also respond well to ministers who know exactly what they want to achieve. Most civil servants agree that the most difficult type of minister to work for is one who refuses take advice but doesn't appear to know what to do either.

From the minute McConnell took over as First Minister, his ability to get to grips with the massive brief was not in doubt.

His private secretary for the first two years of his time as First Minister was Derek Feeley, with whom he is said to have had an excellent working relationship. Those who have worked closely with McConnell all talk of their frustration at his refusal to take decisions on matters which sometimes appear relatively minor. Civil servants, political advisers and close friends all told me of his stubborn approach to issues which he does not feel he has grasped fully. He has held up decisions for weeks because one detail is niggling him. Those who have experience of working with him say they have to work hard to discover what it is that is irritating him and then find a way to reassure him, either by finding a new fact or statistic, or the right person to talk him round – otherwise the issue will become stuck. One former adviser said, 'It can be incredibly frustrating working for him when he just refuses to make a decision.' But another explained:

> Usually, when he is holding on to something, it is because there is a one per cent doubt in his mind which tends to be something which nobody else has thought about and that one per cent turns out to be a problem.

The First Minister is also noted for his attention to detail. He will rarely allow a letter to be sent from his office without making a change or adding a personal sentiment. Jack rarely loses his temper and is quick to give praise when it is due but, if he is unhappy with work done by the civil service, he is equally quick to let them know it is not up to scratch. Although he tends not to shout and bawl, one former member of staff said:

> He doesn't have to. You can see his face go a bit redder and you know he is furious and you will have to fix whatever has annoyed him but he bites his tongue and takes time to calm down. I have never seen him throw a tantrum.

He added:

> He takes a great pride in detail. If a letter goes out from his
> office, he takes the view that how it is presented will affect the
> way the public will view him and the Executive and that it
> must be right.

Similarly, if he believes a minister is on top of their brief, he
will leave them to get on with it but, if he suspects they are not,
he is, according to one civil servant, 'all over them'.

There are few comparisons to be made between Jack
McConnell and the former Tory Prime Minister Margaret
Thatcher but one thing they share is an ability to catnap. When
Jack needs a break, he tells his staff to leave him for half an hour.
He is capable of sleeping at his desk or in a car for a short period
of time. One friend even complained that, during times when he
had been working hard, Jack would invite him for dinner, only
to fall asleep at the table in a restaurant in mid conversation.
When Derek Feeley left his office for another job, Jack joked at
the leaving do that Feeley had woken him up far more times
over the two years they worked together than his wife had.

After settling into the job, McConnell was to enjoy a
honeymoon period in office. He largely succeeded in steadying
the Executive although he won little praise for doing so.
McConnell's promise to 'do less, better' soon rebounded on
him as his critics accused him of lacking vision. With the
benefit of hindsight, the First Minister believes he suffered by
not having to face a contest for the leadership in November
2001 – it would have given him a month-long campaign in
which he could have spelt out what he stood for.

Just eighteen months after taking office, Jack was to face the
electorate and he was worried. He feared that the voters would
punish Labour for the early mistakes made in the parliament
and over the cost of the new building. He was plagued by

insecurity. In his darker moments, he thought that, if there was
a low turnout, he could become the first Labour leader since
the 1950s to lose an election in Scotland. An opinion poll in the
first week of the campaign showed Labour and the SNP
running neck and neck. Jack was feeling the pressure. There
were tensions between McConnell and staff within Labour
Party headquarters during the campaign. They wanted him to
run a campaign based on Labour's achievements after private
polling showed that the voters were not aware of any.

Jack strongly disagreed. He wanted to use the phrase 'on your
side' and was determined that would be the hallmark of his
second term. Jack took to the road in a battle bus for the duration
of the campaign. He toured Scotland giving speeches, meeting
voters and delivering his 'on your side' message in sixty-nine
constituencies in just four weeks. But the Labour campaign for
the 2003 Scottish elections was seen as lacklustre. Despite the fact
that it was Henry McLeish who was responsible for the policy
of free personal care for the elderly, the party was forced to
champion that as one of its biggest achievements while in office.

Jack McConnell made the economy his top priority but
figures released during the campaign showed the Scottish
economy heading towards its second recession in two years.
McConnell knew that he had a difficult task if he was to limit
the punishment the voters wanted to dish out to his party after
the first four years of the parliament. The high expectations the
public had had, prior to 1999, had not been met. The new laws
that had been passed in the early years did not, in the main,
appeal to the voters. And there was fury over the escalating cost
of the parliament building.

One of the smartest moves of the campaign was McConnell's
decision to announce a public inquiry into why so much
taxpayers' money had been wasted on Holyrood. That took
some of the heat out of the situation but the results for Labour
in May 2003 were not good. The Labour group was cut from

fifty-six seats to fifty. Jack has lost 10% of his group overnight –
including cabinet minister Iain Gray and former minister Angus
Mckay. The result showed there was a reaction against the main
parties and the Scottish Socialist Party, the Pensioners Party and
the Greens were the main benefactors.

The election of 2003 was a watershed for Jack McConnell.
He had faced the voters for the first time and had suffered
some damage as a result of his party's performance in the
early years of the Scottish Parliament. But the First Minister
realised that he had carried out his aim of introducing some
stability and it was now time to move on. He needed a new
slogan and his advisor, Rachel McEwen, came up with 'Smarter,
Quicker, Sharper'. It was a take on a phrase from the *Harry
Potter* books – 'Smarter, Quicker, Stronger' – but it signalled
what was to come. In a speech to the parliament, following his
re-election as First Minister, it was clear McConnell had got the
message from the voters. He did not take his success as a ringing
endorsement of success and, instead, he promised, 'We will
raise our game.' He recognised that 'people are impatient for
change'. And he told them that he was eager for it to happen too.
Jack McConnell admitted that the Executive had reached a
turning point – that the first term had been about delivering
devolution – but he acknowledged the time had come for
devolution to deliver. If any speech can define a politician, this
one came close to explain what McConnellism is all about.

As has been noted, the First Minister has often being
criticised for lacking vision. His vision may not extend to areas
some people would like it to and his critics may not like some
of what it contains but it seems wrong to say Jack McConnell
does not have any vision. In that speech of 15 May 2003, Jack
McConnell speaks as a politician who is clearly comfortable
with coalition politics. He said, 'No party or individual holds
the monopoly of representation of ideas.' He sets out a vision
of a confident Scotland in which young people are taught the

skills of entrepreneurship while still at school and are given the opportunity to realise their potential. He outlines ways of making people feel safer through tackling antisocial behaviour – even if that means punishing parents who don't control their kids. Jack McConnell wants people to take pride in the communities they live in and believes those who try to wreck them with graffiti or loutish behaviour should be held to account. In another speech to the General Assembly days later, he said, 'I stand against violence and antisocial behaviour – not to condemn or stereotype people but to speak for those who are the victims and who deserve more respect.'

One of the issues he feels most strongly about is the stain of sectarianism. He gets particularly angry about the abuse he hears at football matches and the sectarian behaviour he has witnessed in his own constituency. Brought up on the island of Arran, it was something he was introduced to relatively late in life but it has affected him greatly. When he went to Stirling University, he was shocked to discover that people ask where someone has gone to school not to determine their academic background but their religious one. Much to his surprise and his disgust, when he married Bridget, there were some eyebrows raised by some distant relatives over the fact that Bridget was Catholic and he was Protestant. When he contested the Motherwell and Wishaw parliamentary selection, he was horrified to hear people tell him there were certain votes he wouldn't get because of his religion and other ones he definitely could count on for the same reason. And when he moved to Wishaw, sectarian graffiti was daubed on his house within weeks.

Critics say the sectarian issue is an easy one for the First Minister to tackle because the vast majority of Scots will say that they deplore it too. One former minister said:

It's hardly a big deal to say you are anti-sectarian. I don't know who wouldn't put their hand up for that one and, until he tackles the issue of Catholic schools, I don't believe he is taking it that seriously.

But Jack's supporters claim his decision to tackle sectarianism head-on has been a brave one and has left some people on the Labour benches concerned that it has been given such a high profile. The First Minister takes the view that sectarianism is still affecting some people's life chances and influencing whether they get a particular job and the friends they have. He ranks it alongside knife crime and street violence as badges of shame that are holding Scotland back and sapping the country's confidence.

In February 2005, he held a summit on sectarianism at which leading church figures and politicians sat down with football fans and members of the Orange Lodge to try to solve the problem being passed on to the next generation. The initiative has come in for some criticism from people who believe that Jack has only served to exaggerate the problem. But just days after the summit was held, a man was murdered in Glasgow because he went into a 'Rangers pub' wearing a Celtic top after an Old Firm game. Jack McConnell has also spoken about his vision of 'one Scotland'. He deplores prejudice – be it religious, ethnic or against the poor.

People may be divided about the extent of political bravery that is required to take on the sectarian issue but one idea has been viewed universally as high risk and that is the Fresh Talent Initiative. Private focus groups commissioned by all the main parties show that voters are afraid of immigration. This is the case not just in Britain but also across Europe. As a result, politicians of all parties have developed an increasingly hardline stance as well as the language to appeal to the voters. In Scotland, Jack McConnell has said and done the opposite and, so far, it has worked.

Much of the inspiration for the Fresh Talent Initiative came from the former Chairman of Highlands and Islands Enterprise,

Dr Jim Hunter, who had successfully helped to boost population levels which, in turn, fuelled an economic revival in the area. Before Jack became First Minister, Hunter was calling for the Highlands and Islands to become multicultural as a way of continuing its economic success. He argued that Scotland should look to American's Pacific north-west, an overwhelmingly immigrant society, to learn lessons. And he advised Glasgow and Edinburgh to adopt a similar outlook. Speaking in September 2001, he said it is only when people are made to feel good about their culture and background that they are motivated to contribute to the area in which they live. He said:

> Until we stop marginalising the inhabitants of Sighthill, Castlemilk, Pilton, Wester Hailes, until we restore these folk's pride in who they are and who they might be, then Central Belt housing schemes will continue to suffer from what our Highlands and Islands communities suffered from for centuries – a complete absence of any reason to think that things can get better.

Hunter's argument gave the First Minister plenty to think about.

Jack looked at the economic success of the Highlands over the last thirty years and Hunter's vision of attracting overseas residents to the area as a way of continuing the boom. The First Minister is aware that one of the biggest problems facing Scotland over the next ten years is the demographic time bomb. Fewer children are being born and talented young people are being lost to London or abroad, leaving an elderly and declining population. It spells economic disaster. If he was serious about making the economy his top priority, Jack knew he could not ignore this problem. However, one look at his party's focus groups would tell him that Dr Hunter's approach could go down like a lead balloon.

The Tories' Michael Howard talks tough on immigration and asylum because he thinks that is what appeals to the voters. And Tony Blair often talks about curbs on immigration but not about how to attract immigrants – even he would consider that political suicide. But Jack's gut instinct told him Scotland has a different problem and this could be the solution. It was a gamble he wanted to take. As with all of Jack's high-risk strategies, he spent a lot of time considering how he could pull it off. The First Minister took the relatively unusual step of calling the then SNP leader, John Swinney, to tell him in advance of his plan. Jack calculated that the SNP would instinctively back the idea but that they could accuse him of hypocrisy given the fears Labour had tried to whip up in the past over an independent Scotland having its own immigration controls.

When Swinney heard of the proposal he gasped. Jack said, 'I trust you will not try to make political capital out of this.' But it was too good an opportunity for the SNP to miss. On 25 February 2004, the First Minister made a statement to parliament outlining how he planned to prevent Scotland's economy suffering as a result of a fast-declining workforce. He made his priority nurturing home-grown talent and attracting Scots who have left the country to work elsewhere back to Scotland. But, controversially, he had done a deal with the then Home Secretary, David Blunkett, to change the immigration rules affecting Scotland so that overseas students are given an automatic right to work there for two years after they graduate in the hope they make Scotland their permanent home. Work permits for people looking to come to live in Scotland would also be easier to obtain. McConnell hopes his plan will boost the population by 8,000 each year, which he calculates will be necessary to stop the population falling below the crucial five-million level in just five years' time.

Swinney couldn't believe what he was hearing – it was exactly the kind of initiative he might have introduced if he was the First Minister of an independent Scotland. However, he couldn't resist having a dig at McConnell for having the audacity to unveil his plan without any mention of 'passport controls at the border or guards patrolling the border with England', both of which were scare tactics Labour had used to discredit similar plans by the Nationalists in the past. The Tory leader, David McLetchie, used Swinney's enthusiasm for the plan as proof that it must be dangerous. But, despite the usual political posturing, there was a realisation that Jack McConnell had come up with a bold vision on one of the biggest issues facing Scotland. Swinney said, 'He used some classic tactics to try to fix the reaction he would get. Basically, he is on the right ground with the Fresh Talent Initiative but that alone will not fix the problem.' From a former SNP leader, that is verging on praise.

And Deputy First Minister Jim Wallace credits McConnell with taking the debate from an academic level onto a pragmatic one. He said:

> He seized the initiative on arguably the most important issue facing Scotland. It will be ten or fifteen years before we will know if it will work but Jack was certainly on to the problem before me or anyone else for that matter.

McConnell's close friend, Neil Stewart, goes even further in claiming that Jack has taken British politics out of a rut on an issue it has been stuck in since before Enoch Powell made his famous 'rivers of blood' speech.

McConnell has also set about trying to be a First Minister for all of Scotland. Coming from Arran has probably helped him to avoid falling into the political trap of concentrating his efforts on the Central Belt. He makes regular trips to the Highlands and to the south of Scotland. He has devoted a great deal of time to taking part in the Highlands and Islands convention and he plans to back a University of the Highlands and Islands – against civil service advice. When Inverness failed to make it on to the shortlist for the European City of Culture 2007 despite running a good campaign full of interesting ideas, Jack announced a Highland Year of Culture so that the work which had been put into the bid did not go to waste.

By the spring of 2002, McConnell was feeling on top of the job but the resignation of Wendy Alexander caused him some problems in the business community. She had been highly rated as Enterprise Minister and business leaders were disappointed to see her go. Jack knew he had a problem and set about trying to address it. He used the election campaign to appeal to his party to become the party of enterprise and, later in the year, he announced his 'going for growth strategy'. He toured Scotland holding business breakfasts in order to meet the country's wealth creators and listen to their problems. He invited the bosses of the 'big six' Scottish headquartered companies, including the Royal Bank of Scotland and Standard Life, to meet him at Bute House to discuss their concerns. And he has forged strong links with entrepreneurs like Tom Hunter and Irvine Laidlaw, whom he has worked with on setting up initiatives to help young people make a success of their lives.

However, many in the business community remain to be convinced that Jack McConnell gives their interests the priority he says he does. While few of them are prepared to speak out publicly, there are general grumblings that the First Minister talks a good game on business but they notice little in the way of a tangible difference. One leading business source said:

Jack McConnell is always saying that the economy is his top priority but, for those of us who work here, it certainly doesn't feel like it. We used to have business rates which were on a level playing field with England. Since the Scottish Parliament was set up, a business in Glasgow has to pay significantly more than a business in Gloucester. And, on planning issues, he will always pander to the protestors rather than take the side of business.

Some leading business figures claim that, when there is conflict between the environment and business, McConnell will always come down on the side of the environmentalists. One of the speeches of which he is most proud is a speech he delivered on 'environmental justice' in February 2002. At the time, it was described by Kevin Dunion of Friends of the Earth as a 'seminal speech'. Some of the language he used provoked a row with civil servants who objected to the term environmental justice but McConnell stuck to his guns. In it, he set a target of 30% of Scotland's electricity coming from renewable sources by 2020.

The First Minister also made it clear that he believes the people who suffer most from a poor environment are the people least able to fight back. One of the issues that has angered him most, since even before he was local councillor, is the poor environmental conditions some people are living with. He has been extremely critical of the effect open-cast mining has had on areas like Muirkirk in Ayrshire. On a visit to the area, he was taken into one home where the tenant showed him a layer of black dust which had gathered on a toothbrush despite the fact the windows were closed. McConnell spent the journey back to Edinburgh lecturing his advisers about the injustice of the situation.

Despite his environmental credentials, Jack had been opposed to the idea of a ban on smoking. However, his advisers sent him to Dublin to see for himself how the ban was working there. He changed his mind overnight. Opposition parties ridiculed him over his lightning conversion but that is exactly what happened. Before he saw the ban operating in Dublin, he was of the view that the government should only legislate to stop people smoking in places such as on public transport and in hospitals where others had no option but to go. Jack smoked around fifteen cigarettes a day until the early '90s, when both he and Bridget decided to give up but several of his advisers smoke around him and it is not something which bothers him personally. The Scottish cabinet was split on the issue – as was the UK cabinet. The public health argument in favour of a ban was overwhelming but McConnell believed that public opinion was against it. However, after speaking to publicans and the public in Dublin, he was convinced that public opinion could be changed on the issue. The First Minister had planned to tell the press that he remained to be convinced that Scotland should follow Dublin's example but, on his way to the press conference, he told his adviser that, instead of struggling to find the justification for doing it, he could no longer justify not doing it. Jack is now convinced that the ban, which, at the time of writing, is due to come into force in 2006, will make a massive contribution towards turning round Scotland's poor public health record.

As Jack developed his 'big ideas', his confidence grew. He saw the opening of the new parliament building at Holyrood as a second chance to win over the electorate and to restore the public's pride in devolution. In the run-up to the opening, he felt under enormous pressure to ensure that he did not squander that second chance. He was mindful of the memorable speech the first First Minster, Donald Dewar, had given when the Queen came to open the parliament on the Mound in 1999. In it, Dewar had spoken of a 'new voice in the land'. That speech was rich with references to Scotland's past and also captured the mood of the nation at the time.

Jack spent hours thinking about the nature of the message he wanted to convey at the opening of the parliament at Holyrood. He finally decided he would make a speech based on the Enlightenment, to point to Scotland's past success and to help build confidence in the great achievements which could lie ahead. Just days before he was due to deliver it, the parliament's Presiding Officer, George Reid, sent a copy of the speech that he planned to make at the opening ceremony to the First Minister's office. The thrust of it was almost identical to the speech Jack had been planning to make. The First Minister did not see it as his place to influence Reid's speech or ask him to change it in any way but it left him with a major problem. He realised he needed inspiration and needed it quickly.

In desperation, he turned not to one of his senior colleagues in the Labour Party but to the former SNP MP, Jim Sillars, for help. A note Sillars had sent him provided the inspiration for an emotional speech he had made in April 2003 about children living in poverty and he thought Sillars was the only person who could come up trumps now. Although the two men do not share a political philosophy, Jack looks upon Jim Sillars as one of the greatest orators of his generation. When Jack addressed the opening of the Holyrood Parliament on 9 October 2004, his MSPs would have been shocked had they known that some of the words he used were not his own but had been written by one of Scotland's best known Nationalist politicians.

> This building is not the Scottish Parliament. This magnificent building can inspire admiration for its design and its detail but it cannot, by its mere existence, influence opinions or judgements on public policy. It is we who are elected to serve who form the human institution that is the Scottish Parliament. It is how we perform our duties, how we advance or inhibit the progress of this nation, in our conduct and the decisions we make, that will chart the future course of Scotland.

The words were delivered by the Labour First Minister of Scotland but they were written by the leading Nationalist, Jim Sillars. Jack's decision to go to Sillars is another example of how the third First Minister is comfortable with the language of nationalism. Unlike many Labour MPs, he does not believe that only the SNP can call Scotland a country or that only Nationalist politicians can wrap themselves in the saltire. As a Labour First Minister, he thinks it is his place to embrace Scotland's traditions and to promote them and is not afraid of using nationalist language to do so.

At around the same time as the new parliament was opened, Jack underwent a minor image transformation. Out went the dull ties he had been wearing in an attempt to look more statesmanlike and in came brighter ones to replace them – Jack wanted to get his spark back. Since taking on the job, he had put on almost two stone in weight as he developed irregular eating patterns and found he had no time left to swim three times a week as he had been used to doing. He got himself a personal trainer who now puts him through gruelling army exercises once a week and this has led to him losing most of the extra weight he was carrying.

His colleagues say he now feels in control of the job. Jack McConnell defined his first term in office by what he didn't do rather than what he did. His second term has marked him out as a politician keen to change the culture of the country he is running. If Jack can help to rid Scotland of the stain of sectarianism, make the Scots a nation that welcomes incomers, boost the confidence of Scotland's young people so they achieve their potential in life and turn around the country's appalling health record, he will have left a legacy of which he will be justly proud. Unlike some of the achievements of his predecessors, be it for the building of the new parliament at Holyrood or for the delivery of free personal care for the elderly, Jack McConnell's vision will take a generation or more to become a reality. If Jack succeeds as a First Minister, it will be only after he has gone that he will get the credit.

Jack McConnell was only forty-one years old when he became First Minister of Scotland. He has already served for four years and has told close friends that he wants to continue as Labour leader for six more years at least. Unforeseen circumstances aside, McConnell plans to lead his party into the 2007 and the 2011 Scottish Parliament elections. If he is lucky enough to remain as First Minister, by then, he will have carried out the job for a decade – nine years longer than either Henry McLeish or Donald Dewar were able to. After the 2011 election, Jack, at just fifty-one years old, will still be a relatively young man. He will be left the option of trying to cling on to power for as long as he can or to get out of politics. In his wilder moments, he has talked of going off to Africa to teach maths. However, he has also admitted that his heart remains in Arran and that he will eventually want to move back there.

# 15

# WISHAWGATE

Real scandal in British politics is rare. The Profumo scandal in the '60s rocked the country but, with the exception of the cash-for-questions row involving Tory MPs and the odd case of perjury, there hasn't been any proven wrongdoing on a significant scale which would shock the public since. However, the absence of such acts does not prevent the press attempting to portray smaller events as more significant than they are. Not for a second did anyone believe that the allegations surrounding Beattie Media's links to the new government was on the scale of Watergate – yet the story was dubbed 'Lobbygate'. When money went missing from Jack McConnell's constituency party, the scandal was referred to as 'Wishawgate' and, when the First Minister chose to go on holiday with his old friend Kirsty Wark to her house in Majorca, it was inevitably hailed as 'Villagate'.

Apart from Henry McLeish's problems over the running of his office accounts which was called 'Officegate', every other recent Scottish 'gate' has involved Jack McConnell. In each case, McConnell was mindful that it is not always the allegations that bring people down but how those involved handle them. Few, if any, political observers believed that Henry McLeish would be forced out of office over the fact that he overclaimed money from the House of Commons which he then went on to spend on his constituents. Despite making no personal gain, McLeish even paid back £36,000 from his own money. It was his failure to appear to come clean from the outset that cost him his job. When allegations of missing money in Jack McConnell's constituency party surfaced less than a year into his leadership, he realised just how serious the consequences could be. Given the nature of McLeish's downfall, the media was never again going to dismiss such a story as a 'storm in a teacup'. The problems in Jack's constituency became public knowledge in October 2002 after concerned auditors in the constituency took the accounts to the Labour Party headquarters. Jack was devastated that the anniversary of him becoming First Minister was to be marred by scandal. He felt he was just beginning to get on top of the job when he was hit by a setback of the worst possible kind.

But it should not have come as a complete surprise. Before the story blew up, there had been months of behind-the-scenes rows over the way the local party's accounts were being run in Motherwell and Wishaw. The first inkling that there could be a problem came in the February of 2002 from one of the people elected to audit the constituency accounts. Hugh Mulholland, a former council education official who had previously been responsible for a budget of £220 million, had spent months trying to balance the books along with another auditor, Sadie Taylor. They could not make the books add up and went to the local party several times to warn that their job was proving impossible because they had not been given adequate information. When they failed to get the information they said they needed, the local party felt it was left with no option but to take the auditors' concerns to the Labour Party headquarters.

Mulholland's friends believe he was given the brush-off for months because he was seen as a troublemaker by those loyal to Jack. He was distrusted by McConnell's allies because he had backed Bill Tynan over Jack becoming the MSP for the area. Mulholland made it clear at the time that he would refuse to back Jack because he believed McConnell was being parachuted into a safe Labour seat. He had also angered McConnell's allies by objecting to the idea of holding Red Rose Dinners in the constituency as a way of raising funds for the Labour Party. Mulholland believed that Labour had been damaged by the revelation that Bernie Ecclestone had donated one million pounds to the party, he disagreed with the gala dinners being organised in London and did not want to see the practice extended to his own area. His view is that those who pay the piper call the tune. He said:

> Tickets are sold to the public for these events. The party cannot control who goes to them and, if the people who buy tables at these dinners then get contracts from the council or government, even if they are totally above board, the perception would be bad. I don't see why the party should take that kind of risk and I don't understand why we need to raise such large sums of money to run a local constituency party.

At the time the decision was taken to hold a Red Rose Dinner, Mulholland's concerns were overlooked but, when the local treasurer Elizabeth Wilson gave the auditors the constituency's books to audit in December 2001, his concerns were heightened. The books covered three separate accounts. One was the general constituency fund, another was the election fund and the third was known as the development fund. The auditors spent two months trying to make sense of the accounts. At the constituency's AGM in February 2002, Mulholland told the local party that he was unable to audit the accounts because there was a lack of detail. He wasn't given the appropriate receipts to show spending and he was concerned that money raised from the Red Rose Dinners appeared to go into the general account from which some was transferred into the development account and then back again.

Mulholland did not think he had stumbled on any wrongdoing but he did think the books were a mess. He says that he returned time and again to the constituency party to warn them that it was impossible to audit the books in their current state. The constituency party then decided the books should be passed to the party's General Secretary, Lesley Quinn, for further investigation. Friends of Hugh Mulholland say that he was victimised as a result of his persistent questioning about the accounts. One said:

> Jack's friends tried to make out that [Mulholland] was someone with an axe to grind and [he was] using the accounts to try to settle a score. But, to his credit, he did not buckle under the pressure and history has proved him to be right.

After the Labour Party received the books, Lesley Quinn decided to call in the police to investigate. There appeared to be an £11,000 black hole in the accounts. At this stage, the auditors had not implied that the money had been stolen but they were furious that it had not been properly accounted for. News of the alleged discrepancies reached several newspapers and Wishawgate exploded on to the front pages. Some within the Labour Party tried to portray the row as the latest example of a long-running feud in the Lanarkshire constituency – nothing more than Mulholland trying to settle a score or two. As the MSP for the constituency, McConnell did not have direct control over the running of the office accounts. His PA, Christina Marshall and another employee, Elizabeth Wilson, were both trustees of the Red Rose Dinner account. However, he knew that, politically, the buck stopped with him.

Some party members in the constituency were furious that the accounts showed that money had been taken from the development fund to pay for Christina Marshall to stay overnight at an Edinburgh hotel so she could accompany McConnell to a party conference in the city. The fact that it was the five-star Caledonian Hotel at a cost of £168 incensed them all the more. The reason she stayed there was that it was the hotel used by Labour Party staff but some party members felt the expenditure should have been agreed by them. McConnell calculated that, if he were to avoid becoming embroiled in the kind of problems that had cost his predecessor his job, he would have to take firm action and he agreed that the police should be called in to investigate. However, if he thought that a police inquiry would clear up the matter, it only served to show that the auditors were right to be concerned.

The black hole they spotted was not the result of botched bookkeeping but something far worse. The constituency's treasurer Elizabeth Wilson had siphoned off money from the accounts over a five-year period. The sixty-two-year-old had failed to get a job in McConnell's office after he became the local MSP – a decision which had left her bitterly disappointed. She confessed to taking £7,000 from accounts, including the Red Rose Dinner account, but said she had paid the money back. The police investigation showed a total of £11,000 was involved in the fraud. The court was told Mrs Wilson embezzled the money because she had been in debt. She was fined £2,400 but escaped a jail sentence. However, it was alleged that, even before Hugh Mulholland started asking questions, some party officials were aware that Mrs Wilson had taken money and paid it back but they were trying to keep the matter under wraps. A Labour Party inquiry into the missing money cleared Jack McConnell of any blame.

With the benefit of hindsight, Mulholland also appeared to have been right to warn the local CLP off getting involved in high-profile fundraising initiatives like the Red Rose Dinners. However, it is not surprising that such an idea appealed to Jack McConnell. He had been instrumental in organising similar events for the Scottish Labour Party while he was General Secretary. His ability to win the support of the business community for such gatherings resulted in him being praised by the party in London. Red Rose events had proved to be successful for MPs like John Reid, who held such an event in his constituency.

In the case of the Motherwell and Wishaw dinner, it attracted unwanted controversy and not just for the missing funds. One of those who attended the event turned out to be Justin McAlroy, a convicted drug dealer. He owed money to two prominent Glasgow gangsters and, in a bid to keep several underworld figures onside, he offered them tickets to the prestigious event. It has now emerged that Paul Ferris was one of those to be offered a ticket but he declined to accept it. However, convicted criminals Stewart Boyd and John McCartney were among those who did dine with Lanarkshire's senior politicians that night. Six days after the dinner, McAlroy was shot dead outside his home in Cambuslang.

Although the controversy over the dinner and the missing funds proved that Hugh Mulholland had a point, there are still those in the local party who claim he is nothing more than a troublemaker who will do anything to harm McConnell or Frank Roy. But a source close to him said, 'He was persecuted over this . . . kept asking questions and he was right.'

Despite the obvious tensions between Jack McConnell and Hugh Mulholland, Mulholland says he remains on speaking terms with the First Minister.

# 16

# A LAPSE OF JUDGEMENT

The First Minister's office receives dozens of official invitations every week but, because of constraints on his time, only around half of them are accepted. Priority is given to invitations which reflect a political priority of the administration, which are for a good cause or which mark an anniversary. In April 2004, a letter arrived from the office of Junior Defence Minister Ivor Caplin, asking if the First Minister would like to join him and the army chiefs of staff for a celebration to mark the D-Day landings on 6 June. There was apparently no mention that the event would be the main commemoration of D-Day or that it was an international occasion. Even odder was the fact there was no mention of the royal family's attendance. Normal protocol dictates that there would be a discussion between the private offices of ministers regarding any event involving the royals. On this occasion, there was no phone call to follow up the letter.

The First Minister's office checked his diary for engagements that day and found that it had been ring-fenced to allow Jack to take time off for a family celebration. It was his son Mark's twenty-first birthday and Bridget had planned to have a party for him in the house that day. As a result the D-Day invitation was declined but an adviser wrote in the diary that the First Minister must mark D-Day in another way. The invitation was then circulated to other ministers and it was taken up by Andy Kerr who, at the time, had responsibility for external relations. Some time after the D-Day invitation had been turned down, Bridget decided to move Mark's twenty-first birthday party to the following weekend when more family members would be able to attend so, when a subsequent invitation came in, asking the First Minister if he would like to attend an anniversary celebration for the Royal and Ancient at St Andrews on 6 June, the diary showed that the day was free again. Given that it was an anniversary to mark Scotland's oldest golf course, McConnell accepted.

Since turning down the Normandy invitation, the First Minister's office had been in discussions with the veterans associations in Scotland over how they would most like him to commemorate the D-Day anniversary. They asked if the First Minister would be prepared to see off the old soldiers who were making the trip back to Normandy for the anniversary. In the week running up to the event, it was receiving publicity on a daily basis across Europe. Men in their eighties in failing health were making the journey back to Normandy to remember their colleagues who had died in the war. When Jack McConnell turned up at Waterloo Place in Edinburgh to wave off those Scots who would be among them, he had no idea that he was about to become engulfed in the biggest row of his leadership.

That afternoon at the daily press briefing, the civil servants were asked why the First Minister was not going to Normandy along with Tony Blair, George Bush and Vladimir Putin. They responded that he had something else in the diary. That something else had initially been his son's twenty-first birthday party but that had been postponed and the only entry was a golf club dinner. The revelation stunned the press corps. For eighteen months, they had struggled to find stories in McConnell's new government. The cabinet was united and the First Minister appeared not to have put a foot wrong. Journalists were desperate for a good story from the parliament and they couldn't believe their luck – on the day that world leaders were making the trip to Normandy to honour the war dead, Scotland's First Minister would be playing a round of golf.

That night, the news coverage of the decision was devastating for the First Minister. Even at this late stage, his office was not completely convinced that it had made a major misjudgement. McConnell and his advisers were confident they had a good relationship with the war veterans and suspected they had offended the Scottish media more than Scotland's soldiers but the next day's newspapers left the First Minister in no doubt about the scale of the anger he was facing. Ironically, that day, he was speaking at a conference in Edinburgh about how to promote Scotland' reputation abroad – over the previous twenty-four hours, he had risked doing it huge damage and, by this time, he realised it. While he spoke about the need for greater recognition of Scotland's achievements on the world stage, his advisers were furiously trying to rectify his mistake. McConnell knew he had to reverse the decision and his biggest fear was that it was too late – that, even if he wanted to go, he would be unable to do so at this late stage. However, the organisers confirmed that he would be able to go and the First Minister announced the dramatic U-turn.

A similar row erupted in Wales where the Welsh Assembly's First Secretary, Rhodri Morgan, had also declined the same invitation but, unlike McConnell, he stuck to his decision not to go. A source close to Jack said, '[Jack] didn't care if it was just a case of annoying the press but he said, if one veteran or one veteran's family were offended, then he wanted to go.' There followed much speculation over who was to blame for the debacle. It was reported that McConnell was furious with his advisers for failing to spot the PR disaster but Jack never blamed anyone on his team – he accepted that, if there was a fault, it must be his. Although he did not point the finger at his own staff, he was said to be angry about the way Whitehall had presented the invitation when it initially arrived. By not highlighting the importance of the event, the First Minister felt it was an easy mistake to make. What he must accept is that, even if he didn't realise the importance of the event when the invitation came in, he should certainly have done so in the week leading up to it.

Immediately after the event, Jack McConnell ordered a post-mortem into what went wrong. The inquest did not focus on the running of his office but on its links with other government departments in London. The First Minister spoke to Constitutional Affairs Minister Charles Falconer to express his concern over what had happened and demand that, in future, his office should be given clearer advice on invitations of such importance.

The disastrous handling of the D-Day invitation did not spoil the event for McConnell. He later told colleagues that it was 'a fabulous occasion to be part of'. At the time, the general perception was that McConnell had tried to get out of going to Normandy because he would only have been a bit-part player and he could, instead, indulge in his love of golf. In fairness, all the evidence is that Jack McConnell attaches a high level of importance to ensuring Scotland is seen as a powerful devolved nation and he tends to take any opportunities that arise to promote the country.

The timing of the row was also bad for Labour. It took place during the run-up to the European elections and the party hierarchy feared the D-Day decision could play badly with the voters. If McConnell had stuck to his plans to attend the golf dinner instead of going to Normandy, it is reasonable to assume it would have lost the party votes. However, Jack McConnell's abrupt about-turn seemed to be enough to prevent any political damage. All the same, it would be used against him for some time to come as an alleged example of his lack of judgement.

Unfortunately, the D-Day storm followed the First Minister's decision to promote a young Scottish fashion designer at the Tartan Day celebrations in New York that spring. In an attempt to boost Scotland's image, Jack McConnell decided to wear what he considered a trendy kilt to a charity fashion show. His outfit certainly grabbed the headlines – but for all the wrong reasons. The First Minister was accused of wearing a skirt and blouse. The papers generally agreed that he looked ridiculous and heaped derision upon him. While the offence caused by his decision to wear a fashion kilt is not in the same league as the offence caused to D-Day veterans, both were public relations mistakes which would haunt him.

With the benefit of hindsight, Jack McConnell very much regrets taking the decision to turn down the Normandy invitation and is furious with himself for not realising its importance. However, he does not regret wearing the much-criticised kilt. The First Minister had agreed to wear a creation by a twenty-five-year-old Scottish designer, Howie Nicholsby, to a charity fashion show in New York. Nicholsby specialises in making trendy kilts and the one Jack wore was a pinstripe design. The designer's company, 21st Century Kilts, also makes leather kilts, tweed ones and kilts made from army combat fatigues. Jack McConnell has worn a kilt since the age of seven or eight and, at every important family occasion he was taken to as a child, he would wear the traditional highland dress. From a young age, he had been told that McConnells tend to wear the MacDonald tartan so that is what he wore until recently. Shortly after becoming First Minister, he discovered that there is, in fact, a McConnell tartan. He had a kilt made in it and he took the kilt with him to New York. For most of the Tartan Day celebrations, Jack wore his McConnell tartan kilt. However, after agreeing to model a kilt for Howie Nicholsby, McConnell failed to arrange any fittings with the young designer. Nicholsby turned up in New York with several kilts in the expectation that one would fit the First Minister. The pinstripe kilt was the one that came closest to fitting but the matching jacket didn't so Jack agreed he would wear the kilt with only a shirt on the top.

The fashion show was a huge success and Jack was cheered loudly for having the nerve to wear such a daring outfit. That night, he went back to his New York hotel room satisfied that he had played a part in helping to promote Scotland and a young up-and-coming Scottish talent. The next morning, he was woken by a phone call from his wife Bridget who had seen pictures of him wearing the kilt in the papers. She left him in no doubt that he was not looking at his best. Jack's bravado from the night before disappeared as it hit him how he was being ridiculed back home. The decision to take part in a fashion show was partly a result of Jack realising that the first months of his leadership had been seen as dull. He felt he had lost a little bit of the sparkle that had earned him his Jack-the-Lad image which attracted supporters inside the Labour Party and among the voters. Jack the Lad was back – but only briefly.

In an act of defiance aimed at his critics, the First Minister opened the new Edinburgh showroom of 21st Century Kilts in January 2005. When the invitation arrived, one of his advisers was heard to threaten, 'If he does this, I'll resign!' But Jack couldn't resist – even if it meant giving the press another chance to dredge up his fashion faux pas. To this day McConnell believes it was a good idea to wear the controversial kilt but he just wishes the jacket had fitted so he could have worn the outfit properly.

Nicholsby has recently designed a plain bright-red kilt and jacket and it is rumoured that the First Minister is planning a purchase.

# 17

## SIR SEAN – A DIFFICULT
## RELATIONSHIP

The Labour Party has always had a difficult relationship with Scotland's most famous son, Sean Connery. The Hollywood actor is not only a Nationalist but also a loyal supporter and funder of the SNP. When the former Scottish Secretary, Michael Forsyth, suspected his party was set to lose power, he suggested Connery for a knighthood knowing that the next Scottish Secretary would be left to say yes or no to the honour. It was a trap the mischievous Forsyth could not resist laying for his successor whom he believed would be George Robertson. Knowing only too well how Robertson despised the Nats, Forsyth believed it would either be a very act hard swallow or the suggestion would be rejected out of hand and Connery would be slighted by the New Labour government.

Despite the fact Robertson did not get the job and Forsyth's successor ended up being Donald Dewar, the outcome was much as he predicted and Dewar dismissed the suggestion to honour the famous Scot. When news of the snub inevitably leaked, Dewar was left looking petty and Connery was furious. Relations between Sean Connery and the Labour establishment were appalling. The row no doubt amused Michael Forsyth but it became a serious problem for Labour.

The 'wrong' was subsequently righted and Sean Connery is now Sir Sean. The initial decision to deny Sean Connery an honour looked all the worse because Dewar had used his appeal during the referendum campaign. The actor came to Edinburgh to take part in the cross-party effort to persuade Scots to vote for a parliament with tax-raising powers. Connery felt he had been able to work with the Labour establishment for the greater good of Scotland but that they had been unable to give him recognition because he was not one of them. It has been a running sore ever since. The second First Minister, Henry McLeish, made strenuous efforts to involve Sir Sean in government events, realising that the actor could be a huge asset in helping to promote Scotland abroad and this is the approach which has been continued by Jack McConnell.

The First Minister met Sir Sean at the Tartan Day celebrations in 2002 but he did not receive a warm welcome. Although relations with the Labour Party were not nearly as bad as they had been, Sir Sean was unhappy over the Executive's Ryder Cup bid. Although Henry McLeish secured the event for 2013, he failed to land the 2009 championship. Connery had helped to push the bid but felt the Executive's presentation of it had been poor. The actor had long been promised that the government would find a fulfilling role for him in terms of promoting Scotland. To his mind, none had ever been forthcoming. His view was that Labour politicians blew hot and cold on him. Jack McConnell realised that it would take some time before Connery would trust a Scottish Labour government fully. But, when they met, they agreed they would try to work together and rebuild Connery's confidence in the Labour administration.

Later that year, the two met up again at the Champions League cup final in Glasgow and dined together that night. In September 2004, Sir Sean and his wife were invited to Bute House for dinner along with several other couples. The issue of his role for Scotland was not discussed – the evening was designed to be another step towards rebuilding the on-off relationship. Jack McConnell is determined to find a role for Sir Sean but believes it has to be carefully thought through. The First Minister knows that Sir Sean will always have a strong loyalty to the SNP but he also thinks he genuinely wants to help his country. Jack has asked both the Presiding Officer George Reid and the former Lord Provost of Edinburgh Eric Milligan, both of whom get on well with Connery, to act as intermediaries in the stand-off.

After years of being shunned by the Labour establishment, Sir Sean is now much sought after. Senior Labour politicians say the problem they have now is that the SNP are reluctant to let their biggest star go. One said, 'We are desperate to use him but the Nationalists are trying to keep him to themselves. He is their biggest asset and they have no intention of sharing him.'

# 18

# CRONYISM

The criticism most often levelled at Jack McConnell is that he is guilty of cronyism. Anyone who works as the General Secretary of a political party is bound to be regarded as a machine politician – particularly if they do it well. It is a job that often results in the holder making more enemies than friends as they carry out the leadership's bidding. It is for that reason that very few people who do such jobs ever successfully make the transition to frontline politics. Helen Liddell and the SNP's Michael Russell are, along with McConnell, two notable exceptions.

Jack McConnell's critics claim he is a machine politician who is not suited to the demands of high office. During his years as General Secretary of the party, he earned a reputation as a party fixer who used persuasion and threats to ensure the leadership got its way. In doing such a job, it was inevitable he would make enemies along the way but he made many more than the average MP would be expected to make during an entire career at Westminster. Jack McConnell was also better known to the Scottish press than many MPs were and this led to a degree of resentment among some high-profile shadow cabinet figures who were bitter about the amount of press coverage the General Secretary would attract compared to them.

Because, when he was General Secretary, he was not an elected politician, McConnell's quotes were often attributed to a 'senior Labour source' or a 'highly placed insider'. Many of the briefings he gave would be off the record and aimed at offering journalists an insight into the leadership's thinking but in such a way that it could not be cast up at a later date in the form of a direct quote. As a result, McConnell came to be regarded as a 'shadowy' figure who operated in the background. Given his role at the time, he did little to discourage the image of himself as an effective backroom wheeler and dealer. However, since making the transition into frontline politics, it is one he has been keen to cast off.

There are still those who refuse to believe that such an effective machine politician can adapt to the different demands of party leader. Frontline politics demands the holder has greater skills as a communicator and an ability to persuade both cabinet colleagues and the public by the force of their arguments and not the threat of the party rulebook. During the first year of the Scottish Parliament, many of McConnell's critics claim that he carried on using the same modus operandi as he did while he was General Secretary. There is a widespread belief that McConnell, as Finance Minister, did not have enough scope in his brief to keep him occupied. He is often accused of using his spare time to indulge in so-called 'politicking'.

While there is little hard evidence that McConnell carried on briefing the press, there is more to suggest that he was using this period to build up a network of supporters and this would stand him in good stead when the opportunity came to stage a leadership challenge. That is why some say the late First Minister, Donald Dewar, remained wary of his Finance Minister. However, after he tried and failed to secure the leadership following Dewar's death, McConnell took advice from his trusted allies on how he should conduct himself under the new regime. He could have been seen as the failed leadership contender, frozen out by cabinet colleagues – a man with his ambition thwarted who had been left bitter and resentful. That was always the risk of going for the leadership but not winning.

Both Professor Mike Donnelly and Neil Stewart told him he must bury himself in the brief. Stewart also told him the importance of sticking by his supporters just as they had stood by him. At Westminster, the smart sacked cabinet ministers are seen to 'walk the walk'. Within hours of losing the trappings of ministerial office, they walk the length of the terrace at the House of Commons, making small talk with colleagues. It is, in almost all cases, the last thing they feel like doing but it serves to give the impression of strength of character. The easier alternative is to curl up and die. Stewart told McConnell to do the Scottish equivalent of 'walking the walk' – to go to the black and white corridor outside the parliament chamber and show everyone that he had not been left battered and bruised by the experience but was stronger as a result of it. Stewart told him, 'You owe it to your supporters – if you crawl away in a corner, they will feel you have left them exposed.'

At the time, McConnell's approach would have been seen as a typical act of bravado. Like so many of his actions, it was carefully thought through. Far from an impromptu chat with colleagues, it was part of a well-orchestrated plan. The new First Minister, Henry McLeish, also realised he was dealing with a smart politician. He had watched him operate under the Dewar administration and came to the conclusion that McConnell did not have enough to occupy him. McLeish thought, if he piled work on Jack, it would limit the time he had on his hands to plot. The fact that McLeish handed him the Education portfolio helped him to knuckle down. If McConnell has a real passion in politics, then it lies in Education. But there is no doubt that, during his year as Education Minister, McConnell continued to network as he has always done.

The backbench group that had gathered round to support him during his first leadership attempt remained close to him. On Wednesday evenings, when most MSPs spend the night in Edinburgh, McConnell would dine with his friends from the backbenches. On one such night, by coincidence, he ended up in the same restaurant as the First Minister, Henry

McLeish. While McLeish sat at a table for three in the dining room of the Holyrood Hotel, McConnell enjoyed the company of seventeen of his parliamentary colleagues.

McLeish tried to counter McConnell's charm offensive by making time to see MSPs on an individual basis. The strategy could have had some impact but one MSP said:

> At first, we gave him a chance but, when we compared our sessions to those of our colleagues, we realised we were all being told the same thing. It didn't help when Henry got in the lift one day along with Bristow Muldoon and, in an attempt to be friendly, said, 'Hi, Ken.' Poor Bristow thought that Ken McIntosh had got in the lift beside him until he realised it was only him and Henry who were there. That was the fundamental difference between Henry and Jack.

McConnell had such a strong grouping around him that it was obvious that, if he ever made it to the top job, he would want some of these people around him at the cabinet table. When his day finally came, there was much nervousness among Henry McLeish's team as almost all of them believed they were for the chop. However, they were lulled into a false sense of security when McConnell authorised his then press spokesman, Tom Little, to brief the papers that, contrary to the rumours circulating, there would be no 'night of the long knives'. The statement was true but only in so far as there then followed a 'morning of the long knives'. Out went Henry McLeish's most trusted allies – the Finance Minister, Angus McKay, and the Business Manager, Tom McCabe, were axed and the Communities Minister, Jackie Baillie, with whom McConnell has been engaged in a stand-off for many years, was another totally expected casualty. The relationship between Baillie and McConnell has been poor ever since she was Chair of the

Scottish Labour Party and he was General Secretary – although, like many feuds in the Scottish Labour Party, nobody appears to know the reason for their fall-out.

The Transport Minister, Sarah Boyack, had been the victim of a hostile press campaign for much of her tenure. She had a massive workload and was never given a junior minister and nor was she blessed with the best civil servants. McConnell decided to drop her from the team – not because he didn't rate her but because he thought she needed a break from the constant sniping. McConnell attempted to demote Susan Deacon from her Health portfolio to the Communities post. Rather than accept what she saw as a lesser job, Deacon told McConnell she would not sit in the cabinet and watch Malcolm Chisholm do 'her' job so she decided to resign, making the reshuffle look even more drastic than the one McConnell had planned. Later that day, McConnell also told the Solicitor General Neil Davidson QC, who had been a big Labour Party donor, he was out so he could replace him with Elish Angiolini.

As Team McLeish headed for the backbenches, McConnell also rewarded some of those who had been loyal to him over the years. Patricia Ferguson, who was his leadership campaign manager, was made Business Manager. Andy Kerr was made Finance Minister and Mike Watson became the Sports Minister. Jack did keep some ministers who had voted for Henry McLeish rather than him in the previous leadership contest. In spite of their allegiance to his predecessor, McConnell gave seats round the cabinet table to Cathy Jamieson, Malcolm Chisholm, Margaret Curran and Iain Gray.

However, the reshuffle resulted in accusations of cronyism that have continued to dog the First Minister. The perception, rightly or wrongly, was that talented politicians had been replaced by people with less skill. At the time, in a jibe at the new cabinet line-up, one of the sacked ministers proclaimed that 'now we are a backbench of all the talents'. The brutality of that first cabinet reshuffle gave the impression that the new First Minister was more interested in settling old scores than in picking the right people to do the job. But McConnell did not wield the axe for fun. He had a difficult calculation to make – should he keep people that he believed would do everything they could to undermine him or make a clean break with the past and choose those he wanted near him?

As he pondered his decision, a spat took place with Wendy Alexander. McConnell had told her he was mulling over plans to give her the job as Enterprise Minister but, instead of linking it with Lifelong Learning as had previously been the case, he was considering joining it with the Transport portfolio. By all accounts, Wendy went berserk. That Sunday, the newspapers were full of criticism of the idea – there were letters of objection from university principals and members of the business community. McConnell was in London ahead of his meeting with the Queen the following day. He was so angry about the reports that he called Alexander, who also happened to be in London, and arranged a meeting to confront her. They met in the lobby of a London hotel off Marble Arch. McConnell looked Alexander in the eye and told her he would not tolerate such briefings. He was particularly angry because, that weekend, he had already come to the conclusion that he would not change the Enterprise brief and felt the public row was an unnecessary one. Alexander agreed she would not use such tactics in the future. After the confrontation the two went on to have a productive meeting during which Alexander made some points McConnell was to take on board.

Those close to McConnell say he conducted an extensive reshuffle of the cabinet because he was very aware of the instability that divided cabinets can bring. In the early days, the First Minister's priority was to end the cabinet infighting which had beset his two predecessors. He deliberately wanted to send a signal that loyalty mattered to him and, more importantly, to the future stability of the administration. He also wanted it to be clear that disloyalty would not be tolerated. McConnell knew all too well the damage that could be done by cabinet colleagues undermining him in meetings or briefing against him to the press. He had seen it done to Donald Dewar and had been accused of doing it, himself, to Henry McLeish. Many of McLeish's supporters think that McConnell was always sniping from the sidelines. It is more likely that any briefing against Henry came from McConnell acolytes rather than from McConnell himself – although it must be admitted that the result was much the same.

However, McConnell's cabinet reshuffle was to play out worse than he could have imagined. According to Sam Galbraith, McConnell was forced to put some of his friends in the cabinet because he owed his position to them. Sam said, 'The difference between him and Donald was that Donald had friends but he was secure in the position and did not owe it to anyone. Jack had people who had done him favours which had to be repaid.'

Although the Industry Minister, Wendy Alexander, had threatened to stand against him for the leadership, McConnell was keen to keep her in his team. He believed that he needed to be challenged and thought Alexander, along with Deacon, would be the best people to give an alternative voice in the cabinet. Deacon's decision to quit at the time of the reshuffle and Alexander's subsequent decision to leave the government were a source of great regret to him. This could have been as much about the damage that losing two high-profile young women from his team would do him as it was about their absence from cabinet discussions. It is also clear that McConnell holds no grudge against Sarah Boyack, his old friend from his days in Scottish Labour Action. He simply felt that she had been unfairly burdened and that, if she was given some time out, she could make a successful comeback.

McConnell's leadership rival, Malcolm Chisholm, was rewarded with the Health brief, sparking rumours that a deal had been done in which Chisholm was persuaded to end his bid for the job. Some of Alexander's supporters were left angry because, at the last minute, she had opted not to challenge for the leadership but she did not appear to have secured any guarantees for her supporters before withdrawing. Ironically, the former Kinnock aide, Neil Stewart, had advised both McConnell and Deacon on how to handle reshuffles, expecting his advice to be taken by his protégés in relation to Henry McLeish when he was First Minister. He had told them how to handle a First Minister who tried giving them a portfolio they didn't want. The message was clear – stay in the building and make it clear you are causing a crisis for the leader. Deacon's decision to resign certainly helped the reshuffle announcement to play badly.

According to McConnell's friend and political ally, Lord Robertson, the First Minister is unfairly criticised for cronyism. He said:

> His first instinct was to form a cabinet of people he could trust – that is natural. In doing that, he only did what Blair, Bush, Clinton and Putin did. That is how you run a government – certainly until you are confident enough to put other people in place.

Since becoming First Minister, McConnell has made changes. He sacked two ministers coincidentally both of Tourism, Culture and Sport, who were close friends and strong supporters. He decided to sack Frank McAveety – not because he was famously late for a statement because he was eating pie and chips but because he felt that he was not displaying strong enough leadership. McAveety was a close friend of the McConnell family and the decision was taken badly by McConnell's son Mark who was bitterly disappointed.

Mike Watson had known McConnell since their days together on the Labour Coordinating Committee in the 1980s. He had strongly urged Jack to stand for the leadership at the time when the McLeish camp were seeking an anointment of their man and had been centrally involved in both leadership campaigns. But Mike had been criticised for putting his constituency interests ahead of collective cabinet decisions and he realised that he may have crossed the line in his support for the closure-threatened Victoria Infirmary in Glasgow. Watson had taken advice from McConnell's special advisers over the dilemma and the First Minister assured him that he had his backing. However, after the 2003 election, the First Minister told him that the Liberal Democrats had been pushing for a third cabinet seat during the coalition talks. He hadn't wanted to give it to them so he was demoting the post of minister for Tourism, Culture and Sport to the junior ranks and there would be no place for Watson in the new line-up.

The idea that Jack was losing the post rather than the minister failed to soften the blow for Watson because he had made it clear he would have been happy to serve in the junior ranks. He said:

I loved the job. It was the best eighteen months of my political life. I had begun to develop a number of initiatives that I wanted to see through to their conclusion. I felt very let down because I wasn't offered the position that Frank got. It took me six months to get over it.

But he adds:

I am still loyal to Jack and the job he is doing. I certainly don't think he is guilty of cronyism. When I think back to the night

Henry resigned, when a group of us met in Sylvia Jackson's house to plan to leadership campaign, very few of us have or have had jobs in the government.

Sylvia Jackson, Cathy Peattie, Karen Whitefield and Janis Hughes were all key members of the leadership team who have been bypassed for ministerial office.

There is some evidence that McConnell is slowly trying to build bridges. After the 2003 election, he brought Tom McCabe back into the cabinet as Finance Minister and he promoted Rhona Brankin to the post of Deputy Health Minister – despite the fact that she admitted she voted against him in the first leadership contest and would have done so in the second if Wendy Alexander had stood. However, there is criticism, mainly from other parties, that Karen Gillion has been overlooked for promotion. Opposition politicians believe she is the victim of Lanarkshire politics. She backed Bill Tynan for the Motherwell and Wishaw seat over McConnell. In West of Scotland politics, that is the kind of decision which is not quickly forgotten – if ever. And some within the Labour group say that Pauline McNeil has never been given a job for no other reason than she is seen as being too close to Wendy Alexander. The former Education Minister, Sam Galbraith, who left the government following Dewar's death, is one of those who think that McConnell is guilty of cronyism. He said, 'He is a typical town-council fixer – he can't help himself. But he shouldn't be because Jack is so much better than that. He does have real ability – he should just give up the machine politics.'

In his last cabinet reshuffle, there was also some evidence that McConnell no longer feels indebted to Patricia Ferguson and Andy Kerr to the same extent. It is understood that Ferguson wanted to remain in her role as Business Manager but was given no option but to move to Tourism, Culture and

Sport. Likewise, Andy Kerr is understood to have been reluctant to move to the Health brief, which will prove extremely difficult if he is to make an impact on waiting lists and adopt the modernising agenda being followed by the NHS in England. But the decision to move Margaret Curran from her job as Communities Minister to the more anonymous territory of Business Manager brought renewed accusations of cronyism. Curran had made a big impact in the Communities brief – so much so that she was awarded the title of Politician of the Year by *The Herald* newspaper. McConnell's enemies claim she was becoming too successful in the job and was moved because she was looking like future leadership material. Curran strenuously denies being the victim of a reshuffle, insisting that McConnell, far from sidelining her, gave her the job she really wanted. He also made her the unofficial 'Minister for *Newsnight*' – the politician he trusted most to get the Executive's message across to the media.

The former SNP leader, John Swinney, who was brought down after a period of vicious infighting in his own party, still believes that a leader has to be more inclusive than McConnell has been. Despite his own experience of back-stabbing, he thinks McConnell has got it wrong. He said:

I don't think there is any question about it – Jack is guilty of cronyism. No matter what I said at the time, I think Donald Dewar made a cabinet selection of able people. He knew that Henry McLeish was a serial briefer, he probably regarded Jack as a young man in a hurry but he would never have contemplated not having them in his team. When I led the SNP, there were people around me whose style of operating I didn't care for but you have to pick the best people whether you happen to like them or not. If you don't, the consequence is that public services suffer as a result.

Swinney's view is not shared by another former party leader. Neil Kinnock was credited with doing much of the work that made Labour electable again. He took on the militants and drummed them out of the party. He also spotted talent coming through the party and used it in his crusade to beat the Tories. He is quick to round on people who accused McConnell of being little more than a party apparatchik. According to Kinnock, Jack possesses a rare combination of political skills as an organiser and communicator and they have equipped him to make the transition from machine politician to party leader. Kinnock said:

> Jack is an unusual combination – a convincing politician, a good speaker and a hell of an organiser – it is very rare to find all of those qualities in one person. He is a bit like Charles Clarke in that respect or John Reid – and, of course, Gordon Brown possesses those attributes.

It was Jack's skill as an organiser which made him a valued General Secretary during the '90s. Kinnock first met McConnell when he made a pre-election visit to Stirling in 1991. McConnell was a young councillor in the area at the time and was asked to coordinate the key visit. He planned it with precision – from organising the transport to deciding whom the Labour leader should meet and what the photo opportunities should be. The high point of the day was to be a visit to a rugby club where Kinnock was to meet the great and the good of the local area, including the Labour councillors. As Kinnock's car drew up to the club exactly on time, inside the councillors were lined up, waiting to shake hands with the leader they believed was about to sweep them to electoral victory. But, as Kinnock walked towards the club, he spotted some kids playing with a rugby ball. Instead of proceeding into the club as planned, he vaulted over a fence to join the youngsters. Inside, the assembled dignitaries waited patiently until their next engagement beckoned. Labour leader or not, they could wait no longer. McConnell panicked and asked his old friend Neil Stewart if he could interrupt the impromptu rugby match, to be told, 'Only if you are very brave!' McConnell then hastily organised a bus to take the councillors on to their next engagement and rearranged the meeting with Kinnock later in the day.

The smoothness of the visit impressed the party hierarchy and, it is said, helped him to get the job of General Secretary. Kinnock said:

> I had no idea I was causing such a problem – I had just assumed that we were going into the club to see some of the lads. If I had known these people were there, then I would have behaved myself. But I'm told we got more votes out of that rugby club than anyone would have thought possible.

The former party leader says, even then, as a local councillor in his mid twenties, McConnell stood out. The same party figures who rated McConnell as a young General Secretary also rate him as a First Minister. On a visit to Scotland in 2004, Kinnock went to the parliament chamber to watch Jack McConnell during First Minister's Questions and was not disappointed. He said, 'He was informative, very agile and highly political which I strongly approve of.' Kinnock worked closely with the first First Minister Donald Dewar and also knows Henry McLeish well. He said, 'Jack is a different kind of guy. He took over in very difficult circumstances and has come out the other side looking very capable.'

While McConnell can impress senior party figures, he has failed to convince some of those nearer home. The cronyism allegation is levelled at McConnell not only by his opponents but also by his friends. When friends who have been on the receiving end of his ruthlessness speak out, it should, in theory, go some way to countering the cronyism charge but, in the case of Tommy Sheppard, who lost his job as McConnell's deputy, it only adds to the suspicion of guilt. Sheppard feels that, despite their friendship, McConnell didn't do as much as he could have to stand by him. He believes McConnell is now guilty of putting loyalty ahead of ability. He said:

> He should have left Susan Deacon in the Health job – they have a shared background and come from the same traditions – but he obviously had promises to keep to other people. The objective is to surround himself with those who share his passion for a quiet life and are keen to fly clear of political turbulence.

It is only when McConnell is actively seen to be burying the hatchet and hands plum jobs to some people he strongly dislikes that many of his critics will be silenced on this issue. They may have a long wait.

# 19

# MY DAD, THE FIRST MINISTER

Hannah McConnell's dad might have the most important job in Scotland, with all the trappings that power brings, but she didn't have the easiest start in life. The twenty-six-year-old is now busy carving out a good career for herself working for the British Council in London. Strikingly tall and slim, she is intelligent, witty and self-assured, with the poise of a woman a decade older. Hannah has a well-paid, interesting job, a wide circle of friends and a great relationship with her parents and her younger brother Mark. From the outside, she looks like a young woman who has it all.

Although she clearly looks like someone on track to make a success of her life, it could so easily have gone wrong for her. By her own admission, she was an unhappy child. Hannah was born to Bridget McConnell and her first husband Richard Brown, a musician with the '60s rock band Procol Harum. It was, by all accounts, a bad marriage in which Hannah's mother was both mentally and physically abused. From the time her children were babies, Bridget McConnell was forced to work long hours. Despite the problems she had at home, she was determined that her kids would not suffer because of them. She fought hard to climb her way through the ranks of local government so she could provide a better life for her family and not see them trapped in an unhappy situation.

Hannah was just four years old when she realised her mum was being abused and it is hardly surprising that she was traumatised by it. However, she now talks about it in a matter-of-fact way, as if she was describing something that had happened to someone else – as if describing another life. Certainly the one she leads today is very different from the one she was born into. Hannah's father was never violent towards her or her brother Mark, now twenty-one, but both children were deeply affected by their mother's unhappiness.

Bridget McConnell was working as a Community Arts Officer with Stirling Council when she made the decision to get out of her marriage. She had just met Jack McConnell who, at the time, was a rising star on the council and shared her interests in the arts. It wasn't long before Hannah and Mark were to meet the man who was to become their father by adopting them. If Bridget McConnell had other relationships between deciding to leave her husband and meeting Jack, then her children were shielded from them. Although Jack met the kids early on in his relationship with Bridget, it was after the couple knew they were firmly committed to each other.

Hannah was six years old when she met Jack but she doesn't recall the first time she was introduced to him. She remembers being taken to visit him in his flat in Stirling and the first time she went to Arran. She said:

> My dad obviously hadn't been round kids that much and he turned up wearing a pair of white jeans, a white shirt and a white jacket. By the end of the boat journey, he was covered in Coke which we had accidentally spilled all over him. He could have lost his temper but he didn't – he laughed it off. He was great with us and we loved him being around.

Hannah and Mark took to Jack instantly. Hannah was impressed that he listened to the same kind of music that she did. And the children were thrilled to discover that Jack's parents owned a hotel. Their grandparents lavished them with attention and allowed them the run of the place. Hannah still talks excitedly about the times they stayed at the Rock Hotel in Blackwaterfoot where they were allowed to help themselves to as much ice cream as they could eat. Hannah paints a picture of a childhood divided in two. The early part was dominated by insecurity and unhappiness and the second part was one of a normal happy family life. It is perhaps because of the first part that she appreciated the second part so much. Although the kids liked Jack as soon as they met him, the most significant impact he made on Hannah's life was to change the way she saw her mother: Hannah said, 'She was happy, relaxed and enjoying herself. I had never seen her like that before. And here was a man who was such a contrast to the man we had had in our lives before – it was great.'

However, Jack coming into their lives did not solve Bridget, Hannah and Mark's problems. In fact, for a time, their new-found happiness may have exacerbated some of their troubles. Bridget had started divorce proceedings against her husband. The process was to be a lengthy and bitter one. Richard Brown fought for joint custody of his children and they were forced to go to live with him in Fife for several weeks. Between Hannah's mother leaving her father and marrying Jack, she went to five different primary schools.

> I wasn't doing very well at school. While we were up north, we had to learn Gaelic. It was a very unsettling time. I never felt that my biological father wanted us for the right reasons. It was as if we were just part of his belongings and nobody else was going to have us.

After the divorce was finalised, things settled down for a time but, when Jack and Bridget decided that he should adopt her children, there were more problems to come. A friend had mentioned to them that they should consider the possibility. At the time, neither of them had realised it would be possible but the more they thought about it, the more sense it seemed to make. Jack set up home with Bridget and the children in late 1987 and they were planning to marry. The process of adopting Hannah and Mark could not begin until after the couple were married. Just as Hannah has no recollection of meeting Jack, nor does she remember being sat down to be told that her mother was going to marry him.

> I think we must just have been expecting it. I don't remember a big discussion about it but we were pleased that they were getting married. My mum felt it was appropriate that we were adopted and we were happy with that. I remember a few sessions with social workers.

There ensued a bitter battle for custody of the children as their biological father contested the adoption. Hannah was desperate for Jack to become their father in the eyes of the law. During the final interview with the social worker who was putting together the case, Hannah feared her brother had blown the chance. Throughout the conversation, he sat upside down on the settee with his legs thrown over the back of it. When the social worker asked whether there was anything about Jack that either of them would like to change if he were to become their dad, Hannah was quick to jump in and reply that there was not. She felt a lump develop in her throat when her younger brother piped up shouting, 'Yes – there is something I would like to change about him!' As the social worker sat with her pen poised ready to take note of Jack's potential failing as a father Mark, said, 'I would like him to change his haircut.' On 5 March 1991, a sheriff ruled that Jack McConnell should become father to Hannah and Mark, who were then aged eleven and seven. It was a highly unusual decision to take parental rights away from a biological father and grant them to another man instead. However, after just one hearing, the sheriff was convinced by the case and found in Jack's favour. It is a date that the family celebrate annually as adoption day. The First Minister has described the first time that Hannah called him dad as the happiest day of his life. She says, 'It was just spontaneous – it seemed natural. Nobody told me I should do it – I just wanted to.'

After the adoption went through, Jack decided that he did not want to have any other children with Bridget. Perhaps because he realised the effect their early childhood had had on Hannah and Mark, he threw himself into making their home life as secure and loving as he possibly could. Some of Jack's close friends believe that, for a man who loves children, it must have been a sacrifice to make the decision not to have any more kids but that it not his view. And it is a decision that, even years later, Hannah McConnell appreciates.

> We had been through a difficult time and were probably quite damaged by it. We were not asked our view about whether they should have more children but I am glad that he made that decision. I think it could have been very difficult for us if another child had come along. My dad made us feel very loved and secure for the first time in our lives and I am extremely grateful for that.

As the children of a former teacher, Hannah and Mark were encouraged in their school work by their father. Despite his hectic life as the Labour Party's General Secretary, he would take time every evening to help the kids with their homework. For many years, Bridget McConnell earned significantly more than her husband but she had to work long hours and endure a long commute to her job at Fife Council. Jack would be the one who got the kids out to school and was home first to look after them. Hannah says:

> I don't think I would have gone to university if it hadn't been for the way my dad encouraged me. He was always keen for us to do well at school and made us study more than we would have.

Unlike her younger brother, Hannah has taken a strong interest in politics since she was at school. She joined the Labour Party when she was sixteen and became active in Young Labour around the time her dad was the General Secretary of the party. At a time when many teenage girls become more distant from their parents, Hannah remained very close to both. With her father's encouragement, she addressed a Scottish Labour Party conference when she was just seventeen years old. She also spent hours on the campaign trail with him.

> I used to love going out canvassing with him and listening to him talk to people and win them round. I would take a note of all the comments we got on the doorsteps so we could analyse them later.

There was some tension in Hannah's relationship with her father around the time she met her first boyfriend. She says, 'He was very protective and became quite strict – I don't think he liked the idea very much.' Other than that, there don't appear to have been many teenage battles in the McConnell household. Hannah believes that it is partly because she has young parents who understood the things she wanted to do and because she shared interests with them.

> Even when I was seventeen or eighteen, I realised that, if they didn't want me to do something, it was because they were

acting in my interests, not because they were out to spoil my fun or that they were out of touch.

Hannah followed in her dad's footsteps by going to Stirling University where she studied Politics and Economics. After graduating, she announced she wanted to go to live in Vancouver for a year, much to her mother's concern. She was just twenty years old and Bridget was reluctant to see her go abroad. Hannah says:

> Dad was much more relaxed about it. I think he knew that I wouldn't end up in jail or do anything stupid and he understood it was a good thing for me to do. It was a good year and they came to visit me there.

Jack is just eighteen years older than Hannah and the relationship they have now is almost more like that of friends than a father and daughter. She confides in him about her personal life, asks for his advice in her working life and dishes out criticism about his when she feels it is needed.

Although Hannah works in London she still takes an interest in Scottish politics. For a time, she worked for the Falkirk East MP, Michael Connarty, in his office in the House of Commons. As a shrewd political operator, Hannah refuses to talk in detail about the political issues on which she disagrees with her dad about. However, she admits raising concerns with him about the Dungavel Detention Centre. 'I have pestered him about one or two things and he certainly listens to what I have to say but I'm not sure that anything I have said has influenced him in any way.'

Hannah's closeness to her parents was emphasised by her decision to spend a New Year holiday with them at the turn of 2005 rather than spend the time with friends. The fact that her parents were going to stay at Kirsty Wark's villa in Majorca probably helped make up her mind. Hannah has known Kirsty and her husband Alan since she was a child and gets on well with both. She is also very fond of their two children Caitlin and James.

> I knew Kirsty and Alan before they were married and I remember going to see Caitlin when she was just a day or two old. They are like an extension of the family. I think of Caitlin and James like cousins.

Little did Hannah realise when she agreed to go on the holiday that it would attract such huge press attention. She was completely surprised by the row that followed her parents' decision to go on the trip. Asked if it angered her, Hannah's response is clearly thought out:

> No, because, if it angered me, then that would mean that it had really got to me and I don't let it affect me that much. I would say it left me feeling very frustrated. This was a story of two families who have known each other for many years choosing to go on holiday together. I think it would be a real story if my dad told them we couldn't speak to them any more now that he is the First Minister. It is laughable to say there is influence there – as if they spent the whole time plotting. The only thing we plotted was which family would win at Scrabble and we spent more time discussing what I would wear to my boyfriend's house and what presents I should take for his family than anything else.

Although Hannah McConnell understands the way the press work, it is clear she thinks that the level of intrusion into her family's life in recent years has gone too far. If she doesn't admit to being angered, then she is obviously irked at some of the areas of their life which attract headlines. She cites her mother's car being broken into as one example. The fact that she dated the TV presenter John Leslie a couple of times is something else that she believes is irrelevant to the public interest.

It is obvious that Hannah finds it easier to live in London while her father carries out the job of First Minister and she avoids reading the Scottish newspapers most of the time.

> I don't think I could live in Scotland at the moment – it's too much of a goldfish bowl. I just wish they would give people their privacy. My mum has her own life but everything she does is scrutinised and I find that very frustrating and unfair on her. It's dreadful reading things about your parents in the papers when you know that it's not true. I see my dad working almost every hour that there is in the day and all people want to go on about is who he is going on holiday with. Sometimes I wonder if his job is worth doing – it seems such a thankless task. But then I speak to him and I know he loves it and gets so much out of it.

Despite seeing the drawbacks and pressures that go with the job of being First Minister, Hannah McConnell has not ruled out engaging in Scottish public life in the future. Asked if she would consider standing for the Scottish Parliament herself, she smiles and says, 'I'm not sure, not at the moment.'

Jack McConnell did not come from a political family but the McConnells may yet end up being a Scottish political dynasty.

# 20

# TONY BLAIR – FROM FRIEND TO PHONEY

On 7 June 2004, Scotland's First Minister, Jack McConnell, sat in his office and contemplated a threat he never imagined he would have to make. It was a tactic of last resort in dealing with a politician he believed he could not trust but it still caused Jack great sadness that it had come to this – threatening a politician he once admired, trusted and considered a friend. In June 2004, just days before the Prime Minister was due to announce that the next G8 Summit of World Leaders would be held at Gleneagles in Perthshire, Jack McConnell felt forced to write to him to make sure that, as First Minister of Scotland, he received a written guarantee from the PM that Westminster would cover the huge cost that hosting the summit would entail. He authorised his closest aides to tell Number Ten that, unless he received a written reply, he would go public and refuse to support the decision.

For weeks before he wrote the letter, Jack had been trying to get an agreement from the Prime Minister that the UK government would pick up the cost of the massive security operation that would have to be staged around the event to be held in July 2005. He knew that tens of thousands of extra police officers would have to be drafted in to protect Tony Blair, US President George Bush, Russian leader Vladimir Putin and the leaders of Japan (Junichiro Koizumi), France (Jacques Chirac), Germany (Gerhard Schroeder), Italy (Silvio Berlusconi) and Canada (Paul Martin).

Previous summits have attracted mass riots and the security bill was estimated at tens of millions of pounds. The UK government would be hosting the prestigious event and, as Scotland's First Minister, Jack McConnell was initially delighted when he was told that it was to be held in Perthshire. However, as the announcement of the venue for the summit approached, he became increasingly concerned that the Westminster government had not made a firm commitment to cover the costs.

Whenever he raised the issue with the PM, Tony Blair would tell him, 'Don't worry about that — it will be taken care of.' If McConnell thought he could have taken Tony Blair at his word, then that reassurance from the PM would probably have been enough to satisfy him. But bitter experience from the previous six years or so meant he knew that he could not rely on Blair to deliver.

Over the previous years, he had suffered one personal let-down after another at the hands of Blair. At first, he brushed aside his disappointments but later, when the PM did not stand by him when he contested senior positions in the party, he felt hurt. Now that it had come to an issue on which he felt the Scottish Parliament and the Scottish people could be let down, it was a matter of betrayal. For weeks, Jack had pleaded with the Treasury for a guarantee that the Scottish taxpayers would not be left with a substantial bill for the G8 Summit — none was forthcoming. McConnell was only too aware of the hostility between Number Ten and the Treasury. He thought that, because it was a commitment that Tony Blair had given informally, Brown could disagree and withhold the money.

What he wanted was written confirmation from Tony Blair — nobody else — that the Treasury would foot the entire bill. Without a firm promise from Blair that the costs would be met, McConnell also suffered the embarrassment of having to own up to the situation at a meeting of the full cabinet. Not only were his own Labour colleagues in no doubt about the state of relations but Liberal Democrat ministers were also made aware of the tensions which existed among their opponents.

When Jack felt he was left no option but to tell Blair that he would make a public announcement about the cash row and the implications it could have for the safety of the leaders of the eight richest countries in the world, he knew he had to be prepared to act on his threat – and he was. McConnell did receive a letter from Number Ten. Tony Blair's senior policy advisor, Alasdair McGowan, replied on 11 June 2004, confirming that extra funding would be made available and, at last, McConnell felt he could welcome the G8 announcement. However, over the following months, the commitment failed to materialise. It appeared to have been caught up in the Blair–Brown feud of that winter. Perhaps because of Jack's past loyalty, the Prime Minister's office continued to put off making the commitment to foot the bill in full in the belief that he would not do anything to damage Blair. McConnell was well aware of just how bad the relationship between Brown and Blair had become and he suspected the Prime Minister was not prepared to speak to his Chancellor to resolve the issue. That fear appeared to be confirmed when one senior aide at Number Ten told Jack's office, 'We are not prepared to use up political capital on this.' What he meant was that Number Ten had bigger battles of their own to fight with Number Eleven and the Prime Minister was not going to go to the wall just to help Jack.

For months, the First Minister was left seething by Blair's attitude but he stopped short of following through on his threat to make a public announcement. Once again, he had been bought off by the promise of further discussions and these either didn't materialise or, if they did, they proved unsatisfactory. The crux of the row was this – the UK government believed that the Scottish budget had money built in to it to reflect the fact that there would be such events from time to time as there were in

England and, because of this, the Scottish Executive should foot the bill. McConnell's argument was that the G8 Summit was no ordinary event and so the UK government should pay the security costs.

The row finally came to a head in February 2005 when Tayside police wrote to the Executive to ask for money to pay for the training of officers who would be working at the time of the summit. The First Minister was not prepared to make the commitment until he had finally resolved the row with the Prime Minister. Jack told a handful of key staff to pencil in a date in mid February when he could make a statement to parliament revealing the Prime Minister's refusal to commit money for Scotland to stage the G8 Summit.

Once again, the First Minister was bought off at the eleventh hour by yet another promise of a discussion on the issue. This time, there was a discussion but, when it did take place, it was not with Blair but with the Chancellor. The two men talked both on the phone and in person and, after months of battling with Downing Street, Gordon Brown finally gave Jack McConnell the promise that he had been looking for. He pledged £20 million from the Treasury to cover the security costs just forty-eight hours before the Chancellor's speech in March.

Since the G8 row, Jack's close friends claim that he feels his 'life would be easier if Gordon Brown was Prime Minister'. Jack McConnell, once one of Tony Blair's strongest supporters, now has a better working relationship with Gordon Brown.

For years, Jack McConnell had been impressed by Tony Blair and his style of leadership but, even before the G8 row, the gloss had worn off their relationship. The personal let-downs he could have dealt with but, since he had become First Minister, McConnell was deeply disappointed by the lack of support he got from Number Ten. As the G8 row came to a head, it was the moment that Jack McConnell decided that being First Minister of Scotland meant putting Scotland's interests ahead of his party's and his government's. Jack was no longer a Blairite but had become his own man.

The extent of the breakdown in relations between Scotland's First Minister and the Prime Minister had never erupted in public. Their relationship has deteriorated slowly and quietly over the years and it will take many in the Labour Party by surprise because Jack McConnell has long been regarded as a Blairite. Some figures in the party did notice that the relations between the two men appeared to be cool at the Scottish Labour Party Conference in March 2005. During his speech, Tony Blair lavished praise on the Chancellor Gordon Brown and on the former Deputy Scottish Secretary George Foulkes who was about to stand down as an MP. He did likewise with the Dundee West MP Ernie Ross and he paid tribute to the Dundee East MP Iain Luke. Yet, when he mentioned Jack McConnell, it was merely to thank him for taking the kicking from the Scottish press that he used to get.

The First Minister was livid that Blair was addressing the Scottish party and did not praise the achievements of his party in the Scottish Parliament. Jack told a confidante, 'I would never publicly humiliate a colleague like that – and he would never do it to anyone else either'. The relationship between the two men who were once so close is described as no more than 'businesslike' in the rare dealings that they now have.

Ever since the leadership contest of 1994, McConnell has been seen as Number Ten's man in Scotland. For many years, the Prime Minister regarded him as loyal and it was the Chancellor who viewed him with some suspicion – something that served to reinforce the idea that Jack had made his choice and was firmly in the Blair camp.

Jack McConnell's relations with Tony Blair and Gordon Brown had been defined for almost a decade by what happened on the 12 May 1994 – the day John Smith died. Prior to that, he had enjoyed good relationships with both men. The day before Smith died, McConnell had travelled to London on a flight with Smith and the then Shadow Scottish Secretary, Tom Clarke. Smith had been in great form and spent the journey laughing and joking with his colleagues. That night John Smith spoke at the Labour Party's annual fundraising dinner in which he appealed for his party to be given a chance to serve. It went down exceptionally well and Smith appeared to be on top of the job − which made his death all the more shocking for those who had seen him on the previous night.

Jack McConnell learned of Smith's heart attack sooner than most in the Labour Party. His pager went off with a message asking him to call Smith's daughter Catherine, which he did immediately. However, the message was not intended for Jack − the family were trying to reach their close friend Murray Elder, not realising that his pager had been passed to Jack when he took over the General Secretary's job. That day, like everyone in the Labour Party, Jack was shocked by the news that Smith had suffered a heart attack. By the time he got off his flight back in Glasgow, it had been confirmed that John Smith was dead. Gradually throughout the day, Labour politicians, from councillors to MPs, made their way to Labour's Scottish HQ to share their sense of grief and shock with others in the party. There was no attempt to organise a gathering − it simply happened. MPs arrived back in Scotland from Westminster and, along with other party figures, they went in search of advice or news of the funeral arrangements.

Smith's death coincided with the Tory Party spring conference being held in Inverness. TV pictures showed Michael Ancram going on to the platform to break the news to the then Scottish Secretary, Ian Lang, whose face visibly drained of colour. Although Scottish politics is often something of a battleground, friendships do develop across the political divide. This is particularly true of Westminster MPs who would often meet colleagues from opposition parties on flights to London and would pass hours sharing harmless gossip in airport lounges. The death of John Smith, like that of Donald Dewar almost a decade later, was felt deeply across the political spectrum.

On the day Smith died, the STUC had been planning to stage a demonstration against the Tories at their party conference. It had been planned for weeks. In light of Smith's death, the STUC's General Secretary, Campbell Christie, and his deputy, Bill Speirs, went to speak to McConnell about how they should proceed. One idea was that their demonstrators should all wear black armbands. McConnell's reaction to the suggestion is unprintable but it is fair to say that Christie and Speirs were left in no doubt that their demo should be cancelled. McConnell had seen the way the Tories had reacted to the news and immediately knew any political activity would be entirely inappropriate.

When the Labour leader's death was announced, Tony Blair, then the Shadow Home Secretary, was on a visit to Scotland. He was being driven from Aberdeen Airport to a Euro campaign visit in the Granite City when the news came through. Like everyone else, he was in a state of shock but he went ahead with the visit before boarding a flight back to London.

Neil Kinnock's former aide, Neil Stewart, was in the office of *The Scotsman* newspaper when it became clear that Smith's heart attack had killed him. In common with many party figures that day, his immediate reaction was to head to Keir Hardie House in Glasgow. To this day, some supporters of Gordon Brown are convinced that McConnell and Stewart spent that day convincing Labour politicians who passed through the office that Blair rather than Brown had to be Smith's successor. However, there is now some evidence which casts doubt on that long-held view. Neil Stewart said:

It is just not true – Jack was trying to work out what to do. His first reaction was to tell Campbell Christie and Bill Speirs in words of one syllable to call off their plans. But people think we were persuading MPs in favour of Blair.

The leader of the House of Commons, Peter Hain, is another close friend of McConnell. The pair met during the late '80s when they were both involved in the Labour Coordinating Committee. Like McConnell, Hain is often labelled as a Blairite. In both their cases, Hain claims, the tag is misplaced. He said:

> Jack is neither a Blairite not a Brownite. I don't like to be labelled in those terms and when people say that I am a Blairite I don't recognise that description of myself. I am loyal to Tony and friendly to Gordon – I think Jack is in the same position. He is not a factional politician. In several years' time there will be a transitional period and, as someone not involved in factionalism, his voice will count.

Tommy Sheppard, who was McConnell's deputy at the time, also said he was unaware of McConnell actively lobbying for Blair or even for his opinion being sought on the matter. By the time of the leadership election, it is true that McConnell had been impressed by Blair's performance and, if asked, he would probably have supported him for the leadership. But friends say any backing for Blair in the past has been political rather than personal. And it is important to remember there is no evidence that anyone asked for his opinion. One party source said, 'The contest was all run in London over a period of seven days.' Another claimed, 'It was over in about seven minutes. Jack McConnell's view was not important during those minutes.'

Large sections of the Labour Party believed that Tony Blair had the best chance of winning for the party in England. That included many Scottish MPs who realised that, no matter how well their party did north of the border, they would never become the governing party unless the performance in the south could be improved. Neil Kinnock lost the 1992 election despite attracting half a million more votes for Labour than Tony Blair did in 2001. This was due, in part, to his support being poorer in England than in the rest of the country.

After Blair had won the leadership contest, McConnell simply saw it as his job to deliver for the new leader. He formed a close relationship with Blair between '94, when he was elected leader, and the election in '97. But, after 1997, Jack's contact with Blair became less frequent for no reason other than Blair was Prime Minister rather than the leader of the opposition and he no longer had the time to devote to his party. But Jack remained firmly on side. He was aware of the fierce competition between the new Prime Minister and his Chancellor.

When he was organising the referendum campaign for a devolved Scottish parliament in 1997, Jack witnessed the extent of the rivalry for the first time. Blair was due to arrive in Edinburgh to meet John Smith's widow, Elizabeth, outside the Caledonian Hotel. TV crews and newspaper photographers from all the main media outlets were there to capture the moment. Gordon Brown was making his way from his home in Fife to join the photocall. As McConnell stood chatting to Alastair Campbell, Blair's spokesman, Campbell took a call on his mobile from the Chancellor, letting him know he was crossing the Forth Road Bridge. Campbell reassured him that he would be there in plenty of time for the photocall. However, just moments before he had taken Brown's call, Campbell had received a call from Tony Blair's car to let him know that the Prime Minister was just round the corner from the hotel. A beaming Blair was pictured on the steps of the hotel with Elizabeth Smith as Gordon was being driven over the Forth Road Bridge. Because of his physical presence at incidents like that, Jack was viewed with more and more suspicion by those close to the Chancellor. Some of their suspicions were, no doubt, well founded but, on other occasions, it is possible that Jack was unfairly blamed for taking sides.

It could be that, because Tony Blair has announced his intention to stand down at the end of a third term, many politicians who backed him for the leadership are now claiming they only did so out of expediency rather than a real desire to see him rather than Brown lead the party.

Relations between McConnell and Brown did not start off badly and there is much to suggest they have improved again recently. When McConnell decided to apply for the job of General Secretary of the Labour Party, Gordon Brown acted as one of his referees for the post and Brown's close friend, Murray Elder, was one of Jack's strongest advocates. But, after Blair's election as leader, McConnell had no hesitation in doing his bidding. He enthusiastically embraced all the changes that Blair pushed through the party and did everything he could to make sure he delivered the leader's wishes in Scotland. He was increasingly seen as pro-Blair and anti-Brown.

During election times, when Brown loyalists were drafted into party headquarters, they were immediately distrustful of McConnell and would often criticise his organisational skills. One Brown source said, 'They would run back to Gordon with stories designed to cause problems for Jack.' In early 1997, ahead of the election, senior Labour figures attended a strategy meeting with Brown to develop the party's key messages for the election campaign. The meetings came up with several important commitments the party would make for Scotland. Gordon Brown devised the plan to promise 'a bonfire of the quangos' as a manifesto commitment. The week after the meeting, *The Scotsman*'s political editor, Peter MacMahon, ran a front-page story revealing Brown's big idea. Inside the same paper was MacMahon's interview with Jack McConnell about his job as General Secretary. Brown was furious that his proposal for the Scottish election had leaked so soon and Brown's allies blamed McConnell for spilling the beans. McConnell claims it was McLeish who told MacMahon of the plan. However, the McConnell–Brown relationship had now reached its lowest point – and was to remain there for the next seven years. But, if Jack thought that his loyalty to Blair would be repaid, he was in for a shock.

The last year of McConnell's reign at Keir Hardie House was particularly difficult. He was in search of a parliamentary seat and it was known that he would have to stand down as the top party official in Scotland. His enemies were keen to speed up the process and have him removed as quickly as possible. When such moves were being made to have Jack ousted from the job, Blair did not appear to stand by McConnell. Number Ten simply got on with the job of identifying a successor for the position. They wanted to install Andy Kerr, then a Glasgow City Council official, as McConnell's successor. Gordon Brown had other ideas. He wanted the Fife Council Leader, Alex Rowley, to take over. Rowley had won great praise during his time as the leader of Fife Council and Brown knew that Alex would always be loyal to him.

As has happened before and since, when Blair and Brown clash over an appointment to a particular post, Brown stands his ground and fights harder for the candidates he supports. Rowley got the job. However, from the moment he took over, he was to become the focus of a nasty campaign to undermine him by both Blairites and Brownites. When, in the run-up to the Scottish elections, Jack decided to publish an account of his time as General Secretary, Number Ten was quick to distance itself from him. Over several days, Downing Street considered blocking McConnell from standing as an MSP if his serialisation in *Scotland on Sunday* played badly. Blair had no intention of supporting the man who had fought to deliver a victory for him on Clause 4 and who had lost many friends by embracing his two-question referendum policy on his behalf.

Ironically, it was Brown who was much more sympathetic to the plight of the former General Secretary. At the height of the row, the party's new General Secretary, Alex Rowley, met McConnell to try to resolve the problem. Rowley left the meeting convinced that McConnell was guilty of nothing more than a genuine mistake. He made a point of speaking to Brown about McConnell's fate and told the Chancellor that, in his view, there was no malice involved in McConnell's decision to publish his memoirs. On the contrary, Rowley believed him when he said he thought it would portray the party in a good light. Brown's view was that the move was a 'misjudgement' but he also thought the row had been blown out of all proportion. While some Blairite politicians were calling on Rowley to 'jump on Jack from a high height', Brown agreed that it would be wrong to hang him out to dry over what he viewed as innocent miscalculation.

The highly publicised *Scotland on Sunday* row came at a time when McConnell was feeling particularly low. He had been frozen out by the party hierarchy, his job with Public Affairs Europe was not going well and he was worried about failing to secure the nomination for the Motherwell and Wishaw seat. That summer, he had decided he would stand for the National Executive Committee (NEC) of the Labour Party, which would boost his profile and put him in a position where he could make a real contribution within the party again. At the time, the deputy leader of the party, Cathy Jamieson, was seen as a radical left-wing activist and she too was keen to get elected to the NEC. Jack and Cathy threw themselves into an energetic campaign to see who could get the most support within the Scottish party. They were running neck and neck.

Jack spoke to his former colleagues at party HQ and in Downing Street. In both places, he received an extremely favourable reaction. Rather than Jamieson, who was seen by New Labour as a troublemaker, they wanted a moderniser from Scotland on the party's ruling body. Jack knew that Downing Street was working on a plan to put together a list of six modernisers who they hoped could stop the six left-wingers from across the UK who were running for the NEC. Given his track record as General Secretary and his loyalty to Blair, he fully expected to be one of the six modernisers. But, just as the contest was hotting up, Jack received a phone call from Downing Street telling him they had decided to back an Engineering Union candidate, Sylvia Tudhope, over him. Tudhope is a party loyalist but she did not have the level of support or recognition within the party nationally to win. By putting her instead of Jack up against Jamieson, the party blew its chance of getting a moderniser. Jamieson was safely elected and Jack was left badly wounded by Downing Street's decision to drop him.

At the time, McConnell was simply hurt by Blair's betrayal but now he sees it as the turning point in their relationship. This was when he realised that, with Tony Blair, loyalty is a one-way street. Because of Number Ten's actions over the newspaper serialisation row and the NEC placings, McConnell believed that he was now on his own. It can, therefore, have been no more than a further disappointment rather than a complete shock to him when, following Dewar's death, he failed to win their backing for the party leadership in Scotland over Henry McLeish. On the night Dewar lay in hospital dying, the Prime Minister's office contacted McLeish but there was no such call for Jack. Following Dewar's funeral, a reception was held at the Kelvingrove Art Gallery and Museum in Glasgow. The Prime Minister and his wife made a point of speaking to Henry and Julie McLeish but they made no attempt to approach the McConnells.

During the short campaign that followed, there is no question that Gordon Brown pulled out all the stops to ensure

Henry McLeish was elected as the next First Minister – the two men had a strong connection through Fife politics. But it is simplistic to say that Brown took against McConnell in the belief that Jack had supported Blair for the party leadership. If that was his 'crime', then McLeish was equally guilty. McLeish admits that, when Blair's aide, Anji Hunter, called him to say that Tony wanted his support, he replied without hesitation, 'He's got it!'

However, when it came to the two men fighting for the biggest job in Scottish politics, Brown did not sit on the fence. Ironically, he did for McLeish what he failed to do for himself back in 1994 – he mobilised his support quickly and put in calls to those he could trust in the trade union movement to secure their backing for McLeish. He was careful not to start canvassing for support among individual MSPs, realising that to do so could turn some people against him and lose support for McLeish if they thought he was exerting undue influence in the contest. With such strong support pledged for McLeish, it didn't matter that McConnell had most of the backbenchers on his side.

In the dying hours of the campaign, the McConnell camp tried to turn Brown's support for McLeish into a 'vote loser'. McConnell vowed to be his own man, free from London control. It is a message that normally goes down well north of the border but the Scottish Parliament was still in its infancy and, back then, many of its MSPs and ministers were more easily influenced than they would be today. Brown delivered for his man. Without the Chancellor's backing for McLeish, it is a near certainty that McConnell would have succeeded Donald Dewar. The Chancellor's role in the contest left some of McConnell's supporters seething and it served to underline the perceived bad blood between McConnell and Brown. Following McLeish's demise, there is little doubt that Gordon Brown would have worked equally hard in an attempt to get Wendy Alexander elected as First Minister rather than McConnell. But, second time around, he would have found it more difficult to influence the outcome. When McConnell fought his second battle for the leadership, he was unstoppable and Gordon Brown realised that as much as anyone else.

The tensions between Gordon Brown and Jack McConnell have been portrayed as one of the most bitter feuds within the Scottish Labour Party. It is often reported that McConnell did everything in his power to stop Brown becoming leader in 1994 and that Brown did everything within his power to stop McConnell becoming First Minister. However, a source close to Gordon Brown has now moved to quash suggestions that the Chancellor is an enemy of McConnell. He said:

> Jack has not put a foot wrong since he became First Minister. Above all else, Gordon Brown wants devolution to work and Jack McConnell is the person who is making it work. The Scottish Parliament is something that Gordon has strived for all his political life and he believes that Jack is delivering the stability the parliament needed. Gordon is very supportive of Jack, they share a common purpose and that can go a long way to overcoming any personality issues. Gordon has no great dislike of Jack.

Over the years, other supporters of the Chancellor have been quick to dismiss McConnell and this has fuelled the idea that there is bad blood between the two politicians. The Brown source added:

> I am close to Gordon – I speak to him every week – and I have never heard him say a bad word about Jack McConnell. There are other people who see themselves as close to Gordon who have briefed against Jack. These acolytes have caused trouble

but they are not speaking with Gordon's authority. It is no secret that Gordon wanted Henry to get the leadership over Jack but there was no malice towards McConnell.

Many of the members of the Brown camp who sought to undermine McConnell while he was General Secretary also turned against Alex Rowley soon after his appointment – despite the fact that Rowley had firm backing from the Chancellor. This made a mockery of the idea that it was a Brown vs Blair battle. With McConnell's camp now claiming that Jack did not work against Brown following John Smith's death and Brown's camp insisting that the Chancellor rates McConnell as a First Minister, there is reason to believe that any feud which existed has now run its course. Both sides seem determined to bury the hatchet and they were encouraged to do so in the summer of 2004 by the Edinburgh-based businesswoman Julia Ogilvy who was speaking to both men about initiatives relating to young people. Struck by how similar their ideas were, she persuaded Brown to invite McConnell to a party at his home and he duly did. However, the real motivation for the improvement in relations probably stems from political practicality. Gordon Brown has accepted that Jack McConnell is the First Minister and he is happier to work with him than against him. Jack McConnell has accepted that Gordon Brown will probably be the next Prime Minister and feels the same way.

But, if relations with Brown have improved, the situation with Blair has gone the other way. Jack McConnell's inner circle believe that the Prime Minister has neglected Scotland since devolution. Communication between Holyrood and Downing Street is poor. McConnell felt badly let down when few of his Westminster colleagues bothered to attend the opening of the new Scottish Parliament building. Despite this, it should be stressed that he thinks John Reid, Charles Clarke and David Blunkett have gone out of their way to be helpful and to assist the

Scottish Parliament. In other European countries with devolved governments, it is not unusual for the Prime Minister to attend the annual opening of the parliament yet Blair declined to turn up for the opening of the new building. One of Jack's colleagues said, 'People would be shocked if they knew how little they spoke. Jack only speaks to the Prime Minister three or four times a year. He has absolutely no interest in what we do.'

Those who surround Jack are clearly angry that Blair has taken so little interest in the devolution project. They point to the fact that even Margaret Thatcher would address the General Assembly of the Church of Scotland and that John Major would regularly stay overnight in Scotland after a visit. Jack's staff believe that it is not just McConnell Blair is letting down through his lack of interest but some of Scotland's most important institutions too. While Jack was first won over by Blair's ability to take tough decisions, he now sees him as someone who will give in to his enemies or to vested interests rather than stand up for his principles. It is clear that he feels personally let down by the Prime Minister and is also saddened because he feels that Blair is also letting Scotland down.

In the most damning indictment of the man McConnell once revered, a friend of Jack said:

> On a couple of important issues, Blair has given Jack his word that he will sort something. A couple of weeks later, we find out that the promise is not going to be kept. Tony Blair has a problem with trust among the voters and, from our experience, it is justified.

By contrast the First Minister has been extremely impressed by the attitude of the royal family towards devolution. The Queen requests a weekly briefing from the Executive and both she and Prince Charles appear to have a good knowledge of the work of the parliament. One of McConnell's team said:

We are always trying to get our colleagues in Whitehall to pay attention to what we are doing and we foist information on them but the royal family actually come looking for it. They are genuinely interested in what is going on in the parliament and how it affects Scotland. If only Blair would adopt the same approach.

# EPILOGUE

It was the Soweto riots in 1976 that alerted Jack McConnell to the importance of politics. As a teenager, living thousands of miles away on Arran, he felt a deep sense of injustice over the killing of black youngsters whose only crime was to protest at their school lessons being taught in Afrikaans and he had a strong desire to play a part in helping to right such wrongs. Thirty years later, as First Minister of his country, he travelled to Malawi in Africa determined Scotland should help those living on the poverty stricken continent. His visit to Malawi could have been seen as a peripheral player jumping on the G8 bandwagon but his interest in international aid goes back decades and his anti-apartheid credentials are strong. As well as going to Africa in person, he invited Bob Geldof to speak at the Scottish Parliament in 2005 because he feels part of the Live-Aid generation and shares Bob's passion that poverty should be eradicated. However, many people will feel that Scotland's First Minister should devote all of his time to tackling the country's own problems – improving the health service and eliminating poverty in Scotland's housing schemes – rather than focusing on Africa.

When Donald Dewar wrote the Scotland Act that was to institute the Scottish Parliament, it is unlikely he would have seen it as part of the First Minister's role to travel to Africa on such a mission. A stickler for constitutional protocol, Dewar, had he lived longer, would have ensured the devolution lines were clearly drawn. He fought hard to ensure the Scottish Parliament was given strong powers but he would also have respected the areas over which his Whitehall colleagues retained control. Jack McConnell is starting to push at some of those boundaries. Under the Fresh Talent Initiative, he has effectively set up separate a Scottish immigration policy as it is now easier for someone from abroad to live and work in Scotland than it is elsewhere in the UK.

He was prepared to weather the anger of his Westminster colleagues by legislating for a tougher ban on smoking in public places in Scotland than will be the case in the rest of the country. And, on European affairs which are the preserve of the Westminster Parliament, McConnell frequently pushes Scotland's case through his involvement in the Committee of the Regions and REGLEG.

When the G8 leaders came to Scotland, it was far from automatic that the First Minister would be the politician who met them on the tarmac at Prestwick airport but McConnell lobbied hard to ensure that it was. The Foreign Office referred to the event as G8 Gleneagles but McConnell called it G8 Scotland in an attempt to ensure the whole country received the maximum benefit from hosting it. Jack went out of his way to say it at every opportunity and it was G8 Scotland that the media adopted.

A politician like McConnell, with such a strong desire to influence global events, would normally be drawn to Westminster or the European Parliament where their interests in foreign affairs could be developed but McConnell is also a strong nationalist so, once the Scottish Parliament was set up, it was always going to be his natural home. Also, his recent bruising battles with Downing Street have ended any desire he may have had to please the UK government.

The First Minster's influence in Downing Street appears to be almost nonexistent and that must be a cause of regret both for him personally and for the running of the Scottish Executive. The Labour Party has always argued that there is strength in Edinburgh and London working together. Now that the relationship between McConnell and Blair has deteriorated to such an extent, that argument is more difficult to make. However, the severing of his once-close ties to the Prime Minister has freed Jack up to pursue those policies and interests which he believes are in Scotland's interests rather than only those which the Scotland Act sets out. Whether you view that as a positive situation or as a serious risk to the constitutional settlement in the UK will depend on your politics.

Some of McConnell's Westminster colleagues have been angered by his description of Scotland as the greatest small 'country' in the world, fearing that there are dangers in using the language of Scottish nationalism. It could be argued that, by wrapping himself in the saltire, Jack makes life more difficult for the SNP. For those Scots who consider themselves to be nationalists with a small 'n', of whom Jack himself is certainly one, his approach is enough to satisfy their demand. But those who wanted a Scottish Parliament primarily as a means of killing off nationalism will feel he is playing a dangerous game which could set Scotland on a slippery slope to independence.

In his first couple of years in power Jack McConnell did very little that was memorable. Over the last couple of years, however, he has grown in confidence and should the election in 2011 be the last one he fights, he will want to boast that he has helped to make Scotland a better place.

McConnellism is not about the best way to tackle hospital waiting lists or to solve the country's transport problems and that could be his undoing. His is not a philosophy that can easily be tagged as right wing or left wing – it is a political outlook that is defined by big-picture issues. Jack McConnell wants Scotland to have a greater voice in the UK and the world and he wants it to be a less racist, less sectarian country, where young people have the best chance of succeeding.

Donald Dewar has gone down in history as the First Minister who made the Scottish Parliament happen – Jack McConnell will want to be remembered as the First Minister who made it work.

# INDEX